RYDER CUP
REVEALED

Tales of the Unexpected

Ross Biddiscombe

First published in Great Britain in July 2014 by Constant Sports Publishing.

A CIP catalogue record for this book is available from the British Library.

For *Ryder Cup Revealed* news, go to golfontheedge.co.uk.

ISBN 978-0-9562850-1-0

Typeset by Leon Harris in Adobe Caslon Pro at 11/13.5pt.

Printed by Dolman Scott Ltd, dolmanscott.co.uk.

Constant Sports Publishing, London, England, a division of Constant Publishing.

Contents

Foreword

The Professional Golfers Association is proud to be recognised as the founding partner of the Ryder Cup, a competition that is fast approaching its 90th birthday. And, as the PGA chief executive and a golf fan, it is true to say that I have an almost obsessive passion for what Samuel Ryder helped create.

The start of these matches in 1927 was of huge significance to the PGA here in Britain. Samuel Ryder was already a well-known golf patron and well connected to the golf professionals of the early 20th century. He greatly respected the pros and, with his help, the Cup elevated those players within society, it gave them a new status. For many decades beforehand, professional golfers had been treated like servants, forced to doff their caps to golf club members, but the Ryder Cup underlined their high levels of skill: these men were the best players in the world, seen to be good enough to represent their country.

The Ryder Cup served the same purpose for professionals in America and the biennial contest has become admired in every country in the world where golf is played. Not only that, but every match keeps us all mindful that there is no greater honour in sport than playing – not for yourself – but for your nation's flag.

So the foundations of the Ryder Cup were laid by a group of like-minded professional golfers and a canny businessman who cared about them. None of those pioneers could have known that the matches would become such iconic sporting events in the 21st century. Neither could they have forecast that a major legacy of the matches is that they act as a bridge between the game as it was and the game as it is today.

For me, that is what *Ryder Cup Revealed: Tales of the Unexpected* is all about, what makes it so different from all those books that have been written before about these matches: it firmly connects the past with the present; it talks about golf as part of society and the professional golfers as honest, working men battling against the problems of money, politics or controversy. That connection is what makes this book intriguing and enthralling and, like the Ryder Cup itself, totally engaging.

Therefore it is an honour and a privilege to write this foreword. Enjoy the book and love your golf.

Sandy Jones, chief executive of The Professional Golfers' Association, *May 2014*

Introduction

It just doesn't make any sense: how can a sport like golf that for so many years was thought to be sedate and gentlemanly produce such frenzied and nerve-wracking theatre? For three whole days every two years, two continents face off on the fairways and greens for the honour of a small golden trophy. No prize money, no second place, nowhere to hide for the losers. It is raw sport, all for glory and there is simply nothing to compare.

The Ryder Cup gets into your blood. Now in its ninth decade of existence, the Cup is a monster of an event, watched by billions and generating colossal amounts of money. Much of the reason lies in its unique history, a story that began as a battle between two nations and now incorporates two continents. In recent times, the tension has been so elevated that it feels like each shot in every foursome, fourball or singles confrontation is a matter of death or glory for the teams. The whole contest is extraordinary in the truest sense: no other competition can equal the to-and-fro of momentum over three long days of sporting struggle; the tales of nerves such as those on the 1st tee of the Ryder Cup are peerless; and nowhere else do tens of thousands of sports fans shout for Europe, for goodness sake. Plus it was Ryder Cup fans who actually invented the chant "U-S-A…U-S-A", such is their passion. The levels of emotion and excitement are off the scale both inside and outside the ropes.

And yet there has always been so much more to the Ryder Cup than the birdies and bogeys that are played out on the greens and fairways of places as far apart as Kiawah Island and Celtic Manor. The fascination of the Ryder Cup dates back to the unofficial attempts to stage international golf team matches between professionals from Great Britain and America in 1921. These were the days when most golf club members came from the upper echelon of society, when magazines for golfers featured stories about new-fangled airplanes and fancy cars. This was a sport ruled by high-class people with a Corinthian code. Pro golfers, by contrast, were members of the 'downstairs' society who had to battle their way into the sporting spotlight.

The social shenanigans, the backroom battles, the craving for money and status were all present as the Ryder Cup came officially into being in 1927. The matches were between two powerful nations – Britain and America – who vied for world leadership in the post-war period and through the social uncertainties of 1930s. Then World War II changed the world and the Cup reflected the rise of the USA into a global superpower and Britain's fading influence on the world stage. Well-heeled American golfers were almost invincible against the impoverished British.

Only one GB victory in the first 36 years of the post-war contests meant the Ryder Cup was becoming a meaningless exhibition with a pre-ordained winner. Is it any wonder that British golfers resented their American counterparts during this time? The seeds of a remarkable rivalry were sown in those years, so that by the time Team GB had become Team Europe in 1979, the needle on the enmity scale was often sky-high.

The compelling nature of the Ryder Cup comes from those feelings, the emotions that have built up over decades and that often spill out into stand-up arguments, inexplicable tears, bitter recriminations and eye-popping celebrations. If the Ryder Cup had not mattered to so many people for so many years then today's matches would be a pale shadow of themselves. In addition, we – that is the many millions of British, European and American golfers of all shapes, sizes, ages and abilities – care so much that the players themselves are even more pumped up. And add to that the professional pride and competitiveness of the best golfers in the world and it is a powerful cocktail.

Given the fascinating history of the matches, *Ryder Cup Revealed: Tales of the Unexpected* delves into the Cup in a way that no other book has attempted before. Instead of just recounting the contests and the personalities who played, captained, administered, and operated them, the book shines a light on the little-known, behind-the-scenes stories that tell the fans how and why the matches are such a spectacle in so many ways.

By taking an original angle on the Cup's history, the chapters provide fresh answers, different perspectives and new talking points. For example, why did Samuel Ryder and not some other patron put his name to these international team golf matches for professionals? Why did the first two attempts to stage the contest fail when the Walker Cup – the amateur version

– had already roared into life so successfully? Why did it take so long for the Ryder Cup to make serious money and how come its future was on life-support at least twice. Or what exactly made the atmosphere at the Ryder Cup turn sour after World War II and who were the main perpetrators? Why was Europe's third consecutive defeat in 1983 perhaps the most significant turning point in the whole history of the event?

The book does contain a few references and stories about the key drives, chips and putts, but the focus is much more on the other side of the ropes, away from the course itself – in the back rooms, the meeting rooms and the locker rooms – where many matches have been shaped and where an equally compelling story can be told. The book also tackles the question of how the contests have changed over the decades: the rivalry, the money, the crowds, the captains, the sponsors, the TV audience and much more. The inside stories come from people directly involved with their opinions and analysis.

Ryder Cup Revealed reveals the political games and mischief-making; the controversial actions and conflicting viewpoints; the ever-changing, sensitive relationship between the players, captains and teams; the early search for money and stability as well as the modern-day means of spending the event's enormous profits. And all this is reported, outlined, contextualised and debated in specific chapters that deal with each key issue that has helped develop the Ryder Cup over a history that covers nine separate decades.

The book aims to surprise, to be insightful and even to shock as it looks both at the past in an alternative way and also projects into the future using original interviews, first-hand research, unique analysis.

I have carried out well over 100 interviews on both sides of the Atlantic, but not just with players and captains past and present. I have also spoken extensively with top golfing administrators; golf historians; psychologists; senior members of the European Tour, PGA of America and the British PGA; match organisers; host club secretaries; sports TV executives; sports commercial experts; and many more people at the heart of the Ryder Cup's often unspoken story.

There is also significant new research and facts about the early matches thanks to the assistance of the British PGA's archives; the USGA's library; the European Tour's information files; the Samuel Ryder Foundation; and memorable stories directly from host clubs both in Britain and America. Analysis – for instance, in areas such as money and finance – is the product of much thought and debate with input from expert sources close to the subject, while all the words have been read by experts who have provided their own opinions and estimations.

Ryder Cup Revealed is the first book to fully explain in-depth both how and why the Ryder Cup – a sporting event once on the point of irrelevancy – is now among the most anticipated dates on the world's sporting calendar.

Ross Biddiscombe, *May 2014*

I

The Three Ages of the Ryder Cup

It was a steamy, hot October day in Florida when the 1983 Ryder Cup match reached its climax. Massive amounts of rain had fallen earlier in the week and the course was still saturated as thunder and lightning began to threaten on the Sunday evening. An unusually large crowd of 15,000 fans lined the fairways of the Palm Beach Gardens course as this most unusual Ryder Cup contest reached its climax. For the first time, the US team was in real danger of losing a home match.

Never before – not even in the days of cloth caps and plus-fours – had a Ryder Cup contest in America been this thrilling. The teams were level after two days and then, as the early singles matches played out on Sunday, neither team could gain more than a one-point advantage. With the last two Americans battling against their European opponents, the overall score was 13-13. The last two points to be decided were in the hands of America's Tom Watson, who was ahead in his game against Bernard Gallacher, 2 up with two holes to play, and Jose Maria Canizares of Spain, who was 1 up as he and his opponent Lanny Wadkins stood over their approach shots to the 18th green. A remarkable 14-14 tie looked the most likely final score.

Then the latest in a long line of Ryder Cup heroes stepped forward. Jerry Lanston Wadkins, Jr. was a good, ol' boy from Virginia, a major champion with 18 professional wins to his credit and two successful Cup appearances behind him. He played his golf with a smile and celebrated his victories with vigour, but he also knew how to stare down an opponent eye-to-eye. Wadkins was playing the tail-gunner role in the singles for a reason – he was a born match player, a street fighter-type of pro golfer who never gave up. In his sights this time was the mercurial Canizares who was playing beautifully and had been 3 up in the match at one point. If the US team was to maintain its record of never losing or tying a Ryder Cup match at home, Wadkins needed to do something extraordinary.

Most of the crowd was now surrounding the 18th green and fairway; the nervous US captain Jack Nicklaus and several members of his team were stalking the Wadkins-Canizares match because they knew it was their best chance of overall victory. The two players both had short pitch shots and their accuracy would decide the fate of this crucial point. Canizares hit first, but caught the ball fat and it landed well short in spongy rough. The Spaniard looked disconsolate and his countryman Seve Ballesteros, who stood next to him in support, knew that the American now had a chance to win the hole to halve this match.

Wadkins was still grim-faced as his wedge lifted the ball high and straight at the pin. It landed a little short, bounced forward twice and stopped 18 inches for a gimme birdie. Canizares had no chance of holing his own birdie attempt from the rough and so Wadkins had stolen a half-point out of the European team's pocket through guts, determination and a chunk of pure skill. Moments later in the other match, Watson confirmed his win and the Americans had sneaked home 14½ to 13½. Nicklaus was so relieved he kissed the ground from where Wadkins had hit his wedge shot.

American pride had been preserved but, for once, the home team's victory was no the main story. It was the narrow defeat suffered by the visitors that prompted the headlines. For the previous 30-plus years, US teams had achieved a near-perfect Ryder Cup record, with just one defeat and one tie since 1947. But this result in Florida heralded a new era for the competition... the Third Age of the Ryder Cup.

It was in the summer of 1927 that the official history of the Ryder Cup began, the start of the First Age of the matches. The initial few contests were relatively friendly affairs played among the best professional players in the world – just what Samuel Ryder envisioned when he became the event's figurehead. This initial era in the Cup's history lasted just 10 years and six matches, from the inaugural contest at Worcester Country Club, Massachusetts in 1927 to the final one before World War II in 1937 at Southport & Ainsdale Golf Club in Lancashire, England. This was a time when Britain and the US were the only significant golfing nations, but plenty of financial and logistical problems had to be overcome each time the biennial match was staged. Establishing an international team competition for the pros on the golfing calendar required plenty of determination from the players and their associations.

Each country took turns to act as host and the first five meetings were all won by the home team. Drama was at a minimum, although the 1933 match in England was won on the final green by the GB squad with the Prince of Wales in attendance creating as much media attention as the golf itself. The sport was hardly a mass participation pastime; far more people played cricket or football in Britain and many more fans followed the results of these sports. In America, baseball was the national sport and sporting superstars emerged from the diamond, the football gridiron, the athletics track or even the boxing ring. However, golf had one advantage: it was the only sport at the time where John Bull regularly faced off against just Uncle Sam, but the Ryder Cup had not fired the passions of whole nations. The contests needed an extra edge to reach the front pages rather than remain just in the sports section. The key would be revenge.

It happened when the sequence of home wins was broken in 1937 as the Americans under Walter Hagen's captaincy (his sixth and last) proved too strong for the GB team. That win was a painful blow to Britain's sporting pride. The US team – with the hugely confident Hagen leading it – seemed smug and the build-up to the next match in autumn 1939 would feature much more patriotic rallying of support for the GB team. After all, pioneers from the British Isles had spread the game of golf around the world – including America – and to be toppled from their perch as the sport's No.1 nation was unacceptable. The temperature of the matches was set to rise as the British media called for a super-human effort to restore lost pride. Then World War II got in the way. Just a few weeks before the 7th Ryder Cup match was due to take place in Jacksonville, hostilities broke out in Europe and a chance for British golfing redemption was put on hold. Thus, the First Age of the Ryder Cup ended.

> **1927: US 9½ Great Britain 2½**
> **1929: Great Britain 7, US 5**
> **1931: US 9 Great Britain 3**
> **1933: Great Britain 6½ US 5½**
> **1935: US 9 Great Britain 3**
> **1937: US 8 Great Britain 4**
>
> **Matches: 8; US wins: 4; GB wins 2**
>
> **1939-1945:** No matches due to World War II

The Americans held on to the trophy throughout the war and even chose would-be teams that played fund-raising matches with the actual Ryder Cup on show. The British had not time nor energy for golf and thoughts of the Cup were put aside. When peace arrived after six long years, there was no guarantee that the GB-US series would resume.

Britain had changed significantly between 1939 and 1945. The war left its mark on sport just as it did on every other aspect of life; the nation was tired and its people listless even in victory. By contrast, over in America, the end of the war prompted an already energetic society to enjoy a period of prosperity and growth. Indeed, it was the get-up-and-go attitude of the Americans that saved the Ryder Cup from becoming a forgotten competition. But perhaps the most pertinent change to emerge in terms of the Ryder Cup's history was that by the time the matches re-started, the edge between the teams had sharpened considerably.

It was only through the generosity of an American millionaire, Robert A. Hudson, who paid all their expenses, that a British team could actually travel to contest the Cup in 1947. But within the atmosphere of American largesse, came the counter feeling of British inferiority and it is little wonder that this GB team was trounced 11-1. Already, a depressing template had been established at the start of the Second Age of the Ryder Cup.

The gap in ability between the American and British teams was not a chasm, but the difference in self-esteem certainly was. Every two years, the best GB players went into the match believing they were closing the gap only to find themselves thrashed once again.

A certain antipathy – whether justified or not – emerged between some of the participants. Feelings of jealousy and missed opportunities were understandable among many British players whose prime golfing years had been lost to the war while many American pros had been able to play and earn money on tour.

The ill-feeling on the golf course mirrored what was felt between the ordinary people of the two nations. The default feeling of the British (reflected in large sections of the media) towards their US cousins was coloured for a long time by the war years when Yank soldiers were characterised as "over-sexed, over-fed, over-paid and over here".

Every time the British Ryder Cup team was beaten in the immediate post-war matches, it was a blow to national morale; the more often the Americans won, the deeper the British resentment. So, after Dai Rees' team surprisingly won in 1957 at Lindrick in south Yorkshire, the home crowd's response was to carry him shoulder-high back to the clubhouse. Rees was an overnight national hero.

But the Lindrick win was the single bright spot amidst another gloomy run of poor British performances. A 16-16 tie in 1969 provided another isolated highlight that temporarily lifted the gloom. The British team was still sprinkled with club professionals who had to hurry home to tend to the needs of their members at weekends while the US squad was filled with world sporting superstars like Lee Trevino and Jack Nicklaus who had no such distractions and could concentrate solely on becoming better players. The contest was basically unfair.

Over three decades, the two PGAs had tried to change the format of the matches to make the results tighter, but nothing really changed – instead, the Americans actually looked like they were getting stronger.

The Ryder Cup was becoming a minor event because it lacked any regular competitive spark. Crowds in America were small and polite (why get excited about another easy win?) whereas in Britain they were larger but resigned to disappointment. By the mid-1970s, the event stagnated. America was an overwhelming golfing power, standing like a Colossus over the newly constituted British and Irish team.

Then in 1977, Tom Weiskopf (a senior member of the US Ryder Cup team and, four years previously, the Open champion) became the first headline American player to refuse to play in the match because, for him, it had become a meaningless exhibition. At that moment, the Ryder Cup organisers had been handed an ultimatum – change or die. Something more drastic than a few cosmetic nips and tucks had to be undertaken.

At Nicklaus's suggestion, the British PGA allowed the introduction of continental European players in 1979, but the American momentum still brought them a comfortable victory. Then at Team Europe's first home match in 1981, the result was even more embarrassing – the US team, perhaps the most powerful ever assembled in Ryder Cup history, won so early on the final day that seven of the 12 singles were still out on the course when the trophy was secured. It looked like the European gamble had failed.

1947: US 11 Great Britain 1
1949: US 7 Great Britain 5
1951: US 9½ Great Britain 2½
1953: US 6½ Great Britain 5½
1955: US 8 Great Britain 4
1957: Great Britain 7½ US 4½
1959: US 8½ Great Britain 3½
1961: US 14½ Great Britain 9½
1963: US 23 Great Britain 9
1965: US 19½ Great Britain 12½
1967: US 23½ Great Britain 8½
1969: US 16 Great Britain 16 (US retains cup)
1971: US 18½ Great Britain 13½
1973: US 19 Great Britain& Ireland 13
1975: US 21 Great Britain& Ireland 11
1977: US 12½ Great Britain & Ireland 7½

1979: US 17 Europe 11
1981: US 18½ Europe 9½

Matches: 18; US wins: 16; GB/GB&I/Europe wins 1; ties: 1

Fortunately for all concerned, the planets had were beginning to align and the one-sided Second Age of the Ryder Cup was about to end. It was the third Europe-US match in 1983 when the American Colossus finally encountered a worthy opponent. The long-time underdogs rose to the challenge because of four crucial reasons: 1. Seve Ballesteros became the team's unofficial on-course spearhead; 2. Europe now had a team core that featured 'The Big Five' – Ballesteros, Nick Faldo, Ian Woosnam, Bernhard Langer and Sandy Lyle – all major champions either present or future; 3. A new sponsor – Bell's Whisky – pumped in a previously-unheard-of amount of money to support Team Europe; and 4. New captain Tony Jacklin used that cash and his own inspirational motivating skills to imbue his team with a new level of confidence and self-belief. So began the Third Age of the Ryder Cup.

To prove that an era of exceptional Ryder Cup competitiveness had begun, Team Europe did not need to win the 1983 contest (the US actually won by a point). The point was that this closest of results underlined the change. Just two years later at The Belfry in the heart of England, the Europeans achieved an historic win (the first in 28 years) and a real rivalry was duly established.

Part of the beauty of this new situation was the fact that the European continent was now joined together to create one sporting team; this was a completely fresh concept. Politically, Europe's countries had been trying to work in harmony for years, but centuries-old differences often prevailed and infighting was as common as agreement. Golf had become the unlikely glue to bring nations together in a common cause; everyone from Catalonia to Caledonia felt like a European at the Ryder Cup. In this contest, the French could no longer hate the Germans nor the Scots show antagonism towards the English. Instead, the common enemy was America.

Europeans like Ballesteros and Langer brought a new attitude to the matches. They wanted desperately to prove themselves on the world stage at every opportunity, both personally, by winning major championships, but also collectively within a successful Ryder Cup team. Suddenly there was a reversal of fortune: decades of British and Irish golfers defeats against a vastly superior US team were consigned to the past and GB inferiority complexes of the previous decades were destroyed as European victories began to rack up – nine in the first 15 matches from the start of the Third Age.

Not only that, but the event was becoming stronger with every dramatic contest – from 1987 to 1999, there was one tie and never more than two points between the teams after three days of fierce competition. The organisers were able to sell more tickets and merchandise, gather in ever-larger television fees and attract more sponsorship and hospitality money. The match that nearly died because of lack of cash had become a veritable cash cow.

The competitiveness put fire in the bellies of the players of Teams Europe and USA, and also their fans; both responded with a patriotism that was fervent and even became so intense that it bordered on the unacceptable. Some US players complained about European crowds cheering their bad shots, but it was in America that tempers really boiled over. In 1991 at Kiawah Island and, more significantly, in 1999 at the Country Club of Brookline (both American victories), the behaviour of the home team and even the home crowds reached objectionable levels. However, that unwelcome development in the Cup's story was put into sharp contrast after the 2001 match was postponed due to the 9/11 acts of terrorism. Angry words on the golf course had been put into proper context and respect between all participants returned.

Since then, Europe has held the upper hand in terms of results while every match has been a huge commercial success as well as being watched by increasing numbers of fans throughout the world. The Ryder Cup has even been copied – by the women's Solheim Cup and the US PGA Tour's Presidents Cup, for example – as well as imitated by the likes of the EurAsia Cup that began in 2014. Such is its power.

The 40th match at Gleneagles – the 16th and latest of the Third Age of the Ryder Cup – was set to break all kinds of records. The future of the competition is seemingly set fair for generations to come, given the current levels of excitement and investment. Samuel Ryder would be amazed.

1983: US 14½ Europe 13½
1985: Europe 16½ US 11½
1987: Europe 15 US 13
1989: Europe 14 US 14 (Europe retains cup)
1991: US 14½ Europe 13½
1993: US 15 Europe 13
1995: Europe 14½ US 13½
1997: Europe 14½ US 13½
1999: US 14½ Europe 13½
2002: Europe 15½ US 12½
2004: Europe 18½ US 9½
2006: Europe 18½ US 9½
2008: US 16½ Europe 11½
2010: Europe 14½ US 13½
2012: Europe 14½ US 13½

2

Birth and Re-birth

Three times during its history, the Ryder Cup has been on life support. The matches played in this era are vast in every sense – the crowds at the course, the massive TV audience across the world, and the huge amounts of money that pour in from sponsorship, hospitality and merchandise. Yet, the Ryder Cup could easily have withered and died long before the 21st century arrived. First, it stuttered from a lack of investment, then it stumbled due to the effects of a world war and, finally, it was almost strangled by overt apathy. But each time it survived and three men can claim to have stood up for the Cup when it was on its knees: the visionary seed merchant who gave his name to the event, Samuel Ryder; the Oregon millionaire whose money funded the first post-war match, Robert A. Hudson; and the golfer who is arguably the world's best ever, Jack Nicklaus. Each of them showed a special affinity for the Cup that changed the course of golfing history.

But the uneasy birth and then the two subsequent re-births of the Ryder Cup were far from guaranteed. Each time the matches were threatened with extinction, there were other possible outcomes and even other possible saviours. For instance, the first questions must be the most obvious: would there have been a Ryder Cup without Samuel Ryder? More accurately, perhaps, would American and British golfers have met in an official professional international team challenge match in 1927 without the input from the seed merchant from St Albans in England?

The key question for the first re-birth in 1947 is why did a man from faraway Oregon think this golf contest could be revived by British golfers taking a 6,000-mile trek to the Pacific North West and, without Hudson's patronage, would the 10-year gap between the 6th and 7th matches have been significantly longer, or could the Cup's absence even have become permanent?

Finally, what if no one had addressed the depressing downward spiral of non-competitive matches that led to widespread American disinterest in the Cup? The Americans had become so dominant by the 1970s that Britain's best player of the time, Tony Jacklin, was worried about the event's future. "I thought there was a danger it might be scrapped altogether," he said. Step forward Nicklaus. But if the Golden Bear had not drawn a line in the sand on behalf of the players and forced the change from a GB&I team to a European one, would the world's greatest golfers have started to decline the invitation to represent their country? Would the Ryder Cup have become a pleasant but meaningless biennial exhibition or even survived at all?

Like so many stories from history, the perspective of time can provide different answers to the same questions, or even raise new ones. However, it is clear that the men who wanted to set up an international golf team challenge match between Britain and America in the 1920s could never have envisioned what would happen to their idea over the next nine decades.

The genesis of international team golf

It is not known exactly when conversations about staging a full-scale, professional team golf contest between Britain and America's best professionals first took place, but it was certainly several years before 1921 when the first of two unofficial matches were played. In fact, it may have happened more than 20 years earlier in 1900 when first the great Harry Vardon and later J.H. Taylor (two thirds of Britain's Great Triumvirate of golfers of the time, the other being James Braid) visited the United States for a series of exhibition matches. Vardon played as many as 80 times in America that year and he galvanised the whole sport as hundreds of thousands of native golfers flocked to watch the world's best player.

At that time, there were very few professional golfers in America and most of them were immigrants from Scotland, young men who were seeking a fortune in the new country. Both Vardon and Taylor were usually too good for all the American challengers – native-born players or ex-pats – and they climaxed the tour by finishing first and second in the US Open in October that year, a result that put American golf firmly in its place as a definite second to the best of British. Nevertheless, the tour led US golf through the next decade and the excited and innovative Americans did not play second fiddle for long. But to be the best, the US players – many of them still amateurs – had to play against and with the best. That meant travelling the length and breadth of the States and, most definitely, abroad.

Perhaps surprisingly, there was one American golfing pioneer in 1900 who had already won an historic international title before Vardon and Taylor had returned home to England. Thirty-four-year-old amateur Charles Sands – who only took up the sport five years earlier – won the gold medal for men's golf at the 1900 Olympic Games in Paris although the title was grander than the event with only just over a dozen competitors on a course built within a horse racing track in Compiègne, 30 miles north of the French capital. There was even a woman's golf event won by another American, 22-year-old art student Margaret Abbott (she was based in Paris at the time), who shot a 47 to win gold in a 9-hole competition she entered at the last minute along with her mother, who finished seventh. Such was the level of international golf at the time.

Back in Britain, of course, international golf meant a contest between English, Scottish, Welsh and Irish players while competition against continental European opposition was extremely rare. Of the countries across the English Channel, France was embracing golf as fast as anyone and staged the French Open for the first time in 1906, the year before the country's best golfer, Arnaud Massy, travelled to Royal Liverpool Golf Club in England to become the first non-British player to win the Open Championship. The British golf grandees actually had a chance to stage the first truly international golf tournament in the world (albeit, of course, for amateurs only) when London hosted the Olympic Games in 1908. Three courses in Kent were willing to stage the tournaments and both the Olympic organisers and the golfing media were excited about many countries being represented, especially after golf at the 1904 Games in St Louis, Missouri, had been contested only by Americans and a few Canadians. However, a letter from the International Olympic Committee to the R&A (who controlled the sport in Britain at the time) went unanswered and golf was dropped from the Games. Over a century later, it was restored to the schedule and will make its return as an Olympic sport at the 2016 Games in Rio de Janeiro.

In 1913, Vardon made his second tour of America and, by this time, the sport had grown globally. A couple of hundred courses, many built by ex-pat Brits, were now operating in countries like Argentina, India and Japan – but the sport was developing fastest in the US itself. From a few thousand players in 1900, when Vardon first visited, there were now an estimated 350,000 golfers across America playing on hundreds of courses, not a few dozen.

American golf celebrated a couple of significant landmarks in the run-up to Vardon's second tour. Firstly, in the summer of 1911, the 19-year-old Philadelphia-born Johnny McDermott became the first home-bred player to win the US Open, at Chicago Golf Club. Then just four days later over at Royal St George's on the Kent coast in south-east England, Chick Evans, one of the most acclaimed amateur players in America, tied 49th to become the first home-bred American golfer to complete all four rounds of the Open. This pair had put American golf on the map and their achievements gave great encouragement to the thousands of US players who were taking up the game every month in the belief that one day soon they could beat the best golfers from Britain. In addition, Evans also reached the quarter-finals of the [British] Amateur Championship that summer to reinforce the message that American golfers were now a force to be reckoned with.

Then in June 1913, McDermott (who had won the US Open for a second time in 1912) made his first trip across the Atlantic to play in the Open Championship at Royal Liverpool. He performed admirably, tying 5th, two shots behind fourth-placed Vardon and 11 shots behind the winner J.H. Taylor. In addition, his countryman Tom McNamara tied 25th on the first occasion there had been two American professionals in the field.

Vardon travelled back to America in September that year along with his great friend and fellow Jerseyman, Ted Ray, to play exhibition matches and climax the trip at the US Open at The Country Club in Brookline, Massachusetts – the same venue that hosted the Ryder Cup in 1999. By now, not only had the number of golfers in America grown, so had their expectations when taking on the mighty British. McDermott was expected to spearhead the native talent, but there was also a promising 20-year-old professional from New York named Walter Hagen. Local amateur Francis Ouimet, also aged just 20, actually lived next door to the course, but wasn't regarded as a serious challenger – until the event got under way.

While the British duo were heavy favourites, they had not reckoned on the dazzling play of Ouimet, whose sensational win – after an 18-hole playoff between himself, Vardon and Ray – became front-page news all over America. Later immortalised in Mark Frost's book *The Greatest Game Ever Played*, Ouimet's victory was as incredible as it was unlikely. The fresh-faced, untested amateur had never faced such esteemed golfing opposition. Hagen's tie for fourth place emphasised the new mood of American golf compared to when Vardon had squashed the local opposition 13 years earlier.

Needless to say, the sense of disbelief among Britain's golfing population was immense and one of the most interested of the country's golfers was 55-year-old Samuel Ryder who had taken up the sport by chance five years earlier because he needed more fresh air to recover from a bout of ill health. As soon as Ryder had taken up this new sport (he was a cricketer in his youth), it became his obsession. He quickly reached a single-figure handicap and became captain of the local Verulam Golf Club in St Albans in 1911. Reading the press reports about Vardon's shock defeat and the subsequent rise of American golf may well have given Ryder the idea that there should be more matches between British and American players. But less than a year after Ouimet had made so many sporting headlines, Britain was at war.

Four years of hostilities ended in 1918 and it was soon apparent to Ryder that a sea change had taken place in the sport: the young American upstart golfers, who had only been full of hope in 1914, could now claim to be the equal of the British. After all, while life in general and golf in particular throughout America were only marginally disrupted from 3,000 miles distance, the Great War had devastated British society. The era of golf's Great Triumvirate was over (neither Vardon, Taylor or Braid won a major title after World War I) and the next generation of British players either suffered four years of golfing idleness or lay dead on the battlefields of Belgium and France. Meanwhile, a group of young American pros, including Walter Hagen, were poised to lead the sport into the future.

Hagen had turned pro in 1912 having graduated from his job as a caddie at the Country Club of Rochester, New York. His tie for fourth behind Ouimet in the 1913 US Open was merely the precursor to him winning the title the following year. Then in 1920, with post-war Europe still struggling to return to normal, Hagen lay down the gauntlet to the entire European golfing establishment. He travelled across the Atlantic for the first time and won the French Open that summer, then played in his first Open Championship at Royal Cinque Ports. The 27-year-old may have only tied 53rd on the Kent links, but he knew America's time was coming because he was now one of the best players in the largest nation of golfers in the world, approaching two million participants.

Jim Barnes, an ex-pat Cornishman who had been playing in America for almost 15 years, was sixth in that 1920 Open Championship, helping to trigger renewed debate about the ability of golfers from the States throughout Britain's golf clubs. Samuel Ryder and his fellow members at Verulam may well have been among those wondering whether Britain or America was now golf's real powerhouse. However, Ryder's role in staging a country vs country team match that might settle the matter was far from fruition.

First rumblings of a contest

The earliest published information about a potential golf match between pros from Britain and America dates back to 1920, two years after the end of World War I and a time when the civilian populations of the two countries were happy to try new and inventive ideas. Many golf historians believe the president of the Inverness Club in Toledo, Ohio, Sylvanus P. Jermain, was one of the early initiators of the notion for such a contest. Both a successful businessman and a hugely important figure in US golf at the time, Jermain helped to persuade Vardon and Ray to travel to Inverness to play in the US Open in August of that year. Of course, Jermain was hoping for an American champion, but Ray defied a strong local field and pulled off a win, with Vardon tied second. While not the result he was hoping for, it was enough for the Ohioan to come up with another plan to provide American pros with an even better chance to prove their potential superiority – an international team contest.

Jermain was an extremely important figure in the history of American golf; he developed the first public golf course west of New York and also served as president of the Ohio Golf, Central States and Western Golf Associations in the early 1900s. He was a lifelong bachelor who devoted his life to the sport. In 1907, he even wrote a book called *American Code of Golf*, which aimed to simplify the rules of the sport that had been formulated across the Atlantic by the R&A (it was the first time anyone in America had dared to challenge the rule-makers from St Andrews). So, given his standing in the sport in America, he soon found supporters for his scheme of a team match.

The leading golf magazine of the day in America, *Golf Illustrated*, was quick to back him. The circulation manager, James Harnett, was especially taken with the idea. His job was to sell more copies and what better way to achieve that than by *Golf Illustrated* promoting a top quality international golf tournament? After all, the publishing industry was by now extremely powerful in sport and Harnett soon attracted the support of the PGA of America. The minutes of its annual general meeting in December 1920 state that the association would partly finance the trip.

Harnett knew the magazine's readers enjoyed the debate about the relative strengths of the two leading golf nations, especially after Ray's US Open victory, so stories about a possible match appeared in the magazine in late 1920. But the genius of Harnett's plan was that the magazine itself did not declare sponsorship, but instead asked readers to make small donations to help the newly-formed PGA of America (it had only been created in 1916) fund the expense of sending the pros on a month-long trip to Britain.

It might have seemed like a brilliantly innovative idea, but it was unsuccessful. Perhaps not surprisingly in this post-war period when, even in America, money was in relatively short supply, the fans could not see themselves supporting their pros. A small amount was raised, but in order not to lose face the PGA of America eventually voted to bridge the funding gap from its own bank account. It was then all systems go for a match in the summer of 1921 with around $10,000 available to send 10 pros to Gleneagles in Scotland. Also, there was a bonus for the American golfers: they could play in both the *Glasgow Herald 1,000 Guinea* tournament and the

Open Championship in St Andrews while in Britain in order to make the trip more worthwhile.

The only question that remained was who would represent the USA? Despite successes by players like Hagen and McDermott, not all the top American pros were home-bred players at this time. There were rumblings from some leading lights among the PGA of America that this contest would have no credibility if the US team was packed with British ex-pats. The question of the Americanisation of the 1921 team was very important to the status of the game throughout the States and to the retiring president of the PGA of America, John Mackie. He was one of the loudest voices in favour of native-born talent and even suggested that any ex-pat Brits on the team would simply be getting a free trip home. It was rather a petty argument, but it won the day. After much discussion, it was agreed that the American team would be made up of a mixture of home-bred players plus, if necessary, naturalised Americans or those who had lived in the States for at least five years and intended to become US citizens. Ex-pat Brits who clung to their connection with the motherland were not welcome.

The match was set for 6 June 1921 at the newly-opened King's Course at Gleneagles. The journey for the Americans was without incident until they arrived at the now-famous Gleneagles Hotel that, unfortunately, was unfinished (it did not open until 1924). The visitors had to stay in five railway carriages a few miles from the course and fetch and carry water for their washing. It was an inauspicious start, but the pioneer spirit prevailed and, in any case, a strong GB team was waiting, including The Great Triumvirate of Vardon, Taylor and Braid plus other top British golfers like George Duncan and Abe Mitchell.

By contrast, the American team could not boast such a long list of storied golfers. Walter Hagen – a loud supporter of this match from the very first murmurings – had made only one previous trip to play in Britain and had not reached the zenith of his career at this point. Three Scots-turned-Yanks, Jock Hutchison, Fred McLeod and Clarence Hackney, had some knowledge of golf in their homeland, but American captain Emmet French (a true home-bred player, born in Pennsylvania) had won only one US professional golf tournament and the extravagantly-named "Wild" Bill Mehlhorn from Illinois none at all to date. However, as they prepared to play, the American pros did gain some cheer from their amateur counterparts who had been able to set up a similar team match against British amateurs in May. The US amateurs, led by Bobby Jones, beat a team representing Great Britain and Ireland 9-3 at Royal Liverpool.

The defeat of the American pros in the match in Scotland was also by six points – 10½-4½ – and, although no disgrace, neither was it exactly a vindication of all the hope and hard work that had gone into sending the team 3,000 miles in the hope of establishing a glorious international legacy for professional golfers (annoyingly for them, the amateurs managed it – the Walker Cup began the following year).

Not only was the result from Gleneagles a disappointment, so was the reaction in Scotland. The *Glasgow Herald* publicised the contest extensively, yet the fans were largely indifferent to the team concept. Most of them preferred the subsequent *Glasgow Herald* event that was won by one of their own, George Duncan. To make matters worse, many of the pros in Scotland had been disdainful of the American challenge in the first place. They saw it as a rather ordinary exhibition match and one vocal pro from the area, Andrew Kirkaldy, previewed the event by saying it would be too one-sided for anyone to get excited about. "The Americans have nay a chance."

In addition, the young King's Course (laid out by Braid and just two years old) was not well received by the players; there were mutterings about the poor condition of the fairways and greens. Meanwhile, *The Times* golf correspondent, Bernard Darwin, bemoaned the state of the bunkers and the rest of his press colleagues were equally unimpressed. In fact, the whole affair fell rather flat and it was soon clear there would be no follow-up event the next year.

But while the professionals scratched their heads and wondered what went wrong, the amateurs' match in Hoylake was deemed a successful experiment and the following year the Walker Cup was established with a GB&I team invited to the National Golf Links of America on Long Island for the inaugural official event. It seems astonishing, nearly 100 years later, to think that an amateur sporting event could flourish while its pro equivalent withered. It felt like the pro team challenge match was the right idea at the wrong time, but there were several probable reasons.

Firstly, the two PGAs, which would act as organising bodies for any pro match of this kind, were still in their infancy – the British PGA was formed in 1901 and the PGA of America in 1916 – and, therefore, unable to underwrite the considerable funds that a team match required on an annual or even biennial basis. Not only were travel and accommodation costs required, but the visiting pros would miss a month's salary back at their clubs, hence the need for sponsorship by *Golf Illustrated* to send the American team over in 1921. By contrast, the top amateur golfers were often gentlemen of some standing with an income to support themselves or, if not, then their own individual patrons to fund such a trip.

Secondly, the professionals and amateur international teams were battling for the same support from both fans and sponsors. Being so close after the end of World War I, there was still not enough money around to finance every new idea and there were very few potential supporters at this time from the world of business who felt they might benefit from an international sporting contest of any sort.

Finally, the most obvious missing link was a figurehead. The amateur team competition had George Herbert Walker (hence the Walker Cup) as its driving force and in other sports there were similar men of vision and influence: Pierre de Coubertin is regarded as the father of the modern Olympic Games; Harvard graduate and future US Secretary of War, Dwight Davis, was an avid tennis player and had helped to create the Davis Cup back in 1900; and football administrator Jules Rimet soon had the World Cup football trophy named after him. The British and American golf professionals had just not found their man in 1921, but in five years time, they had.

The second attempt

At the start of 1926, five years after the Gleneagles match, the old idea of an international team challenge match for pro golfers was re-cycled. In the intervening years, individual pro golfers had begun travelling to foreign countries on a more regular basis. Hagen (twice) and Barnes (once) had won the Open Championship on visits to Britain; golfers from countries including South Africa, Australia, France, Spain and Argentina had all played for the claret jug; and British pros like Duncan and Mitchell had been frequent visitors to America since 1921. So the concept of international golf competition was no longer a rarity.

In addition to the developments in the pro game, the Walker Cup had been up and running successfully since 1922 with both Britain and America taking turns as hosts. So it was high time for the professionals to return to the same idea and by now it had become a question of when a pro team challenge match would take place rather than if.

The obvious problems were fourfold and very much the same as they had been for the match at Gleneagles in 1921: timing, funding, team selection and finding a co-operative venue. The two PGAs were now better organised and their members showed a growing desire for the match, but what they most needed was a benefactor and there were not many of them around.

Nevertheless, there were moves afoot and in March 1926 the British PGA received a letter from St George's Hill Golf Club in Surrey "setting out the conditions of a match to be played against a team of four American professionals selected by Walter Hagen and asking for approval of same also requesting the Association to select the British team and to fix a date for playing the match", according to the association's committee minutes. In addition, the PGA was approached by *Car & Golf* magazine to offer a trophy and prize money for such a match, while Stoke Poges Golf Club in Buckinghamshire wanted to stage a Britain vs America team match but only if it was to be watched exclusively by their own members and guests.

The PGA offered dates in early June to St George's Hill for the planned two-day match that would allow time for the Americans to play in the Open Championship towards the end of the month. The other two offers by the magazine and Stoke Poges were dismissed. There was also speculation in the press that two other courses – Wentworth in Surrey and Waterloo GC near London – were possible venues (also offering to host the match for free with any gate money going to the PGA), while *Golf Monthly* magazine was already speculating about a series of matches and hoping that money for a return fixture in America "might be largely raised from the money drawn at the gates of this match". British golf was clearly excited.

Over in America, however, there was not quite universal support for the match. There had been no formal support from the PGA of America (still a young organisation only exactly a decade old and with just 1,548 members) and no correspondence between that association and its British counterpart because both groups were still maturing (the British PGA had celebrated its 25th anniversary in 1926 and could still only boast around 900 members). The power of the two PGAs was still in the future, so this attempt at an international pro team match was largely player-driven, in fact more accurately, one-player-driven.

Hagen had travelled over to Britain for the Open Championship four of the previous five years and the topic would have been openly discussed by him, but he did not care much for the politics of any association. Hagen was a wealthy man by this time (mostly from exhibition matches for which he could earn as much as $10,000) and certainly the shining light of American professional golf (he had already won seven majors which was as many as Vardon). Hagen's status in the American game meant he could ride roughshod over any dissent, problems with money or potential internal politics. Once it was clear that enough of his colleagues wanted to re-create the match, and after learning that the British PGA was even going to select a GB squad, Hagen decided to increase his team from four to 10 and got his men ready.

With just a few weeks to go, the *Daily Express* reported that Hagen would be bringing a strong group of players to Britain with foursomes on the opening day followed by 10 singles on the second. The newly-opened Wentworth club was finally chosen as host venue and the course owners would use the contest as a marketing tool to attract members. It was all systems go.

However, despite the best possible intentions, the match suffered from both bad luck and bad planning. Firstly, the General Strike of 1926 began on 4 May, just before the Americans were due to set sail. The industrial action was aimed at bringing the whole of Britain to a standstill and, given the potential widespread chaos, four of the US team decided not to travel.

Suddenly there was uncertainty that the Americans would be able to field a large enough team – eight was the absolute minimum because it at least had to match the Walker Cup – let alone how the General Strike would impact such a match. The media on both sides of the Atlantic continued its backing as the match date approached, but it was now hard to convince the public that "the Walker Cup for the pros" had not turned into an informal pre-Open Championship exhibition rather than the beginning of a great golfing spectacle.

The 10-man American team that eventually turned up at Wentworth was the weak link for the credibility of the contest. It was led by Hagen but contained a mixture of non-naturalised ex-pats (like Barnes) and home-bred players plus an Australian, Joe Kirkwood, who was best known as a trick-shot specialist rather than a tournament player. The British team was much stronger, led by three Open champions – Ray, Duncan and Arthur Havers. Cancelling altogether must have been an option, yet by the time the strike ended on 13 May, the players had arrived from the States and common sense prevailed; everyone made the best of a bad job.

Despite all the glitches, crowds in their thousands lined the fairways for the match because, after all, this was still the most star-packed international pro team contest that had ever been staged anywhere in the world. If it was Britain vs a hotchpotch American team rather than the real thing, then so be it. However, there was no hiding behind the one-sided result: a 13½-1½ win for GB. This had hardly been a contest to set the pulses racing, nor was it a reflection of the relative strengths of the two golfing nations.

The American players – particularly Hagen – were unhappy they had taken such a beating; all their reputations were at stake here. However, three weeks later at the Open Championship a record number of 11 US golfers teed off in the 116-strong field at Royal Lytham & St Annes along with a handful of Argentinians, Australians, French and Irish. In the end, the championship was dominated by Americans like never before – they filled seven of the top 10 places with the world's No 1 amateur Bobby Jones as the champion and two of the professional team from Wentworth – Al Watrous and Hagen – second and third.

Perhaps the Americans' performance at Lytham helped keep the idea of an international team match on the agenda because while the British may have gloated at Wentworth, they were embarrassed in Lancashire. A third attempt to decide which of the world's two golfing nations was the strongest needed to be made and it could not wait another five years.

The emergence of Samuel Ryder

The international team challenge match at Wentworth between GB and the US would eventually enter the record books as an unofficial contest, an interesting exhibition just like the one in 1921, but nothing more. But without the 1926 contest, the future of this match would have looked very different because it was then that Samuel Ryder emerged as a key figure. However, exactly how Ryder came to be at Wentworth, what he said or did to align himself so closely to the future of the tournament, and what else happened around him are the topics of debate for historians and golf fans. There are no definitive records of what went on before, during or immediately after the Wentworth event, and this has led to a certain amount of conjecture, even mythology. As is often the case with important historical events, the absolute truth will never be fully known because it died with the man himself. But time can offer a fresh perspective.

It is worth taking a few steps back from Wentworth in 1926 to see what was happening to golf in both Britain and America. There is little doubt that for the first two decades of the 20th century both the golfers and the administrators in Britain and America were trying desperately to grow the sport. In the post-World War I era, the professional golfer was fighting for his rights and his status in society just like every other working man. Individual players – like Harry Vardon and, later, Walter Hagen – crossed oceans and won titles with the support of sponsors, but to organise an official team match between Britain and America would more planning and lots of money (approximately £3,000 for the British and $10,000 for the Americans).

The two PGAs had their fingers burned in 1921 when the Gleneagles match failed to spark enough interest, yet the following year, the Walker Cup got officially started – a galling development for the pros. Although PGA memberships on both sides of the ocean were growing steadily, the professional player's status was still submerged under the weight of society's customs. In 1925 when pros were first allowed into the clubhouse at Prestwick GC alone – that is without being accompanied by a member – it was a major social breakthrough. Plus it was a sign that the international pro team match could now happen.

Around this time, Samuel Ryder had become recognised as a pioneer in terms of supporting golf. He had moved south from Manchester in the late 1890s and set up his seed company in St Albans, Hertfordshire. The company sold penny packets of seeds, an innovation that proved hugely popular and made Ryder a great deal of money.

Ryder was a major employer in St Albans and running a successful business provided Samuel with a standing in the community that enabled him to become mayor of the town in 1906. However, two years later (around the time of his 50th birthday) came his eureka moment when he took up golf as a counter to his ill health and promptly fell in love with the game. But Ryder was not a man to indulge his own pleasure of the sport and not give something back. In fact, philanthropy was a way of life for him. In St Albans, he supported the World War I effort and various city charities either for the poor and the elderly. Soon he turned his attention to the professional golfer.

One of Ryder's concerns about the sport was how the pros were undervalued. He realised that these were men of great skill and dedication, yet in the Britain of the 1920s they were treated more like working-class lackeys, manservants to the upper-class members of the country's golf clubs. He was first made fully aware of the pros' problems at the beginning of the 1920s on one of his annual holidays to Weymouth in Dorset. There he regularly met the talented Whitcombe brothers, Ernest, Charles and Reg. During many rounds with the brothers at Came Down Golf Club, Ryder heard their rather sad story. A lack of money was preventing them from playing in all the top tournaments, sometimes they even missed the Open Championship. Ernest was particularly passionate about his situation and, more particularly, that the rival American players seemed much better funded. "The Americans come over here smartly dressed," he said, "and backed by wealthy supporters. The Britisher *(sic)* has a poor chance compared to that."

Ryder then made two key moves to help the British pro. Firstly, he began to sponsor pro tournaments, something normally done in that era by newspapers or club and ball manufacturers rather than elderly businessmen. The Heath and Heather tournament (named after Ryder's herb company that he set up with his brother James rather than the seed firm) was first staged in July 1923 and attracted most of the best pros in the country, including six Open champions. The event set high standards with prize money (the winner received £50 at a time when the Open Champion himself was only given £75) and even paid every entrant £5 appearance money, something that was unheard of at the time. Ryder would sponsor as many as 17 similar tournaments, many at Verulam Golf Club in St Albans where he would be captain on three occasions.

Secondly, he appointed Abe Mitchell as his personal coach in October 1925. The two men had become good friends and Ryder paid Mitchell £1,000 per year in salary and expenses (a princely sum) plus the golfer was lodged for free in a house within walking distance of Verulam. With this money, Mitchell was free to practice as much as he could because Ryder – himself a great patriot – believed that, with proper financial support, this was the man to rival the coming generation of great American golfers and eventually win the Open.

Both these moves brought Ryder into the family of professional golf very quickly. The current chief executive of the British PGA, Sandy Jones (himself a historian of the Cup), believes Ryder became a fan of all the great players. "He was enthralled by the pros. The game of golf shared his principles: honesty, integrity, fairness, fair play, respect for your opponent, all the things he admired. He was a church leader with strong beliefs, so all his principles in life led him to love golf and to want to give something to the sport." Jones also understands that golf pros of every era have known how to make friends with their potential patrons, and the leading figures of the British PGA back in the 1920s expressed their appreciation of Ryder's financial commitment by playing in his tournaments.

Of course, Ryder would have talked to Mitchell as well the likes of J.H. Taylor, George Duncan and other leading figures in the professional game at that time about his tournament ideas. Facing off against the Americans in another match like the one in 1921 would certainly have been a topic of conversation. British and American pros had challenged each other in occasional fourball matches since then, but these were small, isolated events and something larger on the scale of the Walker Cup was needed. These discussions even led to a report in Ryder's local newspaper, the *Herts Advertiser*, that "Heath and Heather (are) contemplating challenging the Americans to a match". Everyone agreed that the professional sport needed the international challenge match, but why did it begin in 1927 and why was Samuel Ryder the eventual catalyst?

Given his standing within British golf (he was actually captain of Verulam again in 1926), Ryder may well have attended Wentworth for the ill-fated second attempt at the international match as a guest of Mitchell and the PGA. Unfortunately, Ryder made no notes of what happened there, so the most noted eye-witness at the Surrey club was his youngest daughter Joan who attended the match with her father and has spoken and written extensively about what she remembers of the events.

Just 22 at the time, Joan recalled that Ryder and several players at Wentworth discussed how the team matches could take place whenever the Americans travelled to Britain for the Open Championship and be followed by "a small, friendly lunch party". In one newspaper article many years later, she also recorded how it was her father's wish that the match should promote goodwill between the players, hence his offer of prize money, the celebration party and also the trophy. "Everyone was taken with the offer," she said, "and we settled down to the champagne and lots of grand talk – all of us making new friends." But the question remains: was the purpose of Ryder's attendance merely as a casual observer or was it part of a grand plan to create a contest to which he could give his name?

There were certainly press reports about Ryder's desire for the match. *The Times*, early in 1926, discussed the strong possibility of the team challenge and announced Ryder's intended involvement, while *Golf Monthly* reported the following statement in the May edition: "Mr Ryder of St Albans, who has done much to further the interests of professional golfers during the last few years, has presented a valuable trophy for a contest between the two nations (Great Britain and America)." But Sandy Jones is one person who questions the factual nature of these reports. "It was gossip that was printed in the newspapers. There would have been all kinds of discussion and various people talking to the press. But if Ryder had wanted 1926 to be 'his match' then he would have made it happen."

Ryder's conversations with the Whitcombes and his support of the PGA and Mitchell were all about finding ways for British pro golfers to beat the Americans, but Jones believes the match idea was only percolating in Ryder's brain before he arrived at Wentworth. After all, there were many other parties at work on the same idea, notably St George's Hill and Stoke Poges Golf Clubs. "Perhaps 1926 was not the right moment," says Jones. "There is enough evidence to say the PGA and the leading players were in the middle of this and bringing Sam Ryder along with them. They felt the right time to start the match was 1927 and the right place was America. After all, we were still building the PGA here and wanted to engage with the Americans."

However, the urban myth about Ryder's Wentworth actions and conversations are quite specific. They revolve around the seed merchant attending a post-match gathering where he noticed the players from the two teams not mixing together as much as he had expected. He is believed to have casually announced over a cup of tea with a few of the combatants that "we must do this again" whereupon, the pros within earshot (including, it is said, Mitchell, Duncan and Hagen) declared that what they needed was a trophy to play for and asked him to provide it. The story then goes on that Ryder quickly agreed and also offered £5 per man as prize money and a celebration party afterwards of champagne and chicken sandwiches. At that moment the Ryder Cup, it has been claimed, was born, as if by a spontaneous impulsive act. It is a delightful story, worthy of any Hollywood film script, but it is flawed.

So what is the most likely truth? Well, Samuel Ryder was creating a win-win situation both for his patronage plans for pro golfers and publicity for his business. He wanted to help others – including the professionals – but he also had a commitment to his staff in St Albans, both those at the seed firm and the Heath & Heather herb company. The tournaments that he organised at Verulam helped fund the pros, but crucially assisted in publicising his herb business as well. An international team challenge would bring him and his company even more headlines and newspaper column inches. Plus, his conceptual plans for a match against the Americans were in tune with what so many other parties were considering and the press reports prior to the 1926 match at Wentworth were probably as much conjecture as they were hard news. A challenge match of some kind between the two great golfing nations was going to happen this year and the press latched on to similar thoughts by the highly regarded Ryder.

It is highly possible then that Ryder used Wentworth as a talking shop to help him make a final decision. After all, this was the perfect moment for discussion with the leading players from both countries and many committee members of the British PGA in attendance. Ryder may have had the idea of a small contribution to the contest when it was formalised, such as hosting the after-match party, but if he had at one time been prepared to hand over a trophy at Wentworth, his presence there would have been more to the fore. No PGA committee minutes mention Ryder's name before the Wentworth match was played and none of Wentworth's own records mention him at all as being involved. The seed merchant was a wise man, able to engage with all kinds of people, and understood the mind of the pro golfer as well as enjoying his company. It is highly unlikely that Wentworth was ever in his thoughts as the venue of the first Ryder Cup and the seemingly casual conversation in the bar about "we must do this again" followed by the spontaneous offer of a trophy and some money for a party do not tally with Ryder's character and general business acumen.

Instead, Samuel Ryder probably had the express intention of helping set up a match in 1927 once the conversations at Wentworth were undertaken. He probably just wanted to get confirmation that he was the right man at the right time to become the patron of the international challenge. What better way than gathering the opinions of all the key stakeholders at a single event? That means any theory about the Cup actually being manufactured in time for Wentworth and then being withdrawn by James Ryder because of the weak American line-up are most likely inaccurate or mischievious. Also Joan Ryder's recollections are somewhat rose-tinted and probably recall only a fraction of the words spoken by her father. Samuel would have had many conversations over the two days of the match and lots of them could well have been in private, out of his 22-year-old daughter's earshot. Ryder was accomplished on many fronts, including negotiating business away from the eyes and ears of others.

There are actual facts that support the 1927 match as Ryder's choice for the inaugural event in his name. Firstly, it was only in July 1926, a month after Wentworth, that the businessman formally met with the British PGA committee. He attended an association committee meeting that month and was thanked for "generously (offering) to provide a Cup for competition at an annual International Match". Ryder told the gathering that the PGA should be in charge of the match and the minutes of the meeting state that he had "no conditions whatever to impose but pointed out that financing a match of this description might present difficulties but that he would be only too pleased to subscribe towards this".

Secondly, Ryder attended that meeting along with George Philpott, editor of the UK publication *Golf Illustrated* (the same title as the publication in America but unconnected). Philpott said the magazine had "already announced their intention of raising a fund for the purpose of sending players to America to compete in the (US) Open Championship". The magazine was happy that their idea be enlarged so the players could play in both the Open and the international match in America, and estimated that £3,000 would be needed, an amount that should include "a substantial balance for a personal fee to each player". It is a good guess that Ryder and Philpott were together at the meeting because they shared the same views on the match and surely would have discussed all this at Wentworth a few weeks earlier.

Finally, the PGA minutes record incontrovertible answers about the question of where and when the match should take place – "alternately in America and in this country, the first match for the Ryder Cup to be played in the first named country next year". Why the Americans as the hosts and not the British who were setting up the contest? And would Ryder not want to present the trophy at the first match on home turf? Well, it was most likely felt that after two attempts in Britain, the Americans deserved a chance to stage the contest, while Philpott's original idea was to send golfers to the US Open anyway, so that fitted in neatly. Soon afterwards, Ryder instructed his own lawyer in St Albans (at his own cost) to draw up a document, to be known as a deed of trust, with the British PGA to set out the rules and regulations for the match. The deed ensured that the integrity of the contest would be maintained because Ryder (or the subsequent generations of his family) would have to agree to any major changes in protocol or rules.

The deed was eventually signed on 25 July 1927, a full year after Ryder's original meeting with the PGA committee, further indication that the match in 1926 was never intended to be official – there had been no such discussion with Wentworth's owners to agree a contract. The Surrey club had merely been the venue used by Ryder to discuss the match idea with all the relevant parties. The meeting with the PGA then came quickly afterwards and the timetable for his version of the third attempt at an international challenge match was underway.

Just like George Herbert Walker had been in 1922 for the amateur match that bears his name, Samuel Ryder was the right man as well as the best man to come along at the correct time for the international challenge between the pros. Ryder was the glue that held together all the various elements that were needed to ensure the contest would launch in 1927 with the best chance of long-term success.

A Ryder Cup without Samuel?

It is safe to say that an officially-recognised match between British and American professional golfers would have taken place during the late 1920s or early 1930s even without Samuel Ryder's support. There were other men able to step into Ryder's shoes. The most obvious one was Sylvanus P. Jermain.

A serial entrepreneur, Jermain was like Ryder in many ways, particularly in how much he cared about the golf professionals. When the 1920 US Open came to his Inverness Club in Toledo, Ohio, the businessman spoke out against the custom of the day and insisted that the pros were welcomed into the clubhouse, something that would not happen in Britain for another five years. Not only that, but the Inverness members were persuaded by Jermain to find accommodation for the players and also offer their cars for transport during the tournament. Ryder would have admired all these things, while the American players acknowledged Jermain's actions and the members' generosity by buying the club a grandfather clock as a thank-you. The clock still stands in the clubhouse lobby to this day.

Meanwhile, PGA of America president from 1921-26 George Sargent lauded Jermain's role as an early advocator of the international contest. He wrote in an issue of the association's magazine: "The credit for the idea (of an international golf team challenge match) should go to Sylvanus P. Jermain. I remember he suggested the scheme to me and I tried to put it across (at first) without success."

That conversation would have taken place some time after the 1920 Open, when Jermain also approached a fellow member of the Inverness Club to act as a patron for a planned US-GB match. Walter L. Ross, president of Nickel Plate Railroad in Cleveland at the time and a man of considerable wealth and influence, took Jermain's request for help very seriously. At one stage, he was willing to fund the manufacture of "a handsome trophy".

Neither Jermain's nor Ross's involvement were widely chronicled at the time and it is uncertain what happened to the conversations about the match between 1921 and 1926. However, another letter from Jermain printed by the PGA of America said that Ross "withdrew (his offer of a trophy) in favor *(sic)* of Mr Ryder…(which) harmonized *(sic)* all international differences".

Nevertheless, if Jermain had been able to establish a greater involvement then either the first or second unsuccessful attempts to get the international challenge series started in 1921 and 1926 would actually have been official. George Sargent surmised later: "Had (the original plan by Jermain) gone through, then the Ryder Cup would probably today be named for an American."

The possibility of British and American pros playing for either the Jermain Cup or the Ross Trophy was therefore a real option at one stage. What ultimately stopped their plans for involvement is unknown, although it was highly unlikely to be money given Ross's position in the railroad industry. Perhaps the two men needed more support from a US player like Hagen or maybe the PGA of America (formed only in 1916) was too young an organisation to latch on to the vision of the match. Whatever, a slightly firmer push from the Americans could easily have pre-empted Ryder's own links with the putative contest.

Just as an American came close to gifting his name to the team event, then there were also several men in Britain who tried to step forward as the event's key patron. By 1926 there was clearly a groundswell of energy for the match and clubs were offering to host the event including Wentworth, St George's Hill and Stoke Poges. All three potential hosts had their own influential, wealthy members who could have assumed Ryder's eventual role, but Wentworth emerged as the leader because the man who owned the Surrey estate had a long-term plan.

W.G. Tarrant was a master builder who had been developing the Wentworth Estate since 1912. He was also an innovative and forward-thinking man whose idea was to build huge, impressive homes on the estate for the growing middle classes who were making their fortunes in London, yet wanted a more palatial home outside the smoky city. With the international match having been secured for his golf course, Tarrant was likely to have realised that this could become a regular – even annual – affair because the American golfers in particular were visiting Britain more often, and especially for the Open Championship each summer. No doubt Tarrant would have discussed this with key people at his club and senior members of the PGA during the match. It would be no surprise then that three weeks later on 26 June the owner of the estate and his board of directors met and decided formally to offer the British PGA a cup for similar contests in the future. Naturally, Tarrant wanted the trophy to have a connection to his club, so he suggested 'The Wentworth Challenge Cup' as its name. The Wentworth board minutes state that a letter from the club would make the offer "without any condition as to where the match should be played". The board also stated that the club members would be asked to subscribe to pay for the cup.

As it was, the PGA declined the offer in a letter dated 20 July (the day after the PGA's first meeting with Ryder), which arrived in time for the Wentworth board meeting at the end of August. According to the Wentworth board meeting minutes, the PGA wanted to keep full control of the event and probably felt that Ryder (who also declared no pre-conditions) was the best person to work with to achieve that. It can perhaps also be assumed that Samuel Ryder's connection to the PGA – probably via Mitchell – was stronger than Tarrant's through former Open champion Duncan who had become the Wentworth club professional that year.

So it is perhaps fair to say that there would have been an international pro golf match without Samuel Ryder, but that his drive and personality helped give it the kind of start that the other two attempts never achieved.

However, one final question remains unresolved: the matter of the trophy. The association's letter to the Wentworth board stated that "a prior offer [for a suitable trophy] from a private individual had already been accepted". So, Tarrant either did not know this or chose to offer a trophy anyway. Either way, his hopes of a Wentworth Challenge Cup were over.

This letter also helps dispel another myth about the Ryder Cup: that the trophy was ready for the Wentworth match because that was supposed to be an official contest (a theory based on a few press reports that suggested that Ryder's support of the match was well advanced by the time of the famous Wentworth conversation.).

However, the PGA's words about the "prior offer" do not say that Ryder's trophy was in their possession and certainly not that it was already manufactured and available. And, besides, Ryder and the PGA only met *after* Wentworth (according to the committee minutes), so why would the trophy have already been ordered before then? Also, there were no official-sounding statements from Ryder before he sat down with the PGA nor are there records of a purchase order, for example, from the trophy makers or even a suggestion from Wentworth that the seed merchant had anything to do with their match or any trophy (hence their own offer). So, even those historians who point to the 1926 hallmark on the trophy as proof that Mr Ryder ordered it in readiness for Wentworth are being misled: the hallmark indicates when the trophy manufacture was carried out, not the delivery of the finished product.

The most likely interpretation of all this evidence is that Samuel Ryder's commitment to providing the trophy occurred at the July meeting with the PGA. Plus, it was probably an off-the-shelf design already available to any customer (there is even talk of a picture of a silver version in a Mappin & Webb catalogue of the time) and so would be ready, in gold, within a few months after being ordered, rather than having to go through an elaborate and long-winded period of design, approval and manufacture (such a process might have endangered the cup even being ready for the June 1927 match in Massachusetts). This in turn supports the more logical theory that Ryder believed 1927 was the best year to start the series of matches and that the Wentworth event was a springboard to that end rather than a missed opportunity.

Sadly, one result of this sequence of events is that another piece of Ryder Cup folklore is under threat: that the figure of the golfer on top of the trophy lid is Samuel Ryder's friend and tutor Abe Mitchell. If Ryder had asked for the entire trophy (or even the lid) to be custom-made, then the Mitchell story might well be true. But if 1927 really was the date on Samuel Ryder's mind for the inaugural contest, then it tends to point to the design already existing. Plus, there is no actual evidence to support the claims for Mitchell's place of prominence on the top of the trophy. As a Hollywood storyline, to have Samuel Ryder's great friend as the model for the trophy golfer is faultless, but the cold reality is probably the more prosaic version of events. Or maybe it is best that no one still knows the truth for sure.

The First Ryder Cup

Given all the faults of the previous two attempts at an international team match,the 1927 Ryder Cup proved to be much better organised. The date was set early – it would take place on 3-4 June – and the venue was the prestigious Worcester Country Club in Massachusetts, a recent US Open venue. Teams would consist of eight players plus a captain and the format would be foursomes on day one (four of them) and singles on day two (eight of them). The winning team would need 6½ points. Both PGAs were heavily involved and Samuel Ryder helped draw up an agreement for the contest (the deed of trust) along with the British association which accepted the fact that it was Britain's turn to raise the money to send their players rather than the Americans'.

Golf Illustrated editor George Philpott had told the PGA committee back in July 1926 that the magazine would assist with finances and "do anything in their power to obtain this (money)". He also stated that he was confident the money could be raised and launched an appeal to the 1,750 clubs in Britain asking each of them to donate. Philpott believed this match was important for the prestige of the nation as well as its golfers who wanted to "avenge the defeats which have been administered by American pros while visiting our shores in search of Open Championship honours". To show his support, Samuel Ryder guaranteed £100 to help start the ball rolling.

It was not a new idea to appeal to the great and the good of the golfing population of a country (the American *Golf Illustrated* had tried it in 1921), but this attempt was not an immediate success either. Philpott was not afraid to show what he felt about the lack of largesse available for his country's golfers. "It is a deplorable reflection on the attitude of the average golfer towards the game," he said in the pages of his magazine. "We fear [the Ryder Cup] must be held to afford definite evidence that the oft-repeated slur against the pastime, that most of its players are selfish, possesses a good deal of truth."

What the editor perhaps ignored was that these were straitened financial times (the European economy was still depressed even this long after World War I). Perhaps a more subtle reason was that there was some resentment among golf club members (all amateur players themselves and almost all of a middle- or upper-class social standing) funding a team of working-class professionals. In a letter to Philpott's magazine, one reader said he would "no more send a professional player to America to play golf than I would send my chimney sweep". Not everyone shared Samuel Ryder's admiration of golf professionals and Britain's amateur golfers would probably rather have funded the Walker Cup team. In the end, only 216 (one in eight) of golf clubs in Britain answered the call to fund the pro team and the fund reached only around £2,700, made up of £5 and £10 contributions. It was left to *Golf Illustrated* and Ryder to make up the difference.

As financier of the team, Philpott was appointed manager and held a practice session for the players at Verulam – Ryder's home club – during May. Soon afterwards, the small party made ready to embark on the *SS Aquitania* ocean liner at Southampton for a six-day sea journey. Ryder had already decided not to travel, then at the very last minute Mitchell (who had been chosen as team captain) fell ill with appendicitis and had to withdraw. The team was waved off by Ryder on 21 May and would not return until the end of July. It was not an auspicious start.

The British pros had been given a month off from their golf club employers, but it would be unpaid leave of absence; the funds from the appeal would pay the players' salaries while they were away. However, there were some add-on benefits for the players. Even in those early days of the Cup, there was great prestige attached to representing one's country and there were a few commercial sponsors willing to show tangible support. They included Izod of London, who provided shirts with a rampant red lion on the left breast; Battersby, also of London, who gave soft, felt "Varsonian" style hats; while a third unknown company provided golf shoes and three players used a new brand of aluminium putter.

The the PGA of America put on quite a show for their visitors including a whirlwind welcome in New York with various receptions and society events. The only piece of bad luck was that the entire nation was transfixed by something else – Charles Lindbergh's recent solo flight across the Atlantic. Every American was agog at this feat of derring-do rather than the country's first significant international sporting attack on the British Empire.

The GB team's arrival, therefore, was somewhat muted while a very rough sea left the British looking a little green around the gills. Then they were also green with envy at the lifestyle of Americans in general and their golf professionals in particular. Arthur Havers commented on the remarkable kindness of his hosts, the luxuriousness of all the American golf clubs and how this compared to the "rundown and shabby" British counterparts. Nevertheless, new captain Ted Ray and his men were seen as the favourites.

Then, on the very eve of the match, the PGA of America added a last-minute piece of controversy by announcing four changes to what the Brits had thought of as the rules of combat. Firstly, the Americans wanted fourball matches rather than foursomes; secondly, the fourball matches would count for two points instead of one; thirdly, no match could end with a half after the full 36 holes, but instead should be resolved by sudden-death holes; and fourthly, teams could choose a substitute player if necessary on day two for the singles. These rules demands might have been relatively slight, but they annoyed the British team who saw no need for changes as the agreement was to play the match under the same format as the tried-and-tested Walker Cup. In the end, only the second-day-substitute rule change was allowed. But with the GB team unnerved and unwell (illness prevented matchplay specialist George Gadd from playing in either day's matches), it was no surprise that the home team were victorious 9½-2½.

Immediately the trophy was awarded, the excuses followed from the British contingent. Though magnanimous in defeat, the visitors had to come up with a reason for taking such a drubbing. George Philpott complained that all the socialising had been a form of gamesmanship, deliberately keeping his players tired and listless. Some press observers commented that American putting was "manifestly superior" indicated by the size of some of the losses by scores like 8&6 or 8&7. *Golf Monthly* described the loss as "disastrous", while much of the British national press chose another response – they uniformly either ignored the match altogether or dismissed the loss as a product of unfamiliar conditions. Their reaction seemed to say that there was no way that American golfers were better than British golfers; those who spread the game around the world were still its rulers.

However, anyone who had looked a little closer at the two teams would see the underlying story: the old had been swept away by the new. The ages of Britain's team said a great deal: their two best players were Ray, aged 49 and Duncan, 44, while most of the others were at least in their thirties. For the Americans, Hagen was the old man at 35; all his teammates were in their 20s with Gene Sarazen the youngest at 25. So the future of golf resided in America, only the British were too proud to see it. Actually a win for the US team was probably the best result for the first Ryder Cup because Britain's pride had been so wounded that a return match – indeed, a sequences of matches – was now virtually guaranteed.

The first re-birth

There might have been limited drama in the inaugural Ryder Cup match, but the biennial contests grew in stature with each staging as both teams took turns in winning. However, the Cup was threatened again when World War II caused the late abandonment of the 1939 match just a few weeks before it was due to be staged in Ponte Vedra, Florida.

The US team members were particularly disappointed because they had just managed their first victory on British soil in 1937 and wanted to underline their dominance with another victory in the seventh match. The US team had already been announced and plans drawn up for the GB team to travel when Commander Charles Roe, secretary of the British PGA, wrote a letter to his American counterpart just after war broke out and made a jovial and optimistic promise: "When we have settled our differences and peace reigns, we will see that our team comes across to remove the Ryder Cup from your safekeeping." He was, of course, unable to know how long it might be before the next match, or in what state the game of golf would be on either side of the Atlantic by then.

Nevertheless, the Americans found a way to keep the flame of the Ryder Cup burning. In the early years of the war, when the US was a neutral observer, there were actually Ryder Cup teams selected by the PGA of America and those golfers then played exhibition matches against a group of challengers (led by the likes of Bobby Jones or Gene Sarazen) to raise money for the American Red Cross. The mock Ryder Cup matches were just one indication that golf in America was relatively unhindered during World War II. The PGA Tour continued uninterrupted until 1942 (the year America finally entered the conflict) and, while the major tournaments like the US Open were cancelled from that year on, there were still plenty of other pro events. In fact, one of US golf's all-time greats Byron Nelson set two remarkable records during wartime: he won 11 consecutive PGA Tour titles and 18 in total in 1945, marks that have never been broken. However, when the world started to return to normal after the Japanese surrender in August of that year, while many strokeplay tournaments re-started with relative ease, the Ryder Cup was going to need some help. All the momentum for the event had been lost and overcome by economic and logistical problems. There was certainly little money in the British PGA's kitty after six years of inactivity and the Cup's patron, Samuel Ryder, had died in 1936, so that particular source of advice and money was no more. Two leading players at the time, Sarazen and Britain's Max Faulkner summed up the situation years later. Sarazen said he was unconvinced about the Cup's future: "It didn't look good. Who knew what would happen, what shape everyone was in? There was little to be sure about." Faulkner concurred: "We hadn't forgotten about the Ryder Cup, but when the war ended, that didn't mean the competition would be on again. [After the war] it looked rather bleak." Perhaps the Ryder Cup would just become a golfing footnote.

The green shoots of recovery were seen in the summer of 1946 when the Open Championship was staged again, fittingly at the home of golf, St Andrews. The only three Americans to travel over for the event (Sam Snead, Johnny Bulla and Lawson Little) finished first, tied second and 10th. Snead's win was significant because, for the first time, America held every professional golf title worth having – the Open, the US Open, which also re-started that same year (Lew Worsham triumphed at the St Louis Country Club), the Ryder Cup from 1937 and also the Masters and PGA Championship (two tournaments where the fields were 99% Americans anyway).

British golf in the immediate post-war years reflected the whole country: it was full of doom and gloom. With food and fuel rationing in place, with money and resources scarce, a few individual players might be slowly returning to their playing best, but the idea of sending a fully-funded team of professionals and officials on a mission to America to contest the Ryder Cup was out of the question. After all, even the first few Ryder Cup trips 20 years earlier had been staged on a shoestring and now, with a nationwide rebuilding programme to support and rationing to overcome, the task seemed too great. The Cup tradition was in danger of collapsing. Then along came the next noteworthy man in the history of the contest, the Oregon fruit packer, canner and distributor Robert A. Hudson.

From six thousand miles away on the far off coast of north-west America, Bob Hudson heard the plea for Ryder Cup funding and stepped up to the plate. Hudson had always been a driven individual, especially from the age of 14 when he began working in a local grocery store. He was promoted to store manager at just 19 and built his empire from there. He became an avid golfer and, in later life, would be seen almost every Thursday at Portland Golf Club where he played with his company managers. The 60-year-old was a late convert to the professional game of golf, claiming that he only saw his first pro event in 1944. But that did not stop him from almost immediately becoming a significant sponsor of tournaments at Portland where he was a member. He explained to his friends that while other men invested in yachts or baseball teams, he was happier becoming a patron of golf matches, so he offered to sponsor the entire 1947 Ryder Cup at his beloved home club.

In normal circumstances, the idea of the GB team travelling 6,000 miles to one of the furthest corners of America to contest the Ryder Cup would have been preposterous (the journey time alone by sea and air was prohibitive), but the fact was that the British could not raise £3,000 or more even for a trip to the east coast, so they had no alternative but to agree to Hudson's plan, something the PGA of America were only too glad to accept as well.

Hudson's largesse started with him paying for tickets for the British party on a trans-Atlantic liner, the *Queen Mary*, and then hosting the visiting team when they disembarked in New York with a lavish dinner at the Waldorf Astoria hotel. *Golf World* reported that the celebration meal cost "close to $10,000 – no cheque was too big for Bob Hudson". The self-appointed fairy godfather of the Cup then took the GB team all the way to Portland – a 3½-day rail journey – all expenses paid. He also gave each British player $100 in spending money, paid for their accommodation throughout the trip and treated the visitors like lords at every opportunity.

"The players – all of the big names or unknowns – must be treated as if they were guests in my home," were Hudson's welcoming words and it is estimated that this golfing benefactor poured as much as $40,000 of his own money into this single event, such was his passion for it. He was a remarkably optimistic man who did nothing in half measures. On one occasion, the GB party was even given a police escort through the streets of Chicago.

The only glitch in Hudson's plan concerned the competitiveness of the British. Six years of fighting in Europe had decimated the sport: many pros had spent years in the forces; courses were used for all kinds of alternative needs from Home Guard exercises to cattle grazing; and all tournaments had been indefinitely postponed, including the Open Championship. The 1947 Ryder Cup was going to be great for the spirit of the game, but not for the spirit of the British players who were now definitely the poor relations of their American golfing cousins.

"It matters not which side shall win – there is honour in even losing," said a dedication in the 1947 Cup programme. However, honour was all the visiting team achieved. "Stiff and worn out," is how Faulkner described the team's condition on arrival in Portland. By contrast, America's team was full of well-prepared, fit and healthy men, captained by the phenomenal Ben Hogan. The match was to be a non-event, the Americans won 11-1. "I felt sorry for the British players," said Nelson, "because they hadn't been able to play golf or do anything since fighting the war over there."

In fact, Hudson was a long-term patron of golf and golfers, similar in many respects to Samuel Ryder. His golfing influence would be established on both sides of the Atlantic. He was manager of the team in 1949 for the first post-war trip to Britain and worked closely with the two PGAs for years, still supporting the Ryder Cup in 1959. Also, his long-term care for the GB players after their visit to Oregon was touching because once the team reached home, Hudson sent every member a Christmas food basket, a gift that was repeated for several subsequent years.

To stage the Ryder Cup just two years after the war ended had been a remarkable feat by Hudson and the PGA of America and both associations breathed a sigh of relief simply because the sequence of matches had recommenced. This was underlined when the state of the British PGA's financial resources emerged: in January 1948, just three months after returning from Portland, the PGA committee's Ryder Cup fund stood at only £176.

There is no doubt that without, the seventh Ryder Cup match would have been delayed beyond 1947, and for who knows how long into the future. What the late Samuel Ryder had helped start 20 years earlier had become Hudson's choice to continue. The first re-birth of the matches was complete.

Snatching victory from many defeats

The Ryder Cup's return to the golfing calendar following World War II was welcomed by everyone in the sport, but the competition soon became very one-sided. In the first 16 matches following the war (1947-77), the Americans lost only once, in 1957, while they were held to a tie in 1969. The solitary victory by GB&I was such a rare and precious outcome that captain Dai Rees was named BBC Sports Personality of the Year. During this 30-year period, solutions were constantly sought to try to make the results closer. The inclusion of other golfers from around the world was one option and five-time Open champion Peter Thomson of Australia was quoted as saying "all the [GB team] needs is two more really good players". That view complemented some of the sport's commentators who supported the idea of a Commonwealth team to take on America. Some media even suggested a Rest of the World team. Geographically speaking, however, continental Europeans would be the more obvious nationalities to assist the British and Irish, but up to the mid-1970s there had been very few great golfers from those countries.

Nevertheless, there were sections of the British PGA and also the tour players who were far from conceding that overseas help was necessary for the Ryder Cup team even as the number of American wins continued to pile up. The naysayers to change argued that British standards were slowly catching up with the Americans and that oftentimes many of the individual matches within the overall contest were close (in 1969, 18 of the 32 points were only settled on the final green). However, that view might have had some credence when the matches were played in Britain, but in America the gap between the two teams seemed only to be increasing (from 1947-77, the best GB&I performance away from home was a four-point loss). The media offered many technical excuses for the poor British and Irish performances such as putting skills and chipping techniques, but the players themselves, like Peter Alliss (a regular in the team from 1953 to 1969), understood that the problem ran deeper. The future World Golf Hall of Famer and topline TV commentator saw the full-time American tour pros arrive for the Cup fresh from another high-quality tournament and click immediately into top form, while too many British players arrived at the matches straight from their jobs as working club pros. "When the Ryder Cup matches ended, we all went back to selling sweaters in our golf shops," explained Allis when asked about the constant Cup defeats. Alliss believed that a British pro could not cope with the heat of a Ryder Cup battle as well as his American counterpart when his regular lifestyle and workplace was so far behind that of his opponent.

One golfer who was fully aware of all this was Jack Nicklaus. After bursting onto the golf scene as the chubby-faced graduate of Ohio State University who shockingly won the in 1962 US Open by beating the legendary Arnold Palmer in an 18-hole playoff, the golfer who would become known as the Golden Bear grew in stature and reputation to become the greatest major winner of all time. Nicklaus made his Ryder Cup debut only in 1969 because the rules at the time required him to have been a full member of the PGA Tour for at least five years, but by the mid-1970s it was apparent to him that the matches were becoming increasingly unattractive to American players as well as potential sponsors and media. He knew the British and Irish had no chance of victory and, while the US team wanted to win every match, having the result settled almost before the final day began was no one's idea of true competition.

As Nicklaus was about to make his fifth appearance as a Ryder Cup player, he bestrode the sport of golf with 14 major championships to his name and the respect of all his peers. He saw that the American Ryder Cup team was beginning to feel like golf's version of the Harlem Globetrotters, playing a meaningless exhibition every two years that they were almost guaranteed to win. What he and his teammates really wanted was a full-blooded fight between great golfing nations.

There had been signs of American apathy and even a certain amount of disrespect for the matches for many years after the war. As far back as 1951, when the Cup was staged at Pinehurst, North Carolina, in early November, the two-day contest was played either side of an American football college game that fans and even the players wanted to watch. The PGA of America agreed not to play on Saturday 3 November because North Carolina was playing Tennessee in Chapel Hill about 70 miles away. US team members may have spoken in patriotic tones about the honour of playing for their country at the time, but their actions spoke otherwise. Even Nicklaus showed a certain disdain for the event in 1973 when he stayed in Florida an extra day to watch a Miami Dolphins NFL game rather than travel with his teammates and enjoy an extra day of pre-match practice in Scotland.

However, these incidents were small beer compared to Tom Weiskopf's actions. The straight-talking Weiskopf had played in the 1973 and 1975 matches and picked up 7½ out of a possible eight points and was a certainty for the next contest in 1977 at Royal Lytham & St Annes. But the smooth-swinging Ohioan declined to play, declaring that he would rather go big-game hunting than turn up for another easy victory against the British and Irish. For a man handy with a gun, the phrase 'shooting fish in a barrel' must have come to his mind. Weiskopf was really only saying aloud what many of his contemporaries in America were thinking. Meanwhile, the same kind of apathy was being shown by fans and the press in the US; only a few thousand spectators turned up at each match and there was little coverage in print or on television because everyone knew who would win. British golf writer Peter Dobereiner mocked the Americans' feelings for the Cup in an article in *The Observer* when he said the matches "rate somewhere between the Tennessee Frog Jumping Contest and the Alabama Melon-Pip Spitting Championship".

Weiskopf's honest declaration of boredom with the Ryder Cup may have been a shock to some people in the sport, but it finally helped jolt the sport's grandees into action. Up until this point, the British in particular had seemed to be playing a passive waiting game hoping for a divine solution to secure the Cup's future, while the US team was just being polite by showing up every two years. But suddenly the natural American get-up-and-go attitude took over the situation and forced a resolution; thankfully, some of the leading personalities had the courage to act. Conversations about the future of the Cup took place in earnest on England's Lancashire coast during the 1977 match that Weiskopf missed.

As the latest overpoweringly strong American team was squashing the minnows of Britain and Ireland (the 1977 match ended 12½-7½ in favour of the US), Henry Poe, a past president of the PGA of America, and Lord Derby, then president of the British PGA, opened discussions. Poe had talked to several members of the US team and they echoed Weiskopf's view. "[Several players] don't care if they ever play another Ryder Cup because there is no competition," Poe told Lord Derby, and added "I hate to say that, but that's the truth". But, although this was a change from the silent denial of the situation, and talks among administrators were helpful, the momentum for change had to come from the players themselves. And not just any player, it had to come from their figurehead.

Jack Nicklaus took on the role of chief diplomatic negotiator like a natural. He could perhaps have left the matter up to Poe and the PGA of America or insisted that someone like his 1977 Ryder Cup captain Dow Finsterwald (a highly respected man, but someone whose period as a serious PGA Tour player had ended 15 years earlier) take charge. However, Nicklaus was canny enough to understand that he needed to grab the spotlight and turn the talk into action. His masterstroke was to avoid the committee structures of golf's administrators and approach Lord Derby directly during Ryder Cup weekend – the best player in America and the British PGA's lord of the realm were not going to be denied. The two had become friends over the years and both shared a love for the ethics of the game and the friendship that a match like the Ryder Cup represented.

In fact, Lord Derby would now become consumed with the desire to make the Ryder Cup more of a success. He was no fan of the matches being exhibitions and had realised that one day soon – when either the money to fund the matches ran out or the interest of spectators in Britain fell away – the Cup in its current format would not just circle the drain, but disappear down it.

When Nicklaus eventually spoke openly to the press, his message was simple and had the backing of Lord Derby: American golfers *could* continue the matches as "a goodwill gesture, a get-together, a bit of fun", but stronger opposition was needed to maintain their full commitment. He pointed out that America was a nation of 15 million golfers while Britain and Ireland could barely boast one million together and that statistic alone underlined the gap between the two professional teams. Nicklaus would play another diplomatic ace when he confirmed his thoughts in a letter. "It's vital to widen the selection procedures if the Ryder Cup is to continue to enjoy its past prestige," he wrote to Lord Derby.

What Nicklaus and Lord Derby refrained from saying was that the Ryder Cup was no longer alone when it came to international team golf in the professional game.

A golfing world cup had been launched in 1953, originally called the Canada Cup. This tournament quickly grew in stature and had several advantages over the Ryder Cup: it was staged every year with a different country acting as hosts (it was launched in Montreal, hence the name); all of the world's top players could take part from all five continents (the inaugural event was won by an Argentinian pair); and, crucially, America took the event seriously early on (they won the third and fourth tournaments) and consistently sent their top players, including Arnold Palmer, Ben Hogan, Sam Snead and Jack Nicklaus, who would all play on winning teams. Then in 1974, the Hennessy Cognac Cup was introduced as a biennial event, originally contested by British, Irish and Europeans, but later expanded to include South Africans and Australia, among others.

The idea of international team matches was becoming increasingly attractive for television and Nicklaus, in particular, could appreciate that because he had long seen golf from a business perspective. He had joined Mark McCormack's sports agency, International Management Group, early on in his career and there was no company better at setting up golf tournaments that the TV channels wanted to screen than IMG. The World Matchplay Championship at Wentworth that McCormack launched under the Piccadilly cigarette company brand in 1964 was a fine example and, given the chance, this lawyer-turned-sports-entrepreneur could surely have either re-invigorated the Ryder Cup with more players from more countries plus lots of prize money or simply invented his own contest to replace Samuel Ryder's version of it ever collapsed and died.

But Nicklaus had seen the answer to the Cup's problem: it was the 20-year-old Seve Ballesteros who had led after three rounds of the Open at Royal Birkdale the previous year and eventually finished second, tied with Nicklaus himself. The dashing Spaniard was not the only young player emerging from continental Europe and expanding America's opposition to include this new breed of players was Nicklaus's suggestion. After all, the European Tour had been officially formed in 1971, so USA vs Europe was the logical next step. "I had no agenda other than the good of the game," said Nicklaus years later. "The change was just something I thought was right."

Of course, the idea did not meet with total approval. There was opposition initially from Samuel Ryder's nephew, Thomas Anderson Davis, when the original deed of trust signed by his uncle had to be altered. Davis believed Ryder would have "resisted the decision", but Lord Derby eventually smoothed that problem, while a few under-the-breath dissenters among the British golfers on tour never emerged as any threat to the change. In the end, by April 1978, Lord Derby headed a delegation that met the PGA of America during the Masters at Augusta National and the adjustment to the format was sealed.

The 1979 match in West Virginia was the first US vs Europe contest, although only two continental players – Ballesteros and Antonio Garrido of Spain – made the team that year. Their presence failed to stop another crushing 17-11 American win. However, by 1983, the US sneaked a one-point win which happened by be with Jack Nicklaus as captain on the Champion Course at PGA National Golf Club in Palm Beach Gardens, Florida. The Golden Bear had forced through a change to the Ryder Cup that he believed would save it and was seeing at first hand that his dream had become a reality. Not only that, but at the next match, at The Belfry, Team Europe notched up its first victory. Since 1985, it has won the majority of matches (9-4 with one tie up to and including 2012).

3

Remarkable Rivalry

"We're all good friends, both sides of the Pond, but there's something about the Ryder Cup which intrigues me…how you can be great mates with somebody but, boy, do you want to kill them in the Ryder Cup." This was the answer to a very common question put to Ian Poulter. The media never tired of asking him to explain the nature of the unique rivalry of this match. Luckily for all the reporters, the former assistant professional at Chesfield Downs Golf Club in Hertfordshire was not yet tired of answering it. Looking thoughtful and trying to be insightful, Poulter was talking in the media tent before the 2012 Ryder Cup at Medinah, Chicago. It was a practice day, so the two teams were still settling in and the media were hunting for a story. Many players are wary of the press, fearing they might be led into unwittingly creating a headline to spur on the opposition. The tall Englishman has no such anxiety. Wearing his trademark visor, 'Poults' – long been a favourite of the press corps – was happy to explain how and why the best golfers of Europe and America had constructed their friendly war.

"I'm passionate about (the Ryder Cup) and I believe in it. I've seen what other players have committed to it and that inspires me. The Ryder Cup inspires me. I want to walk away from it knowing I've represented my teammates, vice-captains, captain and a whole continent and not disappointed anybody. There's no other atmosphere like it in golf." When Poulter talks about the Cup, his audience remains silent. This is a man searching his soul for words of explanation on behalf of hundreds of others who have gone before.

"With the golf I play week in, week out, the only person I can disappoint is myself – because if I haven't performed I've let myself down. I've got myself to answer to, no one else, and I'm hard on myself when I disappoint myself. But you can't fist-pump and create (a high) level of intensity and inner burn when you've rolled in a 10ft birdie putt in a strokeplay event at 7.15 on a Thursday morning. You can try, but you can't outwardly express it like you do in a Ryder Cup. There, you've got 25,000 travelling European fans waiting with bated breath to see you hole that putt and when you do, you feed them and they feed you. You don't get that in strokeplay." Unlike so many of the 300-plus men who have played in the Ryder Cup's first 40 matches, Poulter finds it easy, even cathartic, to discuss why a team golf match can develop such a magical quality.

The Hertfordshire man is the manifestation of the rivalry that has grown up between the teams. In fact, he can be dubbed the modern-day Mr Rivalry, the spokesman for all those other players unable to put their Cup feelings into meaningful words. The rivalry Poulter talks about in the 21st century, though, is much different from how it appeared in the inaugural match in 1927. The tone and style of the competitiveness has adapted like everything else in the sport – just as golf club shafts are now made of graphite not hickory, so the Ryder Cup teams view each other with more sophisticated sensibilities than 80 year ago. But, although the rivalry has morphed, it remains one of the most compelling elements of the matches. The Ryder Cup is all or nothing, there are no prizes for second place. It is simply unlike any other tournament a professional golfer takes part in year-on-year: its rarity quickens the pulse rate and the team matchplay format heightens the challenge for victory.

And thanks to characters like Poulter, the Cup is even more remarkable. He is such an interesting individual within the history of the event for two main reasons: firstly, his background echoes that of the British players who played in the matches a couple of generations earlier; secondly, he is playing the wrong sport. Poulter wanted to be a footballer. An Arsenal fan from an early age, 'Poults' (golfers did not usually have football-style nicknames before Poulter – if Jack Nicklaus had played soccer, his teammates would not have called him 'Golden Bear') loved to kick a ball around with his friends and actually was good enough to have a trial with Tottenham Hotspur. His cocky demeanour went down well in the football dressing room where the banter can be brutal. The team atmosphere was like a drug to him and so was the thought of playing in front of massive crowds of screaming fans. "To be part of a team is very special," he once told *The Guardian*. "There is nothing like being amongst 50,000 people all cheering on your team. It's truly inspiring. I was such a big football fan. I miss the buzz, I miss going in the crowd and being a football fan. I do miss my football."

So, when Poulter enters the Ryder Cup team room, he brings team spirit with him. He understands how to motivate his fellow professionals with a joke here or a quiet chat there; he feeds off the encouragement of others; he's a lover of the pre-match huddle; and, like Europe's iconic mentor Seve Ballesteros, he is the most fearsome competitor on either team. This is a man who has a temper and is prepared to show it: a loud curse, a swish with an offending club. He wears his emotions openly, but also knows how to use them, how to channel them to a series of incredible shots. The rivalry he feels for "the opposition" comes from the football field. Poulter enjoys football's 11-on-11 more than golf's strokeplay format of 1 vs 155. Even better is one-on-one.

As a footballer, Poulter would love nutmegging a defender or sliding his penalty shot between goalpost and goalkeeper. He could look in the eyes of the player on the opposing team and defeat him with a pass. The Ryder Cup is his football field, a place where the intensity is ramped up as a result of every single drive, pitch and putt. Strokeplay golf tournaments that operate week-to-week on every professional golf tour in every part of the world are set up to establish the best golfer of the week, not the one who can outfox his opponent over a mere 18 holes. Only occasionally are the very best strokeplay exponents actually playing directly opposite each other when a title is on the line in that last round of four.

For the golfers of the early Ryder Cup era of the 1920s, matchplay was their bread and butter; strokeplay tournaments certainly existed, but they only became dominant only after World War II. Nowadays, mano-a-mano affairs on the golf course are an exception and that means today's golf rivalries are often fought out via league tables of ranking points or Tour money lists. Unlike a sport such as tennis where the greatest players often face each other in grand slam finals, golf's greats only occasionally battle against each other in the final group on the final day for one of the four major titles. The famous Duel In The Sun between Tom Watson and Jack Nicklaus at Turnberry in the 1977 Open Championship is a perfect example, Nick Faldo beating Greg Norman at The Masters in 1996 is another. But these are hardly commonplace occurrences. In recent years, every major championship tournament director has prayed for Tiger Woods and Phil Mickelson to stare each other down in the same two-ball on a Sunday afternoon? Yet Woods and Mickelson have managed such a spectacle only once during their 19 combined major title victories up to the summer of 2014. It was at the 2001 Masters.

However, this is a situation that Poulter would relish, a scenario where second place is all but meaningless, where the rawness of a matchplay atmosphere adds a special level of anticipation to every shot. Many years before Poulter played in the Ryder Cup, he could sense that it was an event totally in tune with his personality.

In an interview with *Kingdom* magazine, Poulter remembered: "I went to the Ryder Cup when I was 17 at The Belfry in 1993. I stayed in a tent three miles down the road with two other assistants. We had a fabulous time, it cost us £3 a night to stay in someone's back garden. (The house owner) let us come in to do the washing up as we were cooking on a little camp stove. I had an absolutely fantastic time – the whole atmosphere, the electricity, the passion and what it meant. That was when I said 'this is what I want to do. I want to be a pro'."

Poulter often thinks back to 1996 as well, his second year of cleaning members' shoes at Chesfield Downs and that experience grounded him for the whole of his career. This is a man at peace with himself and particularly the team environment of the Ryder Cup and the rivalry it entails. Poulter knows his Ryder Cup showings could end up as his golfing legacy. "[The Ryder Cup] might be my majors and that's fine," Poulter said before his remarkable Medinah performance. "If they are, if this is it, I'm a happy man. I've got more pride and passion to play in the Ryder Cup than I have to win a major. I want to win a major, don't get me wrong, I'd like to win all of them. I've been close and, who knows, Sunday at Medinah might be that little changing factor to get me over that line. But if I don't win another golf tournament from here, this will go down as the highlight of my golfing career." There can be no greater testimony to the power of the Ryder Cup than a statement such as this.

The rivalry begins

Back in the 1920s, Ryder Cup teams representing the Stars and Stripes and the Union Jack with a special kind of patriotic pride was uncommon in a sports team environment.

The idea of a trans-Atlantic golfing rivalry probably began in 1913 when callow American amateur Francis Ouimet beat the world's greatest player Harry Vardon to win the US Open at Brookline in Massachusetts. Before that, the only significant rivalry between golfing nations was that of England and Scotland. But after World War I, America was itching to prove itself the home of the world's top players, so the emergence of a team contest was the obvious way to prove it.

When the inaugural Ryder Cup took place, Britain's amateurs had already lost the first four editions of the Walker Cup, so national pride was at stake in Worcester, Massachusetts, in 1927. The match was deemed a success although the margin of the American victory (9½-2½) was rather one-sided. A sigh of relief was breathed because the contest had finally begun after two false starts.

The follow-up match in 1929 was perfectly timed because it took place six months before the New York stock market crash triggered the Great Depression. The Americans were keen to show off their superiority and easily raised the $10,000 necessary for the trip for the first ever defence of the Cup at Moortown Golf Club in Leeds, Yorkshire in April. The money would almost certainly have not been raised after the financial collapse had happened in the autumn.

The timing was ideal for the Americans, but not for the British team whose season would only normally start in the spring. American golfers could play throughout their winter in the southern states and were likely to be well practised at Moortown. However, the weather beat both teams because it was very cold and snow even fell during one of the practice days. This would be a contest of character as much as golfing talent.

These opponents were not friends, but respectful enemies, representatives of two countries with a history of conflict. At this time, Americans like Walter Hagen wanted to rule the world of golf; this was their moment to show the pompous British that the US was producing the top professionals. The Americans came with Hagen as their captain and the team were treated like champions, spending some pre-match time relaxing at the steam baths in Harrogate. However, Hagen prompted the first real Ryder Cup skirmish when he insisted on ignoring the rules of the contest that each team should field only eight players. Instead, 'The Haig' demanded all 10 players who travelled from America should take part at some point during the two-day event.

Still, it was not the only pre-match tussle between the teams in 1929 – there was a disagreement about club shafts. Most top American pros had taken to playing with the metal shafts that had become fashionable, and legal in their country, over the previous three years. However, the R&A did not lift the ban on this new technology until November 1929, remaining loyal to wooden-shafted clubs (usually made from hickory) for as long as possible at the behest of the British pros who felt their livelihoods would suffer. When the Americans were told that local rules applied for the Ryder Cup, most of the visiting team had to take to the practice ranges with old-style shafts and re-learn how to swing with them. This problem was not eased by the cold weather that kept both teams indoors for long periods. The tension was mounting and this was only the second ever Ryder Cup.

A few off-course clashes were one thing; to light the blue touchpaper of a real rivalry, the players themselves had to take the matter inside the ropes. Easily the most contentious individual contest was between the two captains, Scotland's George Duncan and Hagen. They avoided each other in the foursomes on day one, but their singles clash in the second match of day two could perhaps be described as the Ryder Cup's first ever grudge match.

The effervescent Hagen, a self-proclaimed peacock with an ego always in evidence, was one of the players who desperately wanted the Ryder Cup to succeed. By this time, 'The Haig', with his characteristic slicked-back hairstyle and colourful golf clothing, wanted to be recognised as the best there ever was. He had already gathered 10 of the 11 major titles he would eventually win and, at 37, he was still in his prime. The only golfer who could attract the same attention was Bobby Jones, the charming amateur from Georgia who was 10 years younger, more handsome according to the ladies and who had won both amateur and professional majors. The American press and public revered Jones because he was a southern gentleman with great natural talent and elegance while Hagen was one of those professional golf hucksters who was brash and full of bravado.

Hagen thought he had put Jones in his place in 1925 after a 72-hole challenge match they played that was promoted under the unambiguous title 'The Match of the Century'. It was rumoured that Jones was thinking of turning pro, but after he was embarrassed by a 12&11 defeat, those plans were overturned and he would remain an amateur for the rest of his career. But although 'The Haig' triumphed, Jones kept winning titles and creating huge headlines. In addition, the one thing that Jones had been able to do since 1922, that Hagen had not, was play on a winning American team against the old enemy, the British. The Walker Cup had taken off that year and Jones had starred in five consecutive American victories, even captaining the team to an unprecedented 11-1 win at Chicago Golf Club in 1928. Every Walker Cup win was like a dagger in Hagen's heart until the Ryder Cup began in 1927 and the inaugural win by the American pros was not enough: 'The Haig' wanted what Jones already had, which was a long run of wins in this international challenge match.

The proud GB Ryder Cup captain in 1929 facing Hagen was Duncan, a grim-faced man from the equally grim climate of Aberdeen who was legendary for playing his golf at the fastest of paces (Duncan thought taking a practice swing was nonsense). The 35-year-old Scot had featured in some of the media build-up between the two teams: a cartoon in an edition of *Golf Monthly* earlier that year illustrated showed a golfing 'George' slaying a US dragon. However, Duncan was depressed by the reality of the build-up because he felt like he was skipper of a listing ship. As had happened in 1927, the Great British public had pretty much ignored a plea to support his team financially. An appeal through the excited British press had raised a paltry £806 to fund the home team's expenses for the match. The British PGA had wanted at least twice that amount and were relying on the gate money being sufficiently substantial. Then, as the match grew near, Duncan's feelings were hurt again as the golf writers noted that the visitors looked fitter and healthier. The story went that while the Americans trained off the course with some running and a little weight training, the British golfers considered playing a few holes as tantamount to fitness training.

Duncan might have felt his team was already a point down when he arrived at Moortown for the second Ryder Cup, but thousands of passionate Yorkshire golf fans turned out to cheer on his troops. Despite this, the Americans went ahead 2½-1½ after the four foursome matches with Duncan failing miserably, losing 7&5 with his partner Aubrey Boomer, and Hagen victorious, by two holes alongside the impressively-named New Yorker Johnny Golden. These were 36-hole matches, so the draw for the singles on day two only took place late in the afternoon and – surprise, surprise – Hagen and Duncan were drawn to play together.

Now there is supposed to be no fixing of the draw in the Ryder Cup and, although it is strictly speaking against the rules, this was probably one of the few occasions when officials turned a blind eye. The two captains had 'history' and were not about to let the opportunity slip to settle a few old scores. Hagen was still seething from the unofficial match at Wentworth in 1926. Twice in two days, the proud American captain had been filleted by Duncan. In the foursomes, 'The Haig' and partner Jim Barnes were beaten by the astonishing score of 9&8 by Duncan and Abe Mitchell, and then the Scot won the singles match 6&5. Great players have long memories and, having missed his chance to reverse the scores in 1927, Hagen was not going to let this latest opportunity slip, particularly as he and Duncan were skippering the two teams. So for them to meet in the singles at Moortown was more than just a coincidence. Having fixed the draw, Hagen then underlined his confidence telling his teammates: "Well, boys, there's a point for our team right there." Legend has it that Duncan either overheard the remark or – more likely – was told about it, but the Scot kept his counsel and would let his play do his talking.

The Duncan-Hagen match was the No 2 singles contest on day two and it attracted the majority of the crowd, including Samuel Ryder who was watching his eponymous Cup for the first time (he hated to travel and had, therefore, declined to sail to America for the inaugural contest in 1927). Hagen was his usual chirpy self at the start of the match, while Duncan played at his usual fast pace. The men had several things in common – they were from working-class families and had learned the game as young caddies – but their golfing careers were on quite different levels. While Hagen racked up titles on both sides of the Atlantic, Duncan would win only one major (the Open Championship in 1920) and a handful of tournaments. The crowd yelled loudly for Duncan, but there was tension behind the cheers; they knew one of the GB skipper's nicknames was 'Miss 'em Quick' Duncan because George not only played his best shots fast, but also his worst. In fact, what was also on the spectators' minds was the 1922 Open Championship at Royal

St. George's. Duncan should have won the claret jug for the second time that season; his third-round 69 was only the third sub-70 score to have been shot in the Open at that time and the title seemed his for the taking. Then on the 18th on the final day, he fluffed a chip shot from the side of the green to lose by a shot. But to whom? Hagen, of course. So, while Hagen thought of Wentworth 1926, Duncan had Sandwich 1922 on his mind when they teed off at Moortown.

The atmosphere was additionally tense during their match because, of course, this was the first official Ryder Cup on British soil. Duncan had given his players what he hoped was an inspiring speech and putting himself out at No. 2 meant he could also lead by example. The man the press labeled as the dragon-slayer knew Hagen was his target all along, particularly because the Scot was the polar opposite in character to the brash American. The closest Duncan got to Hagen's flamboyance was to wear a bow tie when he was on the links. The GB skipper also knew the consequence of defeat. The press had warned that to lose to the Americans would be disastrous. *Golf Illustrated* had moaned about the lack of financial support from the British public, but the magazine's biggest concern was that if the GB team lost their first home match the Ryder Cup would "either die or develop into a private match with little or no interest".

What happened in the No.2 singles match, therefore, was crucial. It actually turned out to be astonishing. Hagen could do nothing right and Duncan could do nothing wrong. The 36-hole match was almost totally one-sided with the Scot delighting himself and the thousands of home supporters by chalking up a massive 10&8 victory. This would be Hagen's only loss (singles or foursomes) in all his six Ryder Cup appearances; although he was gracious in defeat, he admitted that Duncan had given him "a terrific shellacking". The GB captain, with his sharp Aberdonian accent and temperamental personality, was not slow to ram home the point. "This man has never beaten me in a serious match and he never will," he said. Duncan's win also helped spark a GB revival as the home side took the singles 5½-2½ and the match 7-5. With a rare broad smile, Duncan confided as he was presented with the trophy by Samuel Ryder: "This is the happiest day of my life."

While Hagen would captain the American team in each of the next four Ryder Cup matches, Duncan only played once more – as a member of the GB team that traveled to Scioto Country Club in Ohio two years later. Hagen was still in his pomp, though Duncan, a fading force, was a late selection. He was not even selected for the singles on the second day, yet both men knew on the morning of day one, when they were opposite each other in the second foursomes match, that there was an edge to this contest. Hagen paired himself with Ryder Cup newcomer Denny Shute, who went on to win the 1933 Open at St Andrews and two PGA Championships, while Duncan could not partner his pal Abe Mitchell (who was not selected) and had to settle for another player rather past his prime, Arthur Havers, Open Champion eight years previously. The grin on Hagen's face after the match was a mile wide – the result was another shellacking, but this time in favour of the Stars and Stripes. Not only did 'The Haig' win, but the score put the cherry on top of the cake – 10&9, even better than Duncan's singles victory two years earlier.

The Ryder Cup enmities were now emerging even though Samuel Ryder sent a convivial radio message to the teams and the fans in 1931: "I trust the effect of this match will be to influence the cordial, friendly and peaceful feeling throughout the whole civilized world". Mr Ryder misjudged the level of passion that the British pros felt, especially after they suffered a heavy defeat in Ohio. The press was more in tune with the feelings: "We are raw with the wounds of defeat," reported the pages of *Golf Monthly*.

There was also a growing bitterness between the teams. Gene Sarazen played in all six pre-World War II matches and was probably second only to Hagen in terms of his stature in the American professional game. During each contest, Sarazen managed to smile along with the rest of his team for the cameras and not partake of any baiting of the opposiiton, but later in life he allowed his real feelings to emerge. He said his team wanted "to beat the British in the worst way... they looked on us Americans as no more than a bunch of caddies".

The early 1930s were a pivotal period for international sport with contests more prone than ever to touch the national conscience. Firstly, there was suddenly more of it (the football World Cup beginning in 1930 being a prime example) and, secondly, these country-vs-country contests provided more food for the increasingly hungry media; newspapers, magazines, newsreels and radio were quick to turn sporting winners into patriotic heroes like never before. Perhaps the most famous example of the time was the so-called Bodyline Series between the English and Australian cricket teams in 1932-33. This series Down Under caused political and economic uproar after the haughty English captain Douglas Jardine told his fast bowlers to bowl round the wicket and direct plenty of short-pitched deliveries at the opposing batsmen's bodies. In the days when neither helmets nor body protectors were worn, the Australians and their hero Don Bradman took a terrific pounding, so much so that bodyline bowling damaged diplomatic relations and trade between the two countries.

International developments in golf at this time saw new courses being built in all corners of the world, including South America and Japan. A Davis Cup for golf (i.e. a team contest involving all the nations that played the game) was even mentioned in the pages of *Golf Monthly* at the start of 1933 because the editorial team believed that in the next 10 to 15 years there could be more than one country to challenge the golfing supremacy of the USA and Great Britain. "We are on the eve of big developments in the game internationally," claimed one article.

That year, 1933, saw the staging of the 4th Ryder Cup and this contest delivered a level of theatre that was new to the sport. With one singles match still to finish at Southport & Ainsdale that year, the teams were level at 5½ points each. The two men left to decide the fate of the Cup were English journeyman Syd Easterbrook and Shute.

Easterbrook was the professional at Knowle Golf Club in Bristol, an accomplished player but by no means a leading name in British sport. Yet here he was level with a man who was a multiple winner on the US PGA tour. By rights, Shute, who less than a fortnight later was crowned Open champion, should have at least been able to halve the hole and the overall match, but instead he fell victim to the pressure of the moment.

The final hole at Southport & Ainsdale is a relatively short par-4 and both men were on the green in three. Easterbrook tried first for his par, but missed, leaving himself a testy 3-footer. Shute then had a downhiller for the win and two putts for a half. Afterwards, Shute's own captain Walter Hagen said he had considered suggesting a lag putt, but 'The Haig' was away from the action in the company of the Prince of Wales and decided it would be impolite to leave his host.

So instead, the bold American went for the win and looked on horrified as his ball rolled fully six feet past the hole. From going for glory, he now had a very difficult return putt to avoid ignominy. Shute took plenty of time, but missed again and took a six. There was a moment of stunned silence, leaving the nervous Easterbrook to attempt to hole his own putt. It had a nasty left to right borrow, according to esteemed British journalist Henry Longhurst who was a 24-year-old newcomer to the Ryder Cup at the time and later became a television commentating legend. "Rather him than me," wrote Longhurst, but he need not have worried because Easterbrook was made of stern stuff and drained the putt to send the crowds wild with delight. Syd Easterbrook had unwittingly become the first poster boy of Ryder Cup.

Some members of the US team were said to be incandescent with Shute for three-putting from just 20 feet, but Hagen defended his player, saying that playing safe in that situation was not the best option. Shute went for the win, but this time it didn't happen, declared Hagen. Perhaps the captain ate humble pie because he had earlier stoked the fires of resentment between the two teams pre-match by announcing: "We had the Cup on our table on the [RMS] Aquitania coming over and we had reserved a place for it on the way back."

No Ryder Cup had managed such a dramatic finish before (in fact, none would do so again until 1991). For certain now, this was a contest of the highest order that could tantalise the largest crowds and send the media into paroxysms of animated delight. Even the supposedly impartial Prince of Wales broke with normal etiquette and showed his colours. "We are very glad to have won," he said afterwards. The "we" revealed the Prince's own love for golf, a sport that he played as often as possible. Meanwhile, for the British golfing community at this time, for such an important member of the Royal Family to take an interest in the sport, and in this event, proved extremely important.

The Ryder Cup media coverage was heightened by all this royal attention: all the newspapers wanted pictures of the prince in such an informal setting and, certainly, plenty of extra fans turned up at Southport more to get a glimpse of royalty than to watch a golf match. The American team, of course, had no royal seal of approval, although Hagen was the self-appointed king of golf. Perhaps the Prince of Wales's remarks could have been interpreted as another old world advantage that the British waved under the noses of their American cousins, but there is no suggestion that defeat was taken in any way other than graciously.

The rivalry was now cemented in a new way, and not just within the golf communities; the two nations as a whole cared. The prince gave the nod the British needed while the American press had already gone wild about their two previous wins. The pressure would be raised every two years for the teams to perform, not just on behalf of themselves, but for the glory of the fans and the flags they represented. Patriotic pride had begun to power the teams and it would prove to be a fuel appropriate, long-lasting and extremely potent.

From close quarters to walkovers

World War II not only postponed the Ryder Cup for 10 years, but it also caused a massive change in the relationship between the two teams. The final pre-war match had been the first one won by a visiting team – the Americans grabbing the trophy 8-4 at Southport & Ainsdale. So the first few post-war contests would set the tone of the rivalry for years to come. When the first three matches turned out to be dismal defeats for Britain's golfers, the rivalry descended into something more aggressive. After six years of fighting side by side in real battlefields, the two nations now had a different kind of cultural connection. This was the time when the 'special relationship' between the nations of Britain and America emerged. Winston Churchill used the phrase in a speech near the end of the war when he talked of "a special relationship between the British Commonwealth and Empire and the United States", who could "work together at the common task as friends and partners". American President Franklin D Roosevelt is said to have used the same words a few years earlier when entertaining King George VI.

Whatever the origin of the idea of the special relationship, it suggested that at least the politicians of both countries would treat each other with respect, but there was no guarantee of any new trans-Atlantic friendliness between the golfers of Britain and America when they convened for the postponed 7th Ryder Cup in 1947. The pre-war matches had been tight affairs and, despite British society in general and sports including golf in particular being hit far more severely than their American counterparts, it was hoped the level of competitiveness would continue.

But once the money – all from American businessman Robert Hudson – was found and the arrangements were made, something had changed the attitudes of the teams. What would appear in the Ryder Cup matches of the post-war period was a new feeling, a kind of underlying resentment between the teams. It was not disrespect, but more like the harbinger of a barely disguised jealousy between the newly buoyant 'haves' and the now-dethroned 'have-nots'. Sometimes this would be covert and unspoken because of the nature of golfing etiquette, yet there were too many examples of friction and fractiousness for these feelings to be coincidence. Captains appeared more likely to challenge the opposition on rules issues in a way that would have amounted to churlishness before the war. Players would suddenly express real anger during matches when they played poor shots and even openly argue with each other and even their captain. It is particularly easy to understand the internal rows in the British camp as the disappointing defeats piled up. Even the fans lining the fairways would not be exempt from this new atmosphere at the matches; they became more raucous than ever before (there were even reports of people booing the opposition) while the British media scratched its collective head about how the matches could again become competitive.

The post-war group of matches would be dominated by the after-effects of the fighting and the consequences reflected the nations they represented. As the two economies moved in completely different directions, so did their sportsmen and sportswomen. While many golfers on both sides took part in the war as active servicemen, tournament golf continued only on one side of the Atlantic. Many of Britain's golf courses were used as grazing land for sheep and cows, turned into areas of fortification against potential invasion (especially seaside links courses) or acted as training areas for the Home Guard. The very idea of spending too many hours on the links rather than defending the nation was almost unthinkable, unless perhaps you were somewhere in the wildest parts of Scotland or Wales and far from the bombs and barbed wire. British pros mostly were in uniform for much of the six-year conflict and rarely swung a club. Times were hard and only youngsters like Peter Alliss (aged eight when war broke out) could find time to hit a few old golf balls around in their spare time. "Of course, there were no new golf balls to be had and, if you had a golf tee, you got grandma to tie a woolly tassle onto it in the hope that you'd never lose it or break it," Alliss remembered later in his autobiography.

The post-war rivalry felt like it was one-way only. Golf was slower to revive itself in Britain than across the Atlantic; by 1950 there were still only 14 main tournaments on the British PGA's calendar compared to as many as 50 in America. Many US players had enjoyed almost uninterrupted play during the war and, for years afterwards, continually underlined their status as the best golfers in the world by winning almost all the major titles. The Ryder Cup merely provided further proof of their dominance. The British golfers, by contrast, were now playing the underdog role and could only snap at the heels of the US team every two years in the hope that their persistence would force the competition to continue. There were few GB team members who felt comfortable with the phenomenal Americans. One, however, was England's Max Faulkner whose irrepressible personality was not going to be shaded by a few arrogant Americans.

The son of a golf pro, Faulkner was an outspoken player with a penchant for lively-coloured clothing (pink plus-fours, salmon-coloured socks and pink shoes were one of his particularly memorable fashion statements) and a personality to match. He played in five of the first six post-war Ryder Cups and won a major – the Open Championship at Royal Portrush in 1951. In golfing terms, he was no slouch. Yet like so many of his GB team colleagues, he was often fighting a losing battle against the Americans. He made his Cup debut in 1947, but had played hardly any golf during World War II when he was an RAF physical training instructor. Without golf, Faulkner (who was 23 when the war broke out) took up boxing instead, becoming a Services champion. Meanwhile, his future American Ryder Cup opponents were able to play on a PGA Tour that was barely affected by the conflict. For Faulkner, this was one reason for his immensely disappointing Ryder Cup record – he only ever won one point from eight pairs and singles matches. Despite being terrifically fit himself, and a powerful striker of the ball (the width of his swing was legendary), Faulkner understood that his opponents in the Cup matches were better prepared and even better cared for. "It was first-class all the way for the Americans… they always had the best in transportation and accommodation. It was a bit irritating."

Faulkner's opponents – the likes of Jackie Burke, Jr. – did not care about any underlying sporting or social reasons for the lack of competitiveness. The Americans were the best players and that was just the way things were. "They [the British] didn't compete with the best and get better. We played each other, best against the best, and then every two years we kicked butt," Burke said without fear of argument.

Because British players were not invited to American majors, men like Faulkner waited like hunters to face their prey every two years. The Brits could only read about the exploits of America's top players in the Masters, the US Open and the PGA Championship, and this situation heightened the importance of the Cup for them. By contrast, the Ryder Cup was just another tournament to the Americans who played for substantial sums of money almost every week of the season and had no need to look much beyond the horizon of their own shores to appreciate that they were successful golfers. Stars like Gene Littler claimed to take the matches seriously – "If we had not done that, I don't think we would've won," he said – but it still felt like the Americans were doing their opponents a favour simply by turning up to play an uncompetitive match. The US team's attitude to the matches had transformed since the earliest days. Back then, they were striving to prove themselves the best against the sport's traditional leaders, now they suffered only from a fear of losing. World War II had put America in the fast lane in terms of developing the game and finding ways for professionals to improve their games; GB players, by contrast, were stuck on the hard shoulder. With the US team now odds-on favorites to keep the trophy every two years, they felt more relief than joy when they won. To lose would have made them look foolish.

British feelings of inadequacy were only heightened when Ben Hogan lifted the claret jug at his first tilt at the Open Championship in 1953 at Carnoustie. He met with the newly crowned Queen Elizabeth II, appeared before millions of TV viewers back in America on *The Ed Sullivan Show*, was honoured with a tickertape parade through the streets of New York and confirmed as a star in the sporting firmament. This was fame that no British golfer could match. If the Americans were supreme in one area it was the elevation of sports people, artists, scientists, politicians and the like into men and women lionised around the world. America led the world in so many ways – economics, political influence, science and social innovation – and golf was just another sphere of dominance.

By the 1953 match at Wentworth (still only eight years after the war and one year before rationing officially ended in Britain), the phrase "them and us" had entered the vocabulary of the two teams. GB golfers were by far the poor relations of their American cousins. Even the best British pros were relying on their pro-shop salaries while their counterparts across the Atlantic were full-time tournament professionals; a metaphorical chasm in both confidence and class had opened up between the two sides.

To counter Britain's inferiority complex, the team bathed in the nation's joy over the Queen's coronation and a number of successes in other sports and areas of human endeavour. England's cricket team regained the Ashes; football's FA Cup final was lit up by a virtuoso performance from the great Stanley Matthews; and Mount Everest was conquered by a British-led team of climbers. Surely, the Ryder Cup would follow?

For the match at Wentworth, the finest British golfer of the mid-20th century, Henry Cotton, took his turn as captain and attempted to invoke a new attitude. Cotton saw that the GB team was being overwhelmed by the Americans' positive attitude as much as by their collective ability. "To be a champion, you must act like one," was one of Cotton's most famous sayings. He insisted on the best of everything for his team, including food (despite rationing) and even relaxing entertainment (the GB players went to a West End theatre on a practice evening to watch the musical *Guys and Dolls*, certainly a first for several of them). Cotton's attitude was more in the style of his American counterpart than anything the British PGA would have suggested.

The press did its best to add spice to the contest, but the Americans were now overwhelming favourites. They arrived at Wentworth wearing confident smiles and looking as resplendent as ever with their bright-red, custom-made golf bags and matching clothing while the Great Britain team looked rather old fashioned and forlorn. At this moment only one team ever looked and acted like winners and that was the Americans.

At the end of the opening day, the match was following a familiar pattern – the Americans led 3-1 (the British had not won the foursomes since 1933) and Cotton's decision to leave out experienced players like Dai Rees and Max Faulkner and blood some youngsters had rebounded. Cotton is supposed to have said he would "kick the team's asses" that night and the rousing words seemed to do the trick. Instead of folding on day two, the GB team for once found some form and brought the score to 5-5 with a 3&2 win by Harry Bradshaw over Fred Haas. Unfortunately for Cotton, he now had the destination of the Cup resting on the shoulders of his two most inexperienced players.

Peter Alliss was the youngest of the British pair of hopefuls at 22 while Bernard Hunt was just a year older. Both were winning assistant professionals' titles only a year earlier, so to be thrown into such a high-profile event as the Ryder Cup was way beyond their level of experience at that time, even though they were both enormously talented prospects. Hunt's opponent was Dave Douglas, an eight-time tournament winner and 12 years older, while Alliss faced Jim Turnesa, the PGA champion of 1952. Cotton tried to give the young Alliss some extra encouragement by pointing out that his particular American foe was probably one of the weakest in the visiting team because he had not been selected for the foursomes on day one. Alliss listened carefully to Cotton's words, but they turned out to give him false hope; at lunch after 18 holes, the Englishman was 4-under par for his round, yet still 1-down to Turnesa.

Nevertheless, Alliss was spurred on in the afternoon and found himself 1-up with three to play. To his enormous credit, here was a young man whose only title at this time was the British Assistants Championship playing under the most intense spotlight and actually leading an experienced major champion, almost 20 years older than him.

On the tee at that 34th hole, Turnesa (who was also making his Ryder Cup debut) was suffering from nerves as well and a wayward drive would have probably flown deep into some trees had it not hit a female spectator. Fortune again favoured the American when Alliss then misjudged a pitch into the green and lost the hole to fall back to level. Showing his inexperience, the Englishman then drove out of bounds on the next hole to go 1-down with one to play. However, all was not lost for GB as Hunt went 1-up with one to play on the same hole.

The destiny of the Cup lay in the hands of GB's two youngest players and each of them would have a single hole to bring glory to the home team. As it stood, the overall match was tied. But if Alliss could pull back and get a half or if Hunt could keep his nerve and maintain his winning position then the GB side would be celebrating a rare and famous victory.

Turnesa hit a bad drive on the 18th and a buzz went around the Wentworth crowd. Alliss knew he was now in the box seat and needed only a safe par-5 to win the hole to guarantee no worse than a tie for the home team. This would be the best GB result since 1933. Alliss's own father, Percy, had been a member of that winning team, so there was a chance the son could repeat the triumph of the father. What a story it would have been for the press. Two mighty blows and the young Alliss had the hole seemingly in his grasp; he was just short and left of the last green and could take three more shots for his par while Turnesa was heading for an almost certain bogey. Then disaster ensued.

Alliss's description in his autobiography *My Life* of what happened next on that 36th hole is characteristically revealing. "As I walked round the ball, even as I stood by it, my mind was full of nothing but feet – brogues, moccasins, sneakers, boots, shoes, spikes, rubbers, the shoes of the people perched on the front seats of the grandstand. All those boots and shoes kept popping idiotically in and out of my mind."

Alliss had a relatively simple wedge to the green, but the nerves he was experiencing caused him to fluff the shot with a sand wedge and the ball bumbled short of the green. It was still his turn to play. Although his next chip with a 9-iron was about three feet from the pin, he missed the putt for a bogey six, the same score as Turnesa who had now won their match 1-up. The overall match score was now 6-5 to the Americans, but if Hunt could hang on to his winning position then the Brits would force a proud draw.

Hunt and Douglas had been all-square at lunch and their match was nip-and-tuck for the next 17 holes. Hunt was buoyant at 1-up with one to play, but heard the groans of the crowd when his friend Alliss failed to secure a half point. The strain was beginning to tell as both men landed on the 36th green in three shots, although they were each a long way from the pin. Douglas, tall and lean with a steady but unspectacular record in America, then made his years of toil on the PGA Tour pay off. While he knocked his first putt close, Hunt fired his just over three feet past the pin and, from there, promptly missed. His three-putt on the last green meant Hunt only halved his match and the Americans had not only retained the Cup (a 6-6 draw would have been enough for that), but they had won it and once again proved too classy for the British. The 6½-5½ match score was the US team's sixth straight win including three away from home.

The plain and simple truth is that Alliss's unfortunate mis-hit was the result of nerves and the pain of it lives on inside him to this day. Decades later he talked of the fateful chip to the 36th green: "I made an awful bodge of it… I feel I've had to live my whole life with the guilt of messing up that chip." Thus the baby of the GB team found the intensity of the rivalry had been too much for him. As a little boy, Alliss may have imagined holing a putt to win the Ryder Cup, but the reality of the situation was altogether different from the fantasy. The tension of the moment got the better of both him and Hunt. It was left to the British press to underline how American players with more experience of such tight situations continued to have the edge because they did not make as many similar mistakes.

During the decades of heavy losses, some British players, Brian Huggett among them, were desolate and depressed. "Making the Ryder Cup was the next best thing to winning the Open. It wasn't the same for the Americans. They won quite easily and it wasn't a great competition back then. I always felt that if it all went really well, we could have won. But looking back, we had no bloody chance. We only had half a team that thought like me, that we could win. There were some players who got the blazer and thought that they could walk around and live off that for the rest of their lives. They didn't care enough if we won or lost. I was naïve to think we could win, especially away from home."

Huggett would boil with anger at his team's inability to turn the tide. The Welshman's feelings for his opponents were clear. "The Americans tried to make you feel inferior. And we were. They loved to give us a whacking. They were very tough about the matches in those days. They never took it easy. It's bloody lovely for us to win now. They might pull out if they get whacked too often. They were bloody arrogant. I got 12 Ryder Cup points and I enjoyed every one of those buggers."

So as the years rolled by and the defeats piled high, the rivalry showed an unusual aggression. Eventually the 'hate' word appeared, ironically just after the rest of the world had enjoyed another romantic summer of love. The Ryder Cup in 1969 took place on an unromantic stretch of the Lancashire coastline where the temperature between the two teams was raised to boiling point by one man who was not afraid to express his feelings, the GB captain Eric Brown.

To describe Brown as a fierce character would be a vast understatement. Alliss once said the Scot "could make trouble in an empty 'hoos'" because Brown had a chip on his shoulder about many things, including Americans. Despite that, he was a fine player, a man who would have won the Open in 1958 at Royal Lytham & St Annes but for a double-bogey six on the 72nd hole when a par would have won him the claret jug. Even though it was an Australian (Peter Thomson) who won that day and not an American, Brown had a deep loathing for players from the United States and what they stood for. Indeed, he was not afraid to tell anyone who cared to listen how much he hated his Ryder Cup opponents.

In his own four Ryder Cup appearances in the 1950s as a player, Brown played tough on every hole. In his singles matches, this hatred worked for him because he won every time, beating four major champions – Jerry Barber, Tommy Bolt, Lloyd Mangrum and Cary Middlecoff. This was a remarkable record for any GB player during the 1950s, yet in four foursomes, Brown's partner never responded to his intensity and, despite trying four different partners, he lost on every occasion.

The fact that Brown could beat the stars of the PGA Tour one-on-one delivered both a powerful self-belief but also feelings of resentment: why should the Americans be able to play in all four majors while he could not (Brown never played in any major other than the Open). His emotions boiled over in a post-match exchange with Tommy Bolt after their 1955 singles match. In Malcolm Hamer's 1992 book *The Ryder Cup: The Players*, he quotes Bolt as saying: "You won, Eric, but I didn't enjoy the game." Brown was quick to reply: "No, of course, you didn't enjoy it because you were ****** licked." The expletive was enough to send the equally volatile Bolt to the locker room in such a temper that he broke a club and refused to attend the closing ceremony.

Brown's explanation of his hateful feelings was rather convoluted. He said in 1969: "An idea has got round that I hate Americans. I don't – off the course. But on the course, I do hate them. I want to massacre them in a golf sense and that's the spirit I want to get through to my side." Oddly, the Scot's hot temper was something that seemed to work in the 1969 match. A more formal and polite style of captaincy had been the norm before this, the classic British "let's do our best, chaps". By contrast, Brown's version of captaincy was more like what football legend Sir Alex Ferguson made famous: "the hair dryer treatment".

With such a background and temper, it was not surprising that the irascible Brown was at the centre of much of the trouble between the teams. It began when he ordered his players not to help any Americans look for golf balls that landed in the long rough near the fairways. His rather disingenuous excuse ("I don't want my players running the risk of treading on an American ball and thereby losing a hole") did little to calm the mood. The truth was that Brown got under the skin of his opponents and, for the first time in over a decade, the GB team matched the Americans.

Even over 40 years later, Brian Huggett remembers the ire in Brown's voice when he talked to the team. "Eric didn't like the Americans at all, maybe because they'd hammered us so many times when he played. All the team knew how he felt and, for some, it got them to try extra hard. He had more of our guys believing that they could win. Eric was strong compared to captains before him. 'We're going to beat this lot,' he said in the locker room, so he was a bold one and he'd say bold things to you. 'Give them a whacking,' he'd say and he'd use pretty strong words to back that up. Maybe we hadn't had enough of that before."

The contests had been unbalanced for years and any rivalry was flawed. Brian Huggett was clear about the reasons. "The Americans were better prepared, they had better weather, courses in better condition and more consistent. Their rough was at regulated heights. The sand would be beaten down in all their bunkers to the same compression, so bunker shots are easier. In my day, in a bunker, there was a good chance your ball was in a footmark. It wasn't a fair competition because of all that."

Neil Coles played under Brown in 1969 and also in 1971 in America. He recalls that his captain made the Birkdale match niggly almost on his own. "Eric was that kind of character. He just said to us 'just go and kill them'. He was very confrontational and generated a lot of the heat."

Yet there were others in Brown's team, like the strapping 24-year-old debutant Brian Barnes, who pretty much hated the man who hated the Americans. "I found him embarrassing," recalled Barnes years later. "He hated the Yanks and it was win at all costs for him, but I was brought up in public school, to be a good loser and a good winner. Eric tried to get in my face and he just buggered me up completely." Barnes played three times at Lytham and lost each time.

If the 'hate' word had been said under today's media glare then someone like the late Eric Brown might have had serious trouble on his hands because his comments would be seen as incendiary. However, in the less intrusive media world of the 1960s, Brown was simply seen as trying to be honest and attempting to galvanise the fans to roar his side to victory.

Brian Huggett reflects now that 'hate' is not a good word for golf matches: "I mean I wanted to beat the Americans, but I didn't hate them. There was some needle in this match, but I didn't hate them. I definitely wanted 100% to beat them, but they're nice people, very hospitable. [Hate is] not the right word for me, but that's the way Eric Brown felt about them and he told us so in very strong words. He said we could win and he had a strong team and maybe if they were a fraction off, yes, we thought maybe we *could* do it."

Whether Brown's words were appropriate or not for the Ryder Cup, his team managed a remarkable 16-16 tie. The Scot is less well remembered, however, than the Jack Nicklaus concession to Tony Jacklin on the last green of the very final singles match that secured the tie. This was a seminal moment in the history of the contests as the two great champions played the final hole of the final match with the destination of the Cup in their hands. Both players had long birdie putts for glory on the last green, but whereas Jacklin left his approach two and a half feet away, Nicklaus was over five feet past. When the American sank his putt – a shot that showed remarkable guts in itself – that guaranteed a tied match; the only other possible result would be for the Englishman to miss his tiddler and suffer the indignity of sending his team to another defeat. The magnanimous Nicklaus – actually playing in his first Ryder Cup match – was having none of it, immediately walking over and picking up Jacklin's ball marker. The warring atmosphere was forgotten as one of the greatest acts of sportsmanship took place. Nicklaus said to Jacklin: ""I don't think you were going to miss that putt, but I didn't want to give you the opportunity."

Immediately afterwards, however, Nicklaus's captain Sam Snead was unimpressed. "All the boys thought it was ridiculous to give him that putt," Snead said. "We went over there to win, not to be good ol' boys." Perhaps to suggest all his team felt the same way was disingenuous, but the notoriously grouchy Snead was not alone in his feelings. One team member Frank Beard wrote in his 1992 book *Making The Turn* that he also wanted to win so much that he would have forced Jacklin to make his short putt because he would have had "the weight of a whole nation on his shoulders".

Nicklaus had his answer ready. "I thought it was the right way to have it end," he said afterward."I felt like what Tony had done that year, winning the British Open, and what it meant to British golf, was something very special. The spirit of the Ryder Cup was as a goodwill match, and if Tony would have missed that putt, I felt like he would have been [labeled] a choking dog forever. Why would you ever want to give him the opportunity [to miss the putt] when he's given Britain a hero? They'd put him up on a pedestal. Leave him on that pedestal."

The fact that this gesture now gives its name to both a golf club (The Concession in Bradenton, Florida, jointly built by Nicklaus and Jacklin) as well as a new competition for top amateur players (The Concession Cup was first contested in May 2014) is testimony to its significance and Nicklaus's flawless instincts.

Back in 1969, the tied result of the match was a first in Ryder Cup history and also it was only the second time the Americans had been denied since the matches returned after World War II (the surprise GB victory in 1957 at Lindrick was the other). Raising the temperature of the rivalry to boiling hot seemed to work for Eric Brown's GB&I team, but it was an act of pure golf etiquette that will always be remembered rather than the clashes of temper. And, at least for one match in that era, the Ryder Cup had a rivalry worthy of its name.

Europe enters the picture

The introduction in 1979 of continental European players to add their talents to those from GB & Ireland provided a renewed impetus to the Ryder Cup and elevated the match rivalry to a new level. There was more competitiveness between the teams, but even more importantly there was a new fire in the bellies of the so-called Euros. The man to light that fire was Severiano Ballesteros. The resentment felt by the GB&I teams of the previous couple of decades because of the sport's unlevel playing field was replaced by the Spaniard's desire to prove himself against the best – the Americans. The year that the Europeans first entered the contest was the one in which Ballesteros won the first of his five majors. He felt the sting of criticism from the American press, however, (and, privately, from a few players as well) about his cavalier style at Royal Lytham & St Annes where he won the Open and how they claimed it was more good luck than good judgment that won him the title.

What the entire world was only just appreciating was the genius of Ballesteros who could look at the ball in a seemingly impossible position and still make the shot, be it from a bunker, behind a tree or a car park, as he had managed atLytham in the summer. Of course, the GB sides of the past had several on-course leaders, but Ballesteros had an in-your-face attitude with his teammates that they found inspiring. Within six years of European involvement, the Americans had been beaten and Ballesteros was one of the main reasons because he had unadulterated belief in his own ability and then transmitted that to his teammates. To be fair to his opponents, the Spaniard also used gamesmanship, his own legendaryknowledge of the rules and every type of cunning move to unsettle the Americans.

Ballesteros's mirror image in the US team in terms of intensity was the equally competitive Paul Azinger. Their battles in singles or pairs matches represented the new rivalry and not just because the matches were now on a knife-edge. Ballesteros and Azinger both hated to lose at anything, but the enmity was also founded in different political standings – the American was a rabid Republican, while the Spaniard was an emblem of the new, free Spain in the post-General Francisco Franco era. So while Ballesteros and Azinger approached the game of golf in the same way, their visions of life in general were polar opposites. Not surprisingly, their Ryder Cup confrontations were classics.

The pair initially clashed in a singles match in 1989 at The Belfry. The first incident came when the Spaniard asked if he could change his scuffed golf ball. Azinger declined, a move that surprised the European superstar who believed golfing courtesy would override the American's rigid interpretation of the rules. On the 18th tee with Azinger 1-up, the American hit a horrid tee shot into water and needed a referee to decide on where to drop the ball for the next shot. Although it was none of his business, Ballesteros stepped into the debate and disagreed with the referee's suggestion for the drop. This was Spanish gamesmanship at its finest, but Azinger held his temper and played a magnificent recovery to halve the hole and win his match 1-up. There were claims and counter claims by the two players after the match, but one certainty remained – a Ryder Cup feud had begun. And although Ballesteros lost his singles, the Europeans held on to the Cup with a 14-14 tie. The British press did its best to pump up the rivalry for the next match in 1991. "Big Mouth Yanks Get Their Own Butts Kicked," was the verdict of the rather far-from-impartial tabloid *Daily Star*.

With such animosity in the air, there were bound to be fireworks at Kiawah Island, especially when Ballesteros and Azinger were drawn against each other in both matches on day one. Firstly, there was The Mystery of the Wrong Ball, an incident that happened in a foursomes between Ballesteros and his compatriot Jose Maria Olazabal and Azinger and Chip Beck.

The complicated rules of Ryder Cup matchplay stated that a player must tee off with a ball of the same compression throughout the alternative shot foursomes match, although, if one player uses a 90 compression ball for all his tee shots, his partner can hit a 100 compression ball. On the 9th hole, with the Americans 2-up, the Spaniards called in the referee because they believed their opponents had played a wrong ball on the 7th hole, that is, one of a different compression than they had started out with.

It was a very unusual accusation and also it came two holes after the incident had allegedly happened, so there was much discussion between the official and the players. The Americans initially claimed that there had been no change and the rules official decided that no penalty could be issued anyway because they now stood on the 9th tee. The kerfuffle might have been forgotten if only Azinger had not then admitted a change of ball had actually been made, but that it was an innocent mistake. Ballesteros, the ultimate competitor, was furious because there had been a clear contravention of the rules and Azinger only seemed to admit this when he knew there would be no penalty. The American was adamant about his innocence. "I can tell you we're not trying to cheat," he said to his opponents, to which the wily Ballesteros replied: "Oh no. Breaking the rules and cheating are two different things."

Three holes later, there was The Mysterious Allergy. Ballesteros was notorious even on the European Tour as a fidgeter, a cougher and a sneezer, sometimes at the most inopportune moments. Azinger made just such an allegation at Kiawah, claiming that the Spaniard made a noise during his back swing. He gave the Spaniard a particularly long stare after he had felt forced to step away from a tee shot on the 12th. The Spaniard famously replied to the allegations that "everyone knows I have allergies". In the end, all this fuss upset the home team more than the visitors as the Spanish pairing fought back and eventually took the match 2&1.

In his 2007 official biography *Seve*, the incomparable Spaniard was still bullish about the injustice of the incident, stating that afterwards Azinger "went around saying 'Seve was king of the cheats'". It is a mark of the depth of some of the wounds from Kiawah that 16 years later, Ballesteros could not forgive or forget. In fact, Azinger tells the story of how before they faced each other in the Ryder Cup, the Spaniard offered him some very generous assistance. "[Seve] almost took me under his wing in the mid-1980s. He helped me with my short game, but after 1989 [in the Ryder Cup] there was no more help for me." The once-respectful relationship between the two had broken down and was summed up by Ballesteros later saying: "The Americans have 11 nice guys and Paul Azinger."

There were many other questions and controversies during the two matches involving Ballesteros and Azinger that set the bar for the animosity between the two teams. This level of gamesmanship-cum-needle was not representative of every match at this time, but the increased level of interest in the matches and the finely-balanced nature of the contests by now were accentuating the intensity. And Ballesteros was probably the latter day king (Hagen being the holder of the title years earlier). Curtis Strange summed up how all the Americans felt about the Spaniard shortly after Seve's death in 2011. He told ESPN.com: "For the players, as aggravating as that can be, it's part of the Ryder Cup. Especially in Seve's case, God rest his soul. You've heard of him coughing – that happened every time. Stretching match play rules. He just got under your skin. And I think he did exactly what he was supposed to do. He thrived on it. I got upset at myself because I allowed him to get under my skin." Gamesmanship has always been a part of sport and, in this era, its exposure via the media added to the needle between the teams.

The Ballesteros no-holds-barred attitude in particular was infectious. The Spaniard and his fellow continental Europeans had none of the psychological baggage of the British who had been defeated for so many years; they were a breath of fresh air for teammates like Eamon Darcy. The Irishman was a teammate of the Spaniard's only once, but recalls: "Seve didn't even want to shake hands with the Americans when he beat them. He was fantastic. He disliked the Americans because they kept him out of their tour for a while and he never forgot. He was like an elephant. You did something on him and he'd never forget. [Seve's attitude meant] we were all up for the job, especially in the early days of Team Europe when we had never beaten them, especially in America."

The power of the crowd

With a European team bringing competitiveness to almost every Ryder Cup, the rivalry also took on a more patriotic flavour with players now performing before increasingly vociferous crowds. This atmosphere outside the ropes would pile the pressure on the players. But the role of the crowd had always been a factor in making the Cup an extraordinary event.

The treatment of the British team in the inaugural match had been exemplary. One GB team member in 1927, Arthur Havers, commented: "Everywhere we went, we were submerged by hospitality and kindness." The Americans won with ease and the visitors' mood was one of politeness and courtesy even though British golfing pride had been bruised. Britain had been the home of golf since the middle of the previous century and yet now the upstarts from the ex-colony held the only professional golf team trophy that existed, so to lose the 1929 match would not really be an option.

In every issue of *Golf Monthly* in early 1929, there were references to the upcoming Ryder Cup: a story about team captain George Duncan wanting his team to undergo extra physical fitness training; a comment from the great J.H. Taylor that the British players should take on extra practice before the match; and an editorial describing how the GB team needed to win back the trophy "so ingloriously lost" two years earlier. Perhaps not surprisingly, the crowds for the second match of the series at Moortown in Yorkshire were more boisterous than the first. Despite a cold snap of weather (snow fell on one of the practice days), as many as 10,000 spectators attended on each of the two match days and the British PGA charged only a small entrance fee to encourage large crowds, thereby enticing along people who were not regular golf fans.

The match had turned into an event unlike any other golf tournament of the era because team golf meant the entire crowd could simply cheer for one side against the enemy from overseas; there was no list of British players to split the partisan spectators; everyone was behind the entire GB team. Whereas the protocol of the crowd was normally to stay largely silent, this Ryder Cup was slightly different, especially after day one when the visitors held a one-point lead.

Needing to come from behind, the British crowd turned up the heat on the Americans and a mild form of golf hooliganism broke out. *The Times* correspondent Bernard Darwin wrote after the match how some of the crowd at Moortown acted more like football fans and, at one time, to his sadness, "forgot themselves so far as to cheer when an American missed a short putt". It was a surprise for the players to hear the fans become so vocal because golf in the 1920s was a sport where etiquette was everything, much more so than today; players showed little emotion and so the crowd was expected to follow suit. Darwin, in fact, was sympathetic to the cause of the American visitors saying how they fought with gallantry and "never gave in and never grudged a victory" as the British won 7-5.

The trend of large, vocal crowds for the British matches and smaller, quieter ones in America had been set, something that became increasingly noticeable after World War II as the US team notched up a series of convincing victories. Of course, the American players maintained their seriousness about winning the contest because they were representing their country, but crowds of only a few thousand began turning up for the matches in the US. Without true competition, the fans were becoming apathetic. The late, great English sports journalist Ian Wooldridge attended the Californian contests in the mid-1950s and wrote: "More people attended the eve-of-contest dinner than ever watched the matches. There was no entrance fee and there were no restraining ropes out on the course. It was an Arcadian stroll (for the players)."

Even by the 1960s, players like Huggett were startled by the difference in the way fans supported their teams. He loved the passion of the British crowds, but his matches in America were at a time when the US teams won almost at their leisure. Huggett believed there was an arrogance about the US players that fed into the attitude of the US fans, not that they watched in huge numbers.

"In my first match on day one of the 1963 competition in Atlanta, George Will and I were the opening pair against Arnold Palmer and Johnny Pott and 75% of all the crowd at the event in those days always watched the Palmer match. On the 16th green, we holed the winning putt and only about 12 people clapped – they were our own PGA officials. I didn't expect the silence from the American crowd. The crowds were respectful back then, but by 1971 in St. Louis I remember they were maybe a little bit noisier. On the whole, the crowds were pretty good in America, they were very friendly, but not when you beat Arnold."

Contrast this with the thronging hordes at Lindrick in 1957 who carried winning captain Dai Rees off the course on their shoulders when the GB team snatched an unlikely win. Tens of thousands of British fans kept turning up even during the 1960s and 1970s when the American team was so strong their victory was inevitable. Their enthusiasm helped keep some level of rivalry between the two teams intact, but the story in America was quite different; golf fans across the States did not share the British love affair for the contest. Renowned golf writer Peter Dobereiner best summed up the state of the US version of the rivalry in 1977 when the Americans again crushed the brave but outclassed GB&I team at Royal Lytham & St Annes. "In America," he wrote, "the Ryder Cup now rates somewhere between Tennessee Frog Jumping and the Alabama Melon-Pip Spitting Championship." Two years later, a European team would face America for the first time and a real battle commenced.

Finally in 1985 at The Belfry, with the GB players supported by a core of Europe's best, the trophy changed hands. The US was beaten for only the second time since 1933 and the home team and the crowd bonded like never before. The scenes of celebration – with the Europeans spraying champagne from the roof of The Belfry Hotel on to the cheering fans below – set a trend for future matches. Half a century of almost uninterrupted hopelessness had been turned around and the enmity between the two teams was now based on true competition where each match could be won by either team.

The extra input from the fans began to heighten the nervousness of the players. America's Brad Faxon recalls his debut in 1995 at Oak Hill. "I played Monday with no crowd and then on Tuesday there were 40,000 people. We walked through this throng to the 1st tee and there was Byron Nelson and President George H.W. Bush. 'You shoot first, Fax, is what [team captain] Lanny Wadkins said and I heard the announcer say 'Brad Faxon, United States of America', but I still can't remember actually hitting that first shot."

The fervour of Ryder Cup patriotism also surprised Faxon. "Even qualifying for the Ryder Cup is patriotic. You can't escape it. It's on your computer when you open it up. It's everywhere. Playing Ryder Cup is the one thing every player wants. It's a goal on the top of your list when you start out as a pro. It's our Olympics and when the matches started getting closer, it was like World Cup soccer, it's up there with the biggest event. It's the only time we have the team spirit in our game. I don't think either team finds it easy [to be rivals]. Every week, you're trying to beat each other's brains out and then you're a team and playing against the other guys you've been with on the range."

For a player like Faxon, there has always been a fine balance between just enough intensity and too much. "It's good for the Ryder Cup to be a contest on a knife-edge. The media comes up with phrases like 'War by the Shore' and it's almost too much. But who doesn't want to see all these pumping fists and Boo Weekley riding a golf club like a broomstick as he did at Valhalla. And I remember when David Duval went crazy at Brookline – he didn't even know how to fist-pump, he'd never gotten that excited before." Faxon's reference to Brookline points to the nadir of crowd behaviour at the Ryder Cup.

By the 1990s, the involvement of the crowd had increased simply because of the vast numbers now wanting to experience the tense tussles between Europe and America. The 10,000 per day attendances were now approaching 30,000, but in Brookline the number of fans and their behaviour was hard to control. Again, the tension within the match itself (the Americans were 10-6 down after two days) caused the atmosphere on the third and final day to be as sharp as a knife. When the home team began their relentless climb to victory and the fans downed a few too many beers, the course was full of people more in tune with the ethos of a football crowd than a golf audience.

Overall, there was still some love and respect between the two teams and the two sets of fans, but a few boorish idiots directed loud name-calling at players like Colin Montgomerie and it reached distasteful levels. Calling Monty derogatory names like "Mrs Doubtfire" could be dismissed as playful if it was an isolated incident, but the Scotsman's father heard much worse and left the course in disgust. "My father is 70 and it's a pity to have him [be forced to] leave because he's embarrassed and insulted by comments towards his son," said Montgomerie afterwards. Monty's singles opponent that day, Payne Stewart, was so upset by his own fans' behaviour that he picked up his ball on the 18th fairway to allow the Scot a 1-up victory.

Several European players, including the 19-year-old debutant Sergio Garcia, were similarly abused on the course and even the European administrators felt the heat of the crowd. European Tour executive director Ken Schofield was shocked by what he heard. "I have never been more scared in my life on a golf course than I was at Brookline. It was frightening to hear people shouting 'Kill! Kill!' and 'Bring out the body bags!'" Europe's captain Mark James later famously described the atmosphere as a bear pit, while others have likened it to a beer garden.

The rivalry had grown ugly and gotten out of hand. Both teams were probably to blame for ramping up the intensity over the previous two decades, but the Americans took the brunt of the criticism for Brookline. The *Washington Post* wrote: "It seems an American team can't get through an international competition without acting like jackasses at some point, and Steve Pate and Tom Lehman led a ridiculous charge to mob [Justin] Leonard. Olazabal was 20ft away and could have halved the hole. Distracted and delayed, the world's greatest putter missed. Had he made it, done that, the match would have been tied and Europe could have kept the Cup. So it was not just a spasm of well-intentioned enthusiasm. It deserved a severe celebration penalty." None was forthcoming. For Europeans like Olazabal, there was a hope that out of adversity would come strength. "After everything was over and we got to the locker-room and the whole team was there, I sat down looked around me, almost every member of the team was crying. That brings the players together and builds up friendship, and that's why that moment has positive things."

The next Ryder Cup had to clean up its act and find a new way for the rivalry to manifest itself. Ironically, it was an action of pure violence against America (and far away from anything to do with sport) that put at least a temporary end to aggressive behaviour on the golf course. The destruction of the two World Trade Center towers by terrorists happened less than two weeks before the American team was due to fly over to play the 34th match in September 2001. The world changed that day in many respects and, for the Ryder Cup, the violent confrontation of 1999 now seemed gauche and inappropriate. The match was postponed for 12 months and allowed further time for reflection on how the crowd and the players needed to react to this golfing competition. Captains Sam Torrance and Curtis Strange – close friends themselves – had already discussed ways of ensuring more decorum, but sad deaths of so many innocent people in New York, Washington and Pennsylvania provided a strong reason why Ryder Cup teams in future would have to find a new way to express their fierce rivalry.

The 2002 match turned out to be no less of a raucous affair than previous editions, yet emotions were in control. The fans for both teams chanted and even cheered the odd missed putt by an opponent, but security had been stepped up and alcohol was no longer sold on the course. The match was tight, the roars were loud and the Ryder Cup rivalry returned to a level that added to the contest rather than detracted from it.

Two years later, Hal Sutton continued the theme of producing a manageable intensity for the match. "Those planes going into the Twin Towers put things into perspective for everybody. I didn't want things to get out of hand when I was captain. You never know what happens when the crowd overreacts and there are personalities involved. Not everyone likes each other and the crowd reacts differently to different players, but this is just a competition and life goes on."

Most recently, there has been a hint that Brookline behaviour might be returning and that the ugly side of the enmity is re-emerging. The 2012 match in Medinah saw some moronic fan conduct. Little was made of the story, but British newspapers reported how a very small minority of American fans reacted to the European team honoring their hero, the late Seve Ballesteros who had died of cancer the previous year. There were Seve badges on the team's uniforms, constant mentions of Seve's relationship with Europe captain Olazabal and even Seve sky-writing messages for extra inspiration.

Then during one of the afternoon fourballs, an American fan near the 16th tee shouted "F*** you, Seve", an obscenity that was clearly heard by millions of TV viewers watching live. Sadly, this incident was not the only one. It was reported that Justin Rose was taunted about his dead father; two fans were actually ejected from the Medinah course for shouting obscenities at Europe's Nicolas Colsaerts; and even some of the European team's wives and girlfriends were the targets of verbal abuse. Neither Olazabal nor any of the European team made formal complaints and, while tournament director Michael Belot was unaware of any anti-Seve comments, marshals were made aware of the situation.

For Lee Westwood, the boisterous chanting of American fans had actually overstepped the mark at Valhalla four years earlier. "All of the abuse that I got was fairly nasty and pretty shameful," he said. "Some people don't know the difference between supporting their team and abusing the opposition team, which is unfortunate."

Inside the ropes, the modern-day Ryder Cup rivalry is changing again to suit the lives and attitudes of the world's leading players who are now often friends, even neighbours living on the same exclusive country-club estates. Many of the Europeans like Ian Poulter, Luke Donald (who even has an American wife and is based in Chicago) and Justin Rose have played mostly on the PGA Tour for several seasons. These Europeans see their American Ryder Cup opponents on the range almost every day or at the same sponsor events. Rory McIlroy and Tiger Woods have undertaken tours of China together and speak openly about their friendship as well as their mutual admiration for each other; for their sponsors, Nike, this is music to their ears, but is such mutual admiration good for the Ryder Cup rivalry? Then there are Graeme McDowell and Keegan Bradley joking with each other in a television advert for Srixon golf balls. The ad pretends the two are bitter enemies until Keegan's scripted comment: "We're actually good friends." Do these two men sound like they want to stamp on each other's throats in order to bring home the Ryder Cup? The players contend that their professional pride, the effects of the team room and the history of the event are enough to maintain an intense level of competition.

And, if the players' commitment to the cause was ever in doubt, then the tens of thousands of raucous, loyal fans who turn up to support the two teams every two years would not allow it. The players these days even talk about recognising different cheers from around the course; a 'home' cheer sounds different to the golfers than an 'away' cheer and they can be inspired or deflated by what they hear.

Paul Lawrie is the very definition of a dour Scot, but the Ryder Cup experience left him tearful in Medinah in 2012 where he was playing only his second match, the first being in the cauldron of Brookline. But it was not his crucial 5&3 victory over Brandt Snedeker in the singles that touched Lawrie the most, it was realising how much the win would mean to his captain. "On the gala dinner night, Olazabal went round each individual telling him what that player meant to him… everyone was just in tears, you can't imagine. I've never cried so much as I did that week with him."

While the relationships between the players themselves can heighten emotions, the fact that thousands of fans can be in tears as well is where the modern-day Ryder Cup finds its most powerful passions. Justin Rose has no doubt where the rawest emotions come from during the matches. "The crowd makes the intensity. It's red vs blue and two sets of fans, home and away; it's less the individuals out on the golf course. Personal friendships are put aside for the week. The Ryder Cup transcends golf and attracts sports fans, not just golf fans. There are different types of behaviour out there. The players have to go and play each other the following week, so there is respect inside the ropes. But emotions run way higher because the crowds charge the emotions so much. The players in recent years have done a great job keeping sportsmanship first and foremost because the lines outside the ropes do get a bit blurry at times."

From a sport, with its foundations in etiquette and personal integrity with the rules, there has come a fist-pumping, player-roaring battle of skill and willpower that takes place in front of a delirious crowd. So the rivalry in professional golf's oldest team event can be harsh as well as generous. On paper, it makes no sense: just 40 matches played bi-annually over 10 different decades between teams that represent countries and continents 3,000 miles apart; the formula has built a match-day intensity that exceeds anything else in golf and is the envy of many sports. And yet, for all the unlikeliness of it ever happening, the Ryder Cup has become a phenomenon.

Interestingly, there is now a plethora of imitations – from the Presidents Cup to the latest international team contest, the EurAsia Cup that began in spring 2014 – yet none of them have the cachet or the passion of the original, and best, international team competition in golf. The Ryder Cup, with its rivalry dating back almost 90 years, produces priceless moments for the fans and for the players who often talk of how this team experience is the most important of their careers. The genuine rivalry between the players – albeit one that has changed over the decades – remains one of the keys to the Ryder Cup's success.

Justin Rose describes it best. "Losing Ryder Cup matches hurts more, winning means more. I've won one and lost one and you come away from it with a great experience whatever happens, but Medinah [2012] was the first time I had ever experienced the elation of celebrating together and collectively feeling the accomplishment of the whole team. That's what bonds our team, and it's amazing."

The last stroke

To fully understand why the Ryder Cup rivalry is unique, it is necessary to establish that the keys to becoming a great Cup golfer are twofold: being able to play within a team atmosphere and the performing well in the matchplay format. One of the reasons that the rivalry has become such a fierce one is that both these requirements are unusual for the top professionals.

The pressure of the Ryder Cup means the pros cannot simply go out and play their normal game. The world's best golfers have become very skilled at playing for just themselves and shutting out the rest of the world for 72 holes of strokeplay (Tiger Woods is the greatest example), but it takes a different attitude, sometimes a different kind of player, to prosper in a matchplay team environment.

For years, Americans were the best Ryder Cup players, but that was more because they were just superior all-round golfers and had benefited from the use of better courses, equipment, coaching and facilities for decades. Those differences no longer exist and the recent Ryder Cups have been ultra-competitive with Team Europe as soon as full competitiveness was established in 1983. But why do Europeans triumph nowadays?

Almost every European participant in the Cup claims their Tour stimulates more togetherness: players travel, eat and socialise more regularly than their American counterparts who favour private jets, hotel room service and early nights rather than late-night drinking sessions. The result is that European players are more friendly to each other at normal tournaments and so can fit into a team more easily. They say that once the post-World War II inconsistencies in the spread of talent were ironed out in the 1980s, this spirit of devotedness to each other proved crucial. It is hard to argue against the players' beliefs, but maybe there is a more emotional explanation.

Paul Azinger was hailed as a hero after captaining the victorious American Ryder Cup team (minus an injured Tiger Woods, by the way) and reflected on his experiences as a Ryder Cup player in *Golf Digest*: "I've always said that the Americans' love for the Ryder Cup is in our heads, but for the Europeans, it's in their blood. There's a difference. The Ryder Cup meant everything to them." On another occasion, the man nicknamed Zinger told the media: "The Ryder Cup can define you." And for many of the British and Irish pros who played during the lean years between 1935 and 1981, that statement was absolutely true.

Perhaps this is the real truth. Players on the European side of the Atlantic, for decades, had just one annual shot at a major – the Open Championship – and very few were successful, whereas the top American players had three major opportunities and racked up those titles. Plus, the prize money comparison favoured US players for decades, many of whom not only acted like millionaires but were actual ones as well at a time when many GB&I team members were club pros. A top British golfer like Tommy Horton who made the Ryder Cup team in 1975 and 1977 ranks that achievement on a par with all his tournament wins. One of Horton's proudest career moments, in fact, was attending a special PGA centennial dinner in 2001 with all the living British, Irish and European pros who had competed in the Cup over the years. Each player was presented with a special blue blazer bearing an exclusive Cup badge on the pocket. "I wear the jacket for formal occasions and I'm very proud of it. We didn't win [the Cup] in our day, but this was European golf's way of saying that we did our bit. One of my old friends, Jimmy Martin, only played in a single match back in 1965 but he broke down in tears when he was given the blazer. The Ryder Cup has always meant a lot to us."

One of Horton's teammates in 1975 was Guy Hunt who played in the Cup on only that single occasion. The Hertfordshire pro won just once on the European Tour, so the Ryder Cup was "just about the best week of my life". Hunt had turned professional at just 16 and was only 28 when he made the team at Laurel Valley in Pennsylvania. He had only played in one American-based major at that point (he missed the cut at The Masters in 1973), so the Ryder Cup was a step-up in standard compared with a normal week's golf in Europe. "I was immensely proud to get a half point with Eamon Darcy in my first pairs match. We got a birdie on the last hole against Al Geiberger and Ray Floyd. Even now when I see Eamon, we call each other 'partner'. The whole thing was a benchmark in my career. Being a Ryder Cup player was one of the key things I wanted to achieve growing up as a young golfer." Sadly and despite recording his only European Tour win two years later, Hunt never qualified for another team.

Another Englishman, Oliver Wilson, is another 'one Ryder Cup wonder' having qualified for the 2008 team despite never winning on Tour at all. In a BBC 5 Live golf documentary after his appearance, Wilson told how he regarded making the team as the ultimate in his career. "[Qualifying for the Ryder Cup] is everything, it was always my main goal in golf. I'm not sure if that's the correct thing to have as your main goal, but I wanted to be there a lot." Wilson even felt that his desire to have a Ryder Cup appearance on his CV sometimes got in the way of him winning actual events.

By contrast, it is difficult to find American players – and particularly fans – who think about the Cup in quite same way. The players' historical memories of great achievements, perhaps understandably, revolve around what happened at major tournaments: Gene Sarazen's "shot heard around the world" from the 1935 Masters, Ben Hogan's classic 1-iron to the 72nd hole at Merion that helped him win the 1950 US Open or Arnold Palmer snatching the Open Championship at his very first attempt.

Actually, that list is almost endless, but iconic Ryder Cup memories are usually in the background of their career histories, even when America was a regular winner of the Cup. The famous concession in 1969 is often quoted and the US comeback victory in 1999, but there are few standouts that sit above major title tales. Prior to Team Europe's emergence, the Ryder Cup was just something the Americans always won, they took it for granted. Nowadays, it is a match the US does not win often enough, so who wants to talk about it.

In Europe, though, every European player today understands the importance of the Ryder Cup from his earliest moments in the professional sport. The past players underline it, the media never lets him forget it and the fans are always talking about it. For the American players, the Cup is just less important. They love their heroes for winning majors not Ryder Cups, the US press corps can be ambivalent about the contest and the regular US sports fan would rather go to The Masters.

Despite all that, the Ryder Cup rivalry is more obvious than ever and produces yet more drama in every match. But who is driving all that rivalry? Maybe the players who feed off it, who enjoy it more, who revel in the competition are on Team Europe. They bleed for the Ryder Cup. Maybe Azinger has got it right.

4

Money & Business

There is one main commercial conclusion to draw when discussing the history of the Ryder Cup: it is a very peculiar business. The event has grown from simple beginnings into an operation that generates millions of dollars, pounds and euros. Of course, like so many major sporting events in the modern era, it really *is* a business, but one that fails to conform to any of the normal rules. There are no comparable businesses, even in the world of sport.

For a start, the Ryder Cup happens every two years – all the world's other great sporting events are either annual, such as Wimbledon or the Open Championship, or quadrennial like the Olympics or FIFA World Cup. Then, there is the unique matter of the event's management: two completely separate organisations operate the Cup, one on each side of the Atlantic, and they generate an income only once every four years. There is no profit share for the 'away team'. TV companies, sponsors and many other commercial partners have to negotiate with two different groups of people who make decisions based on their own needs and the state of the marketplace in their part of the world. After that comes the deal with the host venue which is often complicated by factors such as other high-profile golf events the host club may wish to stage in the future or the level of support from local and national government. Add to this the fact that the increasingly large profits from the matches are disbursed through a complex network of companies, golf-related development projects and charitable donations. And there is not even any prize money for the players if they win.

The question of compensation

One of the unique aspects of the Ryder Cup is that the golfers take part for pride alone and not prize money. Strictly speaking, that is the truth, but it is not quite the whole truth because the players have always received some form of compensation. In the earliest matches, every Ryder Cup budget included a line that provided payments to the golfers not only for their expenses (in home matches that might mean travelling to the golf course), but also a salary that recompensed the pros who took unpaid leave to represent their country.

In the earliest matches in the 1920s, selection for the contest overseas could mean a month away from the pro shop, so in effect the two PGAs had to find the money to pay the players' wages while they were on Ryder Cup duty. For example, in 1927 for the inaugural match in Massachusetts, the nine British players shared £906 9s. 8d., while for the 1929 contest at home, the British PGA committee records state GB team members each received "£3 10s. 0d. per day for expenses to include all railway fares and that claims for refund of expenses must be accompanied by a statement of expenditure". Given a day to travel and a couple of practice rounds, a British player was given something in the region of £20 for expenses. In addition, there was also what was called "a kit allowance" for golfing equipment, possibly worth as much as £50.

Such monies from the Cup were not insignificant. Although Walter Hagen, at this time, could boast an annual income of hundreds of thousands of dollars, a top British player like George Duncan was receiving around £100 per year as the professional at Wentworth Golf Club.

However, the players were not always happy about the small amounts of money coming their way. The profits from the 1933 match at Southport & Ainsdale still left the PGA £1,200 short of their target amount, so there was no chance of paying the GB players to attend a celebratory dinner a few months afterwards. The PGA's own minutes, however, state: "The honour and publicity of representing their country in an International of the importance of the Ryder Cup should be ample inducement for the players to accept the invitation." Even so, some of the golfers did not attend and did not even reply to the invite.

Their situation in the 1930s had not really improved and several – including Henry Cotton – were tempted by jobs overseas. Percy Alliss, for example, is said to have taken home £800 per year from his job at the fashionable Wannasee Golf Club in Berlin, Germany, and was prepared to miss out on his Ryder Cup place because he lived abroad.

The golfer compensation system remained largely the same for decades, but as the honour of being a Ryder Cup player grew larger, so there were more chances for the player to earn indirect income by improving deals with sponsors or charging more money for lessons or exhibition matches. Also, the freebies the players received began to increase beyond some golf balls, a few items of equipment or clothing and a blazer to wear in the clubhouse.

The problem was that after World War II, the finances of the two PGAs started to diverge and while the American players were encouraged to behave like sporting superstars, the British team members were treated more like second-class citizens. It was cashmere and leather for the US against nylon and plastic for GB, and those differences became rooted in the players' minds. Levels of prize money were indicative of the trans-Atlantic differences. In 1946, for example, The Masters prize fund was $10,000 (the equivalent of £2,500 in Britain) compared to just £1,000 at the Open Championship. The champion's cheque at the American major was $2,500 (approximately £650) while the claret jug winner took home only £150. Not only that, but US golf had already been operating its PGA Tour for 17 years and, by 1946, pros could benefit from near-year-round golf, dozens of events and a total tournament fund of $454,000 (£110,000). In contrast, the British pros barely managed a six-month season, were playing for fewer titles and with prize funds barely in the hundreds of pounds.

Even by the 1960s, the situation for British professionals had hardly improved. Neil Coles was a 27-year-old debutant for the GB team in 1961 and delighted to play in the match, but also baffled by how he was treated. "I was still young to make the team," he says now. "Coombe Hill Golf Club had a dinner for myself and Ken Bousfield because we were both linked with the club and had both made the team. We were each presented with a gold watch, inscribed on the back because in those days it was a personal victory just to make the team." But the glow of recognition was soon forgotten when Coles reached Royal Lytham & St Annes. "The PGA gave us a special uniform with a jacket to wear off the course, four golf shirts and one blue pullover to play in and the plastic golf bag with head covers. But my pullover was too small and I asked for a bigger one. The PGA people said they didn't have one even after I told them it felt restrictive when I swung and I couldn't play in it. They said I just had to wear it." Coles, however, was not to be deterred. "I went into the Pringle tent in the golf village and asked if they had a bigger blue pullover. They said they didn't have one, but they had a cardigan. I said: 'That'll do.' So I played the entire tournament in that, with no badge on it. You can see it in the photos."

By the late 1970s, the prize fund differences were starting to decrease between the two sets of golfers and European players in the Ryder Cup were at least given some decent expenses for the week – sources put the figure at between £2,000 and £3,000 – to match the Americans. By the next decade, with Team Europe enjoying notable success and the matches becoming more competitive, the British PGA achieved much betters deals for their players.

For instance, the arrangement with clothing company Austin Reed – owner of golf brands Glenmuir and Proquip – was worth £60,000 and provided each member of the team with a £600 cashmere jacket, eight cashmere jerseys, a £400 suit and a dozen shirts. The players were also given fitted waterproofs, warm-up jackets, golf shoes, street shoes and much more. The team that had felt like ragamuffins for so long left for PGA National in Florida in 1983 with £4,000 worth of goodies. This was a huge confidence boost and a far cry from the cheap and cheerful uniforms of the past, like the white jackets with blue-edged lapels worn by the 1973 GB team that made them resemble a comical gang of Eton rowers.

The issues between the two teams about levels of earnings were settled during the 1980s and 1990s. By then the top American and European players were banking small fortunes. In the year of Team Europe's famous victory at The Belfry in 1985, Curtis Strange won $542,000 as the top money earner on the PGA Tour compared to Sandy Lyle's £162,000 on the European Tour – the one-time underdogs were inexorably catching up as the two Tours mixed more overtly. Thanks to improvements in air-travel efficiency and a more welcoming attitude Stateside, a greater number of international players had the opportunity to earn far more prize money in America than ever before. The PGA Tour's first prize money millionaire (again, Strange) came in 1988, while the European Tour's equivalent (a euro millionaire) was Colin Montgomerie in 1994.

With prize money now flowing on both sides of the Atlantic, it was a surprise that financial griping became a topic of dispute within the Ryder Cup. The American team had fewer complaints over Cup expenses (by Brookline in 1999, their payment for the week was up to $5,000), but they did start to question the lack of payment for their services, not so much prize money as appearance money. This caused a rift with the PGA of America, but the two sides eventually agreed that the captain and each player would receive $200,000 from the match income to donate to their own charities and golf projects. To millionaire golfers, this was a reasonable compromise.

British and European golfers never had such a dispute. Instead, the players have more likely valued the priceless memories from the team room or even the extravagant gifts from the captains (of course, paid for by Ryder Cup income). Tony Jacklin began that trend and every European skipper has continued it, including Sam Torrance in 2002. "My wife, Suzanne, and I prepared the gifts," the Scot told *Golf Today* afterwards, "so that when they returned to their room every night they had one waiting there for them. And I mean a very special gift… [like a] dinner set, the main gift that went on display on the Tuesday night. I had it presented in an oak case, a 12-piece setting with the names of all the players engraved on the cutlery, captains and vice-captains on the carving knives and forks, and so on. It really was something."

Captains also take on the job without formal payment although they are compensated for their time promoting the match, attending official functions and various meetings. The smarter the captain (or his agent), however, the more the job translates into money in other ways such as contracts for clothing, equipment or cars; fees for exhibitions, TV commentating or after dinner speeches; and even the cost of having the ex-Ryder Cup skipper's name attached to a golf course design. The likes of Nick Faldo and Colin Montgomerie have been among those to make the most of the captain's status.

But 'twas not always thus. Mark James says he managed one exhibition that brought him £10,000. "Luckily I had a good year on tour," he now recalls. Tony Jacklin has speculated that "there's at least a million in it now". The four-time captain found the job to be not so lucrative in his day. "No more than £50,000 and a case of Johnnie Walker whisky," was the extent of Jacklin's compensation.

Location, location, location

Even though the players have – and always will be – central to the fortunes of the Ryder Cup, selecting the venues has often caused the most hassle, particularly when the matches have been staged in Britain or Europe.

The early Ryder Cup matches on the British side of the Atlantic were the sole responsibility by the PGA. Samuel Ryder bought the trophy, added some cash to the pot at the outset and helped put together the deed of trust that defined the rules of engagement. But it was the association that had to make each contest a success and the most important job was to find a host club to generate the most cash.

The situation was the same both in Britain and America, but the British PGA found the task much harder. There were two reasons for this: the British had fewer potential clubs to partner with and also there was no culture in Britain at the time to invest in professional sport, certainly not to the same degree as in America's thriving meritocracy. Neither the PGA of America nor the British association made losses from the matches they staged, but rarely did they create enough of a surplus to pay the expenses for the team to travel to the "away" match, and that was the overwhelming need.

The British PGA was formed in 1901 by 59 full-time pros and 11 assistant pros and its first reported war chest of funds was just over £47. By the late 1920s, the association had around 900 members and still lacked any real commercial acumen. The pros believed in the Ryder Cup as an event that would add prestige to their organisation, but they needed the expertise of a prestigious club and the business contacts of their senior members to help. The PGA definitely did not have enough money to send their team to the inaugural match in America in 1927 and had to rely on donations from some of Britain's 1,750 golf clubs as well as sympathetic groups and individuals from around the world, like the London Stock Exchange Golfing Society who sent £210; a golf club in Nuwara Eliya, Sri Lanka, that contributed £25; and anonymous donors such as "A Boy Golfer" who chipped in two shillings and seven pence. When the total fell short of the necessary £3,000, Ryder and *Golf Illustrated* magazine put in the final £300 or so to enable the team to travel.

But after that, the pressure would be on the venue of first "home" match in 1929 to make enough money to pay for the team to return to America in 1931. The profit required was £3,000 and, without it, either the PGA could be left bankrupt or the match simply would not take place.

Many fans thought the most obvious option for a venue partner was one steeped in the history of the sport, somewhere in Scotland perhaps, like St Andrews or one of the regular Open Championship venues in Lancashire such as Birkdale. However, staging the Open with all its heritage and tradition was a far cry from an untried and untested team event that had already twice failed to capture the imagination of the golfing public. The PGA was not in a strong position to open negotiations with any club and needed a partner that shared its vision for the Cup while still being credible in terms of its reputation. Both unofficial matches – at Gleneagles in 1921 and Wentworth in 1926 – had new courses to publicise and jumped at the chance to host a large number of the best golfers in the world. For them, the Ryder Cup was a publicity stunt as much as anything. For the 1929 match, the PGA wanted a similar partner, but this time there could be no question of failure.

With all this in mind, there were few options. The association's minutes from December 1927 show that only Moortown Golf Club in Leeds, Yorkshire, and Gleneagles made offers to act as host. The committee selected Moortown for a very simple reason: it believed more spectators would come from the surrounding English towns and cities than travel north to Scotland and thereby deliver more cash from ticket sales. Even from that early moment, money was on the Ryder Cup agenda. "The match should not be played further south than Lancashire or Yorkshire," said James Braid, five-time Open champion and a commanding voice on the PGA committee. Moortown it was then.

Built on moorland in 1909 and designed by the great Dr Alister MacKenzie, the Moortown course had little history of top-line golf events, but it did boast a large contingent of businessmen members from Leeds and the surrounding area. Moortown was also well known to the players – Braid and Harry Vardon played an exhibition match there as early as 1910 to mark the course's opening.

However, the man behind the Moortown bid is thought to have been a local bank manager named Kolin Robertson, a well-known member of the Yorkshire club and someone of rare far-sightedness who was instrumental in organising the well-respected *Yorkshire Evening Post* professional event at the club every year. Robertson suggested that Moortown's rough and windy conditions would give the home team a significant advantage and the regular staging of a pro tournament proved the club's ability to both handle the practicalities of the Ryder Cup and, crucially, the finances of the event. Plus the *Post* not only agreed to provide plenty of local publicity (the support of the print press was a critical factor for sports events in the 1920s), but also invited the two Ryder Cup teams to play in its pro event the week before as a warm-up that would put extra cash into the players' pockets.

And so it came to pass. The American team came over to Yorkshire in April 1929 and Joe Turnesa from New York won the *YEP* event before the two teams battled for the Ryder Cup before a crowd of several thousand fans. The match raised around £1,300 for the PGA's coffers, an amount that was short of the intended target but still deemed a success. Still, the PGA committee knew that profits from other tournaments would have to be diverted to a Ryder Cup fund if the team was actually going to set off for America two years later – a strategy that continued for many years.

At the time of the next match in Britain in 1933, the country was in a state of economic despair. With a quarter of the country's workforce (2.5 million people) unemployed and cash in very short supply, the PGA needed a Ryder Cup partner even more willing than Moortown. Luckily, interest in the Cup was increasing and Southport Town Council contacted the PGA about being the next host almost two years in advance. The burghers of the Lancashire seaside town had been active supporters of professional golf for several years: the likes of American legend Walter Hagen had already played an exhibition in Southport; and the national newspaper, *The Sunday Dispatch*, had also co-sponsored the Southport Professional Golf Tournament in 1930 to the tune of £1,500, prize money that was believed to be the highest of any similar event in Britain at the time. Eventually, Southport & Ainsdale Golf Club was chosen as the host club and backed with £400 from the council.

The club members set up a committee that made plans for marquees and purchased a new motor tractor to aid course preparations. Crucially, a tight rein was kept on finances and a tidy profit of around £1,800 was banked by the PGA after the match, an amount which the association's Board minutes state was "highly satisfactory" and compared "very favourably" with the 1929 profit. In fact, Southport Town Council and Southport & Ainsdale made such a success of the match that it returned there in 1937 when a £2,600 surplus was achieved. The PGA's own chairman J.H. Taylor then stated in his post-match speech that he hoped the Ryder Cup contest would return again to the same club in four years time in 1941. It was even a thought within the PGA that the club could become the Cup's permanent home. There was certainly a paucity of suitable alternative courses at that time and to have a regular, vibrant partner prepared to invest time, effort and money into the Ryder Cup would have been a huge relief for the PGA. However, World War II began in September 1939 and destroyed many things in the ensuing six years, including the connection between the Ryder Cup and the Southport & Ainsdale links which had to be downsized and redesigned so new houses could be built for the families of returning soldiers.

Good win for Goodwin

For the next three matches in Britain – 1949, 1953 and 1957 – the PGA hopped around the country to whichever golf club offered the best financial prospects for the Ryder Cup. Yet the association's strategy was at least set: find a hosting partner that will underwrite any loss. That meant an upfront payment into the Ryder Cup Fund that covered expenditure like staging costs and team expenses, and then any surplus was shared once the host had been repaid their initial outlay. So, for example, the 1949 match went to Ganton Golf Club after the local Scarborough Corporation offered a £5,000 guarantee.

Ganton was one of the country's best-regarded courses. Both Harry Vardon and Ted Ray had both served as club professional there and its course had been tweaked over the years by designers such as Harry Colt and Dr Alister MacKenzie. It had a fine golfing pedigree, was and the necessary finances were in place to bring the Ryder Cup back to Yorkshire. At a time when the PGA's Ryder Cup balance sheet showed a paltry £176, the guarantee clinched the deal, setting the template for venue choices for the next three decades.

In 1953, with Britons still subject to post-war rationing, Wentworth Golf Club – the venue of the second unofficial match 30 years earlier – stepped into the Ryder Cup spotlight. The venue fitted the PGA's desire to spread the matches south and involve a club within London's wealthy Surrey stockbroker belt.

The next contest would be a landmark event for several reasons, one of them being the personal patronage of Sir Stuart Goodwin. Finding Goodwin was a lucky break for the PGA because the elderly steel magnate was at a loose end one day in the early 1950s after a cancelled lunch and decided instead to go and watch an exhibition match at Lindrick Golf Club, near Sheffield, South Yorkshire, where he was a member, between Dai Rees and former Open champion Fred Daly. Goodwin was not much of a golfer himself, yet he ignored the heavy rain and suddenly found himself entranced by the contest and enjoying the company of the two great champions.

A proud and generous Yorkshireman, he then decided to put his birthplace of Sheffield on the golfing map. From 1952-54 he spent £15,000 on the Sir Stuart Goodwin Foursomes tournament. That was enough to get the PGA's attention because he was promptly made a vice-president of the association. But the industrialist did not stop there.

In late 1955, the PGA secretary, Commander Charles Roe, approached Goodwin to solve the association's latest problem: the 1957 Ryder Cup. After so many defeats (the run currently stood at seven in a row dating back over 20 years), the PGA's options were narrowing, so it was a huge relief when the industrialist quickly agreed to be the match's benefactor and wrote out another cheque for £10,000 to underwrite the costs with his only requirement being that a course near Sheffield should act as host. The PGA felt that the rather unfashionable but remarkable Lindrick course was the only one in the area that was suitable, but even then there were issues. Firstly, Lindrick had no history of staging any kind of international event, but then that drawback had been solved before by other Ryder Cup venues. The more practical snag was that the course straddles the busy A57 trunk road between Liverpool and Lincoln; holes 1 to 11 along with the 18th are on the south side with12 to 17 to the north. This would mean a road closure and major diversions during the competition to ensure both player and spectator safety.

However, the PGA overlooked the issue because they had a £10,000 gift while the autocratic Goodwin was not a man to let such things stand in his way. He even made the agreement with the PGA without the knowledge of some members of the club's committee. They had to read about the Ryder Cup coming to Lindrick in the local newspapers. When the official announcement came, the committee was again unhappy to find that Goodwin had handed over all the profits – from ticket sales through to car parking and catering – to the delighted PGA. This meant that Lindrick's officers and volunteers would be working hard to stage an event from which the club was unlikely to benefit, at least in immediate financial terms. And the amount of work turned out to be huge, including creating two new back tees on the 2nd and 13th holes, block-booking all the nearby hotels for players and officials, recruiting hundreds of marshals from other local clubs and then negotiating with the highway authorities to close the A57.

As the work piled high, the relationship between the association and the club became a little fraught. The most awkward moment came when the PGA asked Lindrick members to pay to park their cars on match days, a request that was eventually rescinded.

Yet the honour of staging the Cup paid off all round because the GB team actually won for the first time in two decades and Lindrick became famous on both sides of the Atlantic. Prior to its Ryder Cup hosting, this unassuming course had been famous because its 5th green straddled three different counties – Yorkshire, Derbyshire and Nottinghamshire – but now it had a different place in sporting and golfing history.

The financial issues were eventually settled. The committee recorded in its minutes that "a few hundred pounds" had been made from the Cup despite no financial help from the PGA "beyond the salary of a part-time typist and a small figure for office expenses". The club had to wait until the following year for the PGA to settle other bills such as for extra work by the greenkeepers to prepare the course, but by then Goodwin and the club committee were basking in the reflected glory.

However, the PGA could not find another Sir Stuart Goodwin four years later and so a new strategy was implemented: it was time to work in partnership with some Open Championship venues that had commercial as well as staging expertise. The next five hosts of the British Ryder Cups would be Royal Lytham & St Annes in Lancashire (1961 and 1977), nearby Royal Birkdale (1965 and 1969) and the Honorable Company of Edinburgh Golfers at Muirfield in Scotland in 1973. The 1961 match at Lytham inadvertently became an even more effective choice because it was staged just three months after American maestro, Arnold Palmer, had won the Open Championship at Birkdale. At the Ryder Cup, attendance was high as Lancashire's version of Arnie's Army gazed open-mouthed at their new hero's aggressive shot-making for the second time in three months.

However, it took the 1965 match at Royal Birkdale to make it clear there was a potential commercial future for the matches. Brian Park, PGA vice-president and former captain of Royal Birkdale, was at the helm for this match and he brought a new level of professionalism to everything outside the ropes. Park, a canny businessman who worked closely with sponsors like the Senior Service cigarette brand, produced a hefty programme for the first time and built a tented village for the fans. Although Park was not involved on the Cup committee in 1969 when the match returned to Royal Birkdale, the blueprint had been established four years earlier and more fans, sponsors and money were attracted to the event. But even though the match was now generating six figure budget numbers and everyone, from players to spectators to commercial supporters, was getting a better deal, the costs of staging the event were also increasing. Thus, there was still a shortfall in the PGA's Ryder Cup fund when the next team went to America.

The Muirfield contest in 1973 witnessed the emergence of the first corporate sponsor in the Cup's history – Sun Alliance – while the match was back at Lytham in 1977, the year of both the Queen's Silver Jubilee and the Ryder Cup's Golden Jubilee. But still there was not sufficient profit for the PGA's liking. Team GB&I became Team Europe in time for the next "home" match at Walton Heath in 1981, but just when this change spread hope that the contests would become closer, there were huge commercial disappointments.

The original plan for this match was for the teams to lock horns on a different course – the infant golf resort in the West Midlands, The Belfry –

but in February 1981, just seven months before the due date, the contest was switched to Walton Heath. This was hardly an ideal situation and, albeit a great course, neither the Surrey club nor the PGA had enough time to organise an international tournament on this scale. When both teams turned up on the first morning wearing dark blue sweaters and looking interchangeable, it was a sign that the 1981 match would hit a low in terms of the Cup's on-course and off-course achievements. In the end, both the PGA and the club did wonders just to stage an event worthy of Samuel Ryder's name, although the US team, perhaps the strongest ever assembled even to this day, showed no sympathy and trounced GB&I 18½-9½ for their 11th Ryder Cup victory in a row. To make matters worse, huge amounts of rain deterred many potential spectators and washed away the income targets. Some estimates forecast the match's deficit at £50,000. To add insult to injury, Sun Alliance walked away as sponsors shortly afterwards and that seemed like the last straw for the Cup's commercial potential. Luckily, help was on the way, back in the West Midlands.

The Belfry to the rescue

When The Belfry was officially re-opened in 1977 with the newly-completed Brabazon course and a re-fitted hotel, it could have been custom-made for the Ryder Cup: millions of pounds had already been spent on the resort and there were plans for further investment; the Brabazon was the ideal course for spectator viewing; there was plenty of space for the fans and their cars; the practice facilities were splendid; a large hotel complex and function rooms were on site; and there was even a nightclub within the grounds. The PGA's executive director, Colin Snape, also signed a deal that year with the resort owners who would build the PGA's new headquarters and give the association a 99-year, rent-free lease in exchange for two Ryder Cups coming to The Belfry, starting in 1981. The Brabazon course even staged a dry run in 1978 when a Great Britain team took on the Continental Europeans for the Hennessy Cup. Everything was in place, or so it seemed.

However, problems then began to emerge as soon as the pros played the Brabazon: the course received heavy criticism – too many stones in the fairway, complained some players; it was a quagmire and too bland, said others – and the fear arose that the resort might not be ready for its first Ryder Cup, even in three years time. The man faced with that decision was Snape.

Snape had joined the PGA in late 1972 as a tournament administrator, but then was suddenly thrust into the key job of the association's secretary the following spring when his predecessor, Major John Bywaters, died of a heart attack while at work in his office. At just 34-years-old and with less than six months in the job, Snape's appointment was unexpected, but the man from

Bury in Lancashire was a wheeler dealer by nature and also someone who liked to make decisions, even tough ones. He knew that one of his first tasks was to change the culture of the PGA from a slow, committee-based one to a more commercially-driven mentality. "The PGA in those days was long on reputation, but short of money," says Snape. "Our offices were two rooms under the main stand at The Oval cricket ground in London and we had £17,000 in the bank. Commercially, it was a shambles." The Ryder Cup was an early priority and, according to Snape, was only "washing its face" in terms of profit and loss, so it was a huge breakthrough for him to bring in major sponsorship money from Sun Alliance (£375,000 for the next three matches) with their chairman Lord Aldington requesting Muirfield as the venue for the 1973 contest. "We were still only just balancing the books. We never made any money from the Cup in those days," remembers Snape whose deal to take the PGA to The Belfry in exchange for two Ryder Cups was a win-win for both sides. But when it became apparent the Brabazon course needed more time to settle, Snape had to find another venue for 1981 (it turned out to be Walton Heath) and push The Belfry's deal back.

So there was a certain amount of trepidation when the Ryder Cup finally arrived at The Belfry four years late. However, as luck would have it, for the first time since the matches began almost 60 years earlier, the PGA finally found the planets were fully aligned in their favour: The Belfry's golf course and its whole facility was considered of a high enough quality to stage the 1985 event; the European team was full of star names (Seve Ballesteros, Bernhard Langer and Sandy Lyle were all major winners by now); Team Europe had been competitive in the 1983 match in America (when they suffered only a narrow defeat), so interest among fans and TV companies had never been higher; and Snape (whose job title had been upgraded to executive director) had signed a fabulous sponsorship deal with Bell's whisky. The breakthrough was imminent.

A record 90,000 fans turned up for the 1985 match (over five times more than at Walton Heath four years earlier); a tented village with dozens of hospitality suites proved hugely successful; and the European team capped it all off by winning the Cup for the first time in 28 years. This was truly the first modern-day Ryder Cup in terms of commercial activity. The gross income shot past the £1 million mark and, for the first time enabled the PGA to pay a huge facility fee to The Belfry of £50,000 (for comparison, it was just £6,000 to Walton Heath four years earlier) and so, from this moment on, the Ryder Cup began supporting the association rather acting as a drain on its finances. "The Belfry in 1985 was really what we dreamt of," Snape said years later. "There was a lot of criticism that it was played there, that it was all about commercial greed, that we were playing on a manufactured course... but when Concorde did a fly-past it was the culmination of a dream."

Europe now had a great team and a venue to match, so before the Cup came to The Belfry again in 1989, its new owners DeVere Group had pumped another £8 million of upgrade work into the facility and now the bar had been raised again in terms of the type of venue that would stage the matches on this side of the Atlantic. Further and greater profits for the PGA were inevitable.

Discussions about the host of the next "home" match for Team Europe began in earnest in 1990 and The Belfry course got the nod for a third European match, but not without controversy. The PGA and the European Tour were working ever more closely on the matches now and three members from each side sat on the Ryder Cup Committee at this time with Lord Derby (the PGA president) having the casting vote. But when the Tour wanted a match in Spain and the PGA favoured a return to The Belfry, there were some harsh words exchanged, especially when Lord Derby plumped for the West Midlands resort and the more powerful Tour did not get their way.

Sandy Jones took over as PGA chief executive in December 1991 and made an early decision to share the Ryder Cup with the Tour. When Jones started his job, the Cup was making around £1 million profit, but the PGA was losing a quarter of that every year between "home" matches so this surplus was being wiped. "The good news was that the PGA was no longer having to fund the Ryder Cup, but we were now spending all the profits to develop the association and the game of golf," Jones said. In order to create more revenue, the PGA would have to employ staff dedicated to the Ryder Cup full-time, but Jones saw that as a foolish option when the European Tour was itching to be more involved and already had all the necessary people and expertise in place. So the PGA and European Tour became 50-50 partners in a new company, Ryder Cup Ltd, and would make all key decisions – including deciding the venues – together.

So, any fractiousness over the decision for the 1993 host venue was short-lived. There was also no argument over the PGA arranging with The Belfry's owners to build a new PGA training centre within the resort and to sponsor the PGA Seniors event from 1996-2000 as part of the deal. It was a unique agreement and the last of its kind. The Cup was now generating tens of millions of pounds in turnover and ever more sophisticated negotiations on all fronts needed to be conducted.

The benefit of the deal for the training centre and sponsorship was estimated at £5 million, so that became the going rate for host clubs pitching for the Cup. Valderrama in Spain was the first continental European course to stage the event in 1997 thanks to its significant support to the Tour over the previous 10 seasons. The course owner, Jaime Patino, was a great friend to European golf; his Valderrama course had staged the Tour's end-of-season Volvo Masters tournament since 1988 and contributed as much as

£10 million in prize money during that time. For the first time, there was help from the nation's government through the tourist board, Tour Espana, while Patino used his wealth (originating from his Bolivian grandfather's tin-mining business) to match what The Belfry had achieved in terms of course preparation. Then the match was scheduled to return to The Belfry for a final time in 2001 to mark the centenary of the PGA. Tragically, the world's most outrageous act of terrorism pushed that date back by 12 month.

The 2006 host was the K Club in County Kildare, Ireland, largely because of massive support from the club's owner Dr Michael Smurfit and local sponsors (AIB Bank, BordBia, Ballygowan water and Waterford Crystal), the Irish Tourist Board and the Irish government. This high level of backing then led to a more sophisticated bidding system being introduced by the European Ryder Cup Committee. The idea of finding a host club was suddenly old hat; the Cup needed the support of an entire nation and also proof of a long-term commitment to the Tour. The level of committed investment had become huge. For example, the unsuccessful bid by Slaley Hall in Northumberland to stage the 2010 match was valued at more than £46 million, including £22.5 million from Sport England as part of a campaign to develop young golfers in the north east of England. While, the owners of Valderrama, the K Club and Celtic Manor had all been long-time supporters of an event on the European tournament calendar (a crucial factor in effective bids), providing something like £50 million in prize money over as long as a decade, the Welsh and Scottish were asked to pay as much as £2 million into a legacy fund to help grow golf. Those levels of outlay have become minimum guarantees where once Ganton GC had guaranteed £5,000 in 1949. The Ryder Cup venue stakes have grown exponentially.

To become the 2018 host, the Ryder Cup Committee insisted on one-club-per-country bids only with criteria including not only the obvious elements of player accommodation, transport for fans, on-course viewing, hospitality capacity and local sponsors, but also plans for a golfing legacy and detailed economic impact forecasting. Six countries initially put themselves forward – France, Spain, Germany, Portugal, the Netherlands and Sweden – and with tens of millions of euros at stake the committee even employed an independent company to police the system and stave off any accusations of impropriety.

The winning French bid for Le Golf National near Paris included mass support from the 400,000 members of the French Golf Federation – that is, all the ordinary amateur players in the clubs around the country – who agreed to pay a levy of €30 each over a 10-year period to finance the project. That meant an initial promise of €1.2 million before a vote had been cast, while the French federation also announced plans for as many as 100 new six- or nine-hole courses to be built in urban areas, a plan that was supported by the then French president Nicolas Sarkozy. The next three European-based matches are all guaranteed for continental European courses and there is no shortage of potential bidders, making the PGA's first 70 years of struggles to find a profitable Ryder Cup venue seem almost impossible to comprehend.

American hosting

In early 2014, PGA of America president Ted Bishop made headlines by suggesting that one day "down the road" one course – he chose Valhalla GC in Kentucky – would be the permanent home for US-based Ryder Cups. This was a left-field comment because not one American course has ever hosted more than one Cup match (unlike Britain where four courses have been multiple hosts), but it does highlight how seminal the choice of the US venue has become.

The pick by the PGA of America has always been based on achieving the best possible partnership, both with a great golf course and club organisation that will help deliver a healthy surplus. For nine decades, the association has moved the event to different cities and states using those criteria. And plenty of courses have usually been keen to play host. There has never been an overt bidding system between potential US Ryder Cup sites, but obviously an interested club would make its own individual case. This would include a financial agreement to allow the club to generate some income depending on its success at selling tickets, local sponsorship deals and hospitality units. The PGA of America also on occasion uses a carrot-and-stick strategy as well because if a club wants to stage a PGA Championship in the future, for example, then they would have to host a Ryder Cup. But whichever course was chosen, the idea would be a partnership with the association with monetary benefits for both sides.

The inaugural Ryder Cup in 1927 certainly fitted the partnership element of the template, but also showed the strong connection US golf still had with Britain because it was an ex-Carnoustie caddie who brought the Cup to Worcester Country Club in Massachusetts. Willie Ogg, who had trained a young Bobby Jones earlier in his career, was the pro at Worcester and initially brought the 1925 US Open to his course, proving that the club's members could support a significant tournament. So staging the Ryder Cup two years later was a natural progression.

Worcester also had the advantage of a course designed by the renowned Donald Ross as well as club members who were wealthy manufacturers and businessmen with contacts with British companies and the seal of approval of America's first golfing President, William H. Taft who was the special guest at the course's dedication ceremony in 1914. Not only that, but Worcester was near the east coast, less than 200 miles from New York where the GB team would disembark after their ocean crossing. Travel overland was therefore minimal, while the perfect June weather would be pleasantly warm rather than extremely hot.

As many as 4,000 spectators turned up for each of the two match days and paid $2 each for the privilege. However, the $10,000 profit target was not reached and the PGA of America was left with only a profit of $1,833.72 and had to stage fund-raising events over the next two years to pay for the travel expenses for their Britain-bound team.

The search then began for the perfect host club that could offer a money guarantee (similar to those that the British PGA was now achieving), a superb course and a suitable climate. In 1931 for the third Cup match, the members of Scioto Country Club in Columbus, Ohio, offered their course the week after the US Open at Inverness Club in nearby Toledo. That meant visiting British players could take part in both tournaments without a hugely long journey in between. The club was also favoured because long-time PGA of America president George Sargent had been a professional there while Bobby Jones had won his second US Open title on the course in 1926.

In fact, just being able to stage the Scioto match at all turned out to be a triumph because the Wall Street Crash of 1929 had sent the country's economy spiraling downwards. After this match, the PGA of America's funds for the "away" match were in dire straits. The association even wrote to the British PGA suggesting that because of the serious financial position, the teams for the 1933 match should be four-a-side and, to add further interest to the match, suggested that countries like Canada, Argentine, Japan, France and Germany might be invited to take part. In the end, this kind of knee-jerk reaction to the financial problem was dismissed and the money was found, but the precarious nature of the Ryder Cup was never far from the surface in those early days.

The 1947 match, for example, was only taken to Portland, Oregon, because wealthy fruit-canning millionaire Robert A. Hudson agreed to pay for the GB team to make the trip. The ever-smiling Hudson's generosity did not stop there: he entertained the GB players on their arrival for the next two matches in America in 1951 and 1955 and also sent Christmas hampers every year to each of the British players throughout much of the 1950s.

The magnificent Pinehurst No.2 course in North Carolina played host in 1951 and remains one of the finest courses ever to stage the event. By then, the PGA of America had its eyes on developing the sport in the fast-growing state of California. Thunderbird Country Club in Rancho Mirage and Eldorado Golf Club in Palm Desert staged the 1955 and 1959 matches respectively in a decade when the grandees of California were trying to attract top sporting events and teams to their state. The first Ryder Cup in the golden state was a forerunner of that strategy, beating the arrival of the baseball Dodgers from Brooklyn (to Los Angeles in 1957) and the NFL

Giants of New York (San Francisco, 1958) as well as the basketball Lakers of Minneapolis (also LA, 1960).

The PGA of America then continued to spread the Ryder Cup around– from Missouri to Florida, from Texas to West Virginia – often to courses without any significant tournament background. Finally came a commercial breakthrough in 1987, two years after Team Europe's first victory. That match – at Jack Nicklaus's Muirfield Village course in Dublin, Ohio – was the first to be a sellout in America and the first US-based match to produce a significant profit, around $500,000. Now the PGA of America had a real contest to offer to potential hosts and there was more money to be made. But with more money at stake came more problems. The next match was originally given to one of its own branded courses, PGA West in California, but as the date for the contest approached, it was clear that the eight-hour time difference for European TV viewers would cause too many problems and the event was switched to the Kiawah Island resort in South Carolina. This, however, led to another glitch because although the resort had been launched in 1974, the Ocean Course on which the Ryder Cup was played, had opened just a few months in advance of the match. The clubhouse was still being made ready in the week before the teams arrived. It would be the first time the choice of an American Ryder Cup venue caused any serious controversy. "The entire decision-making process for the 1991 Ryder Cup could be called crass, craven and ill-considered," said James Y. Bartlett in an article in *Forbes* magazine at the time. He was just one observer who claimed that the Cup in America could now be the victim of a search for bare-faced profit rather than an event staged at a venue worthy of the name and with a superior golf course.

The lesson was quickly learned and, after that, the PGA of America returned to its criteria of opting for an experienced host: Oak Hill (1995), The Country Club at Brookline (1999), Oakland Hills (2004), Valhalla (2008) and Medinah (2012) had all been major championship venues in the recent past. All contributed to the popularisation of the contest across the whole country and, during this time, the profits from the match grew enormously, thus justifying the venue choices.

Clubs in 17 different states of the Union have so far staged the 20 matches in America (Massachusetts, Ohio and California have seen it twice). The chances are that, so as long as the PGAA is in charge, the Ryder Cup will continue its tour of the country.

A question of value

Despite only 40 Ryder Cups ever being played, the value of the name – the brand, as marketing folk would call it – has risen dramatically in recent years.

One measurement of this is the economic impact the Cup has on the course, the region and even the country where it is staged. Since the 1990s, the sports tourism industry has been particularly interested in producing forecast figures for economic impact.

The 1997 match in Valderrama was the first to be staged outside Britain or America, so it was of special interest in terms of the economic effect on the region. The area of southern Spain where the course was situated had long been a destination for golfers in search of good weather and research indicated an economic impact of around £52 million, an amount certainly on a par with a corresponding event like the Open Championship. The next three impact numbers from European Ryder Cup venues all saw an increase: The Belfry generated as much as £62 million in 2002; the K Club managed £95 million in 2006; and Celtic Manor £85 million in 2010. The Belfry's figure was affected by the 12-month postponement of the event due to 9/11, while the Irish match had the benefit of thousands of Irish-Americans simply extending their trip a little more than usual because they were visiting "the homeland". Even though Wales's numbers were down, they were still ahead of original targets. For the 2014 contest at Gleneagles, the Scottish nation and its golf industry estimated £100 million of impact almost immediately their hosting was confirmed.

The benefits the Ryder Cup offers in America are based on regional rather than national numbers. Brookline was the first host club to generate an economic measurement – their study estimated $150 million worth of benefit to the Greater Boston area. The figure for the Oakland Hills match near Detroit in 2004 dropped to $77 million, but the Louisville numbers bounced up again to $115 in 2008 and the study for Medinah showed the highest ever impact of $135 million for Chicago.

However, another figure emerged in 2005 in the search to find the value of the Ryder Cup when an Irish company, the Quinn Group, bought The Belfry golf courses and resort complex, paying a staggering £186 million. The financial wizards stated that the so-called book value (that is the bricks and mortar, the land, the calculation of the return-on-investment of the business and its assets) was £125 million of the total purchase price. That left £61 million which could be listed as the brand value of The Belfry and, given that the Ryder Cup and The Belfry are so closely associated, the vast majority of that figure can be assigned to the Cup.

That was almost a decade ago and the cash turnover of the Ryder Cup matches and its awareness around the world has kicked on since then, so the current estimated value could be anywhere between £75-£100 million or $125-$150 million.

Television, the income giant

Ryder Cup matches in the modern era have five significant streams of revenue: TV broadcasting fees; spectator ticket sales; event sponsorship; on-course hospitality; and logo-itemed merchandising. From the moment when the matches became highly competitive in the mid-1980s, TV executives on both sides of the Atlantic suddenly wanted the Ryder Cup and the broadcast rights they pay the organisers have grown ever since to become the largest single source of net income. From being worth almost nothing as recently as 25 years ago, the amounts paid is today have soared into the multi-million range.

However, before there were any televisions in British or American homes, the interest in filming the contest came from newsreel companies. In 1929 the Gaumont Company (more famous for making movies and owning chains of cinemas) bought the first newsreel rights for a match from the British PGA for £15 15s. at a time when golf was a very difficult sport to film. Spread over so much ground and with costly technical difficulties to overcome, the early Cups were filmed just by a couple of newsreel cameras fixed on top of small trucks or set firm on the first tee.

The Ryder Cup finally came to television in Britain in 1953 with the BBC filming at Wentworth and then televising match highlights. It was a development prompted by the huge number of TV sets sold for the Queen's coronation that summer. The first TV coverage of the Cup of any kind in America was in 1959, just two hours of highlights on the NBC network, while the first live pictures were broadcast from Royal Birkdale in 1965, but the action was limited because there were only cameras on the final few holes. The attitude of TV to the Cup was largely one of apathy and rights fees were "virtually nothing", even in in the 1970s, according to Snape, with the Ryder Cup acting as a kind of sweetener within a larger deal involving several other European Tour tournaments. "We were just happy to get the event televised so that we could then sell that on to the sponsors," he says.

Meanwhile in America, the Cup had become television poison. In 1983, Roone Arledge, the president of ABC Sports at the time, is reported to have made a rather unusual offer to the PGA of America: he wanted to pay them back $1 million in order that he did *not* have to broadcast the Ryder Cup from PGA National Golf Club in Florida. It was not an offer the association accepted, but it demonstrated the low level of interest in the one-sided matches.

However, the win by Europe in 1985 was a breakthrough moment for all the television channels. The BBC showcased this tournament with extra live hours, while American broadcasters (who had previously only been interested in the US-based matches) finally screened an "away" match, although it was only one hour of highlights broadcast on the cable sports channel, ESPN, seven weeks after the event. The BBC upped its game after that and provided its first live pictures from a match in America at Muirfield Village in 1987 while US viewers saw a record 6½ live hours that year. The matches were still not always treated as broadcasting royalty, though. For example, US coverage was so haphazard in 1987 that viewers were watching a commercial break when Seve Ballesteros holed the winning putt for the Europeans and the BBC often chose to switch to live horse racing during the Saturday afternoons. Two years later in 1989, the BBC managed to have cameras on all 18 holes for the first time and American viewers saw live TV pictures from Britain for the first time.

By the 1990s, sports broadcasting rights had become a real hot property as cable and satellite channels like ESPN and Sky Sports had grown large enough to bid either against or alongside their larger, terrestrial rivals. In Britain, Sky Sports had outbid the BBC for exclusive live rights to the Cup in time for the 1995 match and showed every shot, from opening drive to final putt, while USA Network, first, then ESPN and The Golf Channel screened all three days plus plenty of special programming from the practice days.

At the same time, the fees were growing enormously. TV income from the 1991 match at Kiawah Island had been around $1 million, but the fee had grown to around $13 million by the 1999 contest at Brookline. In Britain, while the BBC were said to be paying less than £100,000 for all its golf programming before 1995 – including around half a dozen tournaments a year plus the Cup – suddenly BSkyB, on behalf of Sky Sports, wrote out a cheque of more than £1 million to the European Tour and agreed to show many more regular tournaments as part of the package.

There is a terrific sensitivity about the current TV value of the Ryder Cup and the absolute numbers are kept a closely guarded secret, but industry experts still try to put a number on it despite the fact that extracting the Cup from within a package of rights fees further complicates the matter. However, the estimated income generated by the US-based matches from TV companies from around the world is $35-40 million, while for the European contests, the total is around £15 million. The slightly larger number for American matches is explained by US networks being willing to pay more for prime time Ryder Cup action in their own country rather than a match that starts at 3am, east coast time, when played in Europe.

The fees for Ryder Cup broadcasting have grown considerably, but there is still a lot more money to come, particularly in the American market where sports like NFL football and basketball have been talking about deals worth billions of dollars – not millions – for a couple of decades. In fact, the advent of Fox Sports has recently galvanised the market for sports TV rights in America as a whole and golf has begun to benefit.

In 2013, the United States Golf Association announced a stunning deal with Fox Sports worth around $1.1 billion over 12 years. Starting in 2015, the

\$93 million per year agreement replaced the previous deal with NBC and Golf Channel and covers the US Open along with its seniors and women's equivalents as well as some amateur and team events also run by the USGA. The PGA of America's current agreement for Ryder Cup broadcasting as well as its other properties (such as the US PGA Championship) is with NBC and the Golf Channel and runs until 2030. However, if the American sports TV market remains as dynamic when the next contract is negotiated, then the PGA can expect a windfall payment perhaps double its current amount.

As the hours of coverage have grown, so have the television viewing figures. The potential audience for the Cup is based on a figure of 500 million homes around the world receiving the various channels that broadcast the action, but the actual number of people who watch is much less. American TV audiences for the Ryder Cup reached a record high of 17 million for the 1999 match at Brookline while the most recent "home" match at Medinah in 2012 managed over 15 million. In a country of more than 300 million people, those figures may seem tiny, however, every US-based Ryder Cup match has to battle for viewers directly against two of America's favourite September sports – both college and NFL football as well as baseball – and, for that reason, the numbers are considered very healthy by industry insiders.

In Britain, the BBC's audiences of 30 years ago were several million strong simply because TV viewers in those days only had a choice of three or four channels. Sky Sports was still building its subscription numbers in the 1990s when it acquired live Ryder Cup rights, so audiences were very low, maybe as small as a few hundred thousand. But now the BSkyB network boasts over 10 million homes as well as audiences in their tens of thousands in pubs and clubs throughout the country. By 2006, the estimated peak audience was over three million and that figure is thought to have doubled in 2012, although because the these figures includes the possible pub and club audience, they have to be treated as unconfirmed estimates.

Those in attendance

Up to the mid-1920s, golf fans watched their heroes for free. At this time, paying to enter a stadium was normal, but golf courses were vast expanses of land that were difficult and costly to fence off so that spectators could be funneled through turnstiles. Besides which, the Open Championship or US Open apart, crowds at most golf tournaments were small and manageable, maybe consisting of just a few hundred people. In general, forcing so few to pay to watch golf is a dumb idea; better to have them watch for free and bring some atmosphere to the proceedings than have even fewer paying fans and no atmosphere at all. Crowds were warm and respectful to their heroes on the links and the idea of security was an anathema. Anyone wanting to watch even the very best golfers at the most prestigious of tournaments at that time was able to do so without any restriction.

Henry Longhurst once reflected about watching golf back in the 1920s, writing that it was "an esoteric pastime and no promoter worried very much about the spectator. If the occasion were important enough, a local caterer might be commissioned to provide food and drink in a tent. If there were any attempt to provide toilet facilities, it was usually limited to a few yards of flapping hessian draped on poles in some obscure woody corner. Crowd control was almost non-existent and, if a really large gallery assembled to watch a particular match, some club members would be recruited to walk around with red flags."

The idea of collecting gate money at golf events and taking better care of the golfers themselves on the fairways and greens only came about because of an unforeseen incident rather than careful planning by the organisers. After 54 holes of the 1925 Open at Prestwick, the American Macdonald Smith was in the lead after rounds of 76, 69 and 76. He needed only something in the order of a 78 to take his first title, but the final day crowds were particularly large; reports stated there was something like 10,000 spectators following his match alone. Simply keeping the players moving and quieting the fans had suddenly become a substantial job. Smith was badly affected by all the fuss and eventually shot 82 to finish fourth.

Something had to be done to stop this happening again, so the R&A decided to charge gate money in 1926 for the first time for both the Amateur and Open championships. At the Amateur at Muirfield, £996 was taken from 9,000 people during a week of matches while at Royal Lytham, 12,000 fans paid £1,365 in just three days.

For the Ryder Cup organisers, the innovation of charging spectators arrived just in time – here was a much-needed revenue stream. Certainly, the PGA of America and the club committee at Worcester Country Club had no inhibitions about charging spectators $2 each to attend the inaugural match, while the British PGA's daily ticket price at the 1929 match at Moortown was three shillings (15p). Then in 1933, an estimated 14,000 people turned up during the two days (many trying to catch a glimpse of the Prince of Wales who arrived on day two) and, although some managed to climb over the rudimentary fencing and watch for free, many more paid three shillings for the privilege of watching legitimately. This was the first instance of Ryder Cup crowd control as the club appointed 250 stewards (nicknamed the Southport Lancers) to use long canes with a red flag on top to marshall the crowds. Also, white lines were drawn around each green indicating where the spectators had to stand and the official programme contained an impressive list of "dont's" to ensure good behaviour by members of the gallery who were not golfers.

The bonanza attendance in 1933 then led the PGA to raise the admission fees four years later to five shillings and the crowds – and their income – were suddenly well down. Nevertheless, attendance at the matches in Britain continued to run into several thousand for the next few decades because fans could usually only see players of such stature in the Open. By contrast, the galleries attending in America were usually smaller than in Britain; there was less attention on the Ryder Cup, especially when the matches become one-sided after World War II, but the PGA of America still welcomed money from ticket sales.

The first ticket controversy came in 1961 at Royal Lytham & St Annes at a time when the British PGA was really struggling to fund the costs. The association raised the ticket price to the sum of £1 per day, at a time when this sum could buy no fewer than 20 loaves of bread. Nevertheless, Lytham St Anne's Corporation was happy because it had guaranteed £10,000 towards the costs and when 35,000 fans turned up, the corporation got its money back. So the actual event was generating a profit, but the PGA still had to find extra money to pay the expenses of the away match. It was a long road to genuine profitability.

As with so many elements of the Ryder Cup, the biggest change came in the mid-1980s. The American fans began waking up to the thrill of the matches in 1983. A record number of over 46,000 attended the three days at Palm Beach Gardens in Florida that year for the closest match so far on US soil – Jack Nicklaus's team won dramatically by a single point. Two years later at The Belfry, another attendance record was set when 90,000 fans came through the gates during the week, even though this was still a time when a few tickets were still on sale each day of the match itself. Meanwhile, the following match at Muirfield Village was a ticketing triumph with spectators travelling from Britain to America in large numbers for the first time, some of them paying for travel packages that included flying on Concorde with the official Team Europe party. For the first time, Ryder Cup organisers sold out all the tickets and, perhaps as a consequence, a heightened partisanship among the two groups of fans was noticeable.

By the 1990s, 25,000 spectators were attending on each day and tickets were gobbled up quickly. Then there was a key breakthrough at the K Club in 2006 when match tickets were sold in week-long packages, including the three practice days. That meant over 260,000 fans attended the K Club compared with 147,000 who turned up at The Belfry four years earlier. All the recent matches have followed the K Club's lead and attracted at least 40,000 fans per day. The daily maximum set by Gleneagles is 45,000 but that figure may well be topped in France in 2018.

Ticket prices have also increased steadily over recent years: at Medinah in 2012, the cheapest was $35 and the most expensive $115; at Gleneagles, prices ranged from £35 for a practice day to a top price for the Sunday singles of £145.

With every increase has come added income and, based on current attendance levels of around 240,000 spectators and an average ticket price of about £50 or $75, the total revenue from ticketing is estimated at around £10 million in Europe and $15 million in America.

Sponsorship meets hospitality

Although in the modern era, the income from sponsorship and hospitality can be split into separate columns, the stories of the two in terms of the Ryder Cup are intricately intertwined. Historically, sponsorship came first and, once those sponsors became more sophisticated and demanding, they would demand some hospitality at the event within their overall deal. Actually, in the early Ryder Cup matches, the word 'sponsorship' could easily be replaced by 'patronage'. In the late 1920s, there were no car manufacturers or drinks companies lining up to put their names to a new golf tournament. In Britain, at least, the most likely sponsor of a golf event would be a newspaper.

Early sponsorship monies were raised via a variety of sources and often by the host club members themselves. Official dinners like the one at the Queens Hotel in Leeds for the match at Moortown in 1929 charged members of the public 25 shillings to dine with the two teams, while local councils (such as in Southport in 1933) would chip in several thousand pounds as seed money. Then there were the Cup's early patrons, the likes of Samuel Ryder, Robert A. Hudson and Sir Stuart Goodwin. While the sponsorship benefits for the players were relatively meager: a few gifts from sporting goods manufacturers and maybe some expenses.

If the idea of sponsorship was rather basic back then, the word 'hospitality' did not even exist in this context. For decades, the clubhouse was the only refuge for what might be called VIPs, while the average fan was lucky to have a few food stands around the course and perhaps a couple of tents acting as outdoor toilets.

Then the 1965 match at Royal Birkdale (the first to be staged over three days rather than two) set a benchmark on both the sponsorship and hospitality fronts. Brian Park, who provided £11,000 of his own money to promote the event and left no stone unturned to make it bigger and better both for companies and general spectators, went to PGA Tour events in America for ideas. He was also inspired by a tournament in Britain three years earlier sponsored by Senior Service. Park constructed the first proper tented village at a Ryder Cup with a special area for sponsors and their guests as well as clean, white canvas tents with flushing toilets, a ladies "powder room", bars for drinks, food marquees, a television pavilion, fashion shows and a Senior Service Festival of Golf exhibition. The cigarette sponsor even introduced periscopes for the fans to allow them to see more of the action and operated mobile scoreboards around the course on little Mini Moke vehicles (the petrol-engined precursor of the electric golf cart).

Record crowds of up to 50,000 turned up in 1965 and Park's innovations won praise from *Golf Illustrated* which was happy to say goodbye to the bad old days for spectators of "a few dirty old marquees in which to eat; toilet arrangements which were little more than four pieces of torn hessian; and a programme which was no better than many a free give-away".

It was not until 1973, when the match moved to Scotland for the first time, that there was a significant commercial sponsor – Sun Alliance, the insurance company. The company's chairman, Lord Aldington, was a self-confessed golf nut and considered the support of the Ryder Cup team as a matter of national duty rather than an event that needed to produce a return on investment. This was, in fact, the decade during which sports sponsorship began to emerge. The organisers of the Olympic Games and football World Cup were putting their first commercial programmes together at this time, so for Sun Alliance to offer money to support the Ryder Cup was totally in keeping with the wider sporting picture.

Lord Aldington's company would eventually put in a total of £375,000 towards three matches in Britain in what was comfortably the Ryder Cup's most lucrative single commercial deal to date. "Before then, the PGA had been used to patronage, not sponsorship," said Snape. "The pros were used to touching their forelocks. But air travel and TV had meant that major companies could see the benefits of sponsorship."

When Sun Alliance decided to withdraw in 1981, the British PGA was in a crisis because without another sponsor, there was again a danger of the Ryder Cup folding. Snape searched the corridors of business for over a year trying to find a replacement, but to no avail. By the end of 1982, a certain amount of panic was beginning to set in. Leading European player Bernard Gallacher, who sat on the Ryder Cup committee, said there could be no question of the players not travelling to the match in Florida the following year and he even believed the players would pay for their own plane tickets if they had to. Sponsorship prospects looked so bad at one stage that the best offers on the table consisted of £80,000 worth of cigarette coupons or £100,000 in Green Shield stamps. Such was the embarrassment of this proposed deal, and also the fact that tobacco sponsorship was not acceptable by now, that no one took it seriously.

Then in the very final month of 1982, with the next match only nine months away, a new sponsor appeared out of nowhere to save the day. The man in question was Scottish businessman Raymond Miquel, the head of Bell's Scotch Whisky. "Ruthless Raymond" was a well-known cost-slasher and autocrat in the business world who preached efficiency over waste. He had been running the whisky brand since the late 1960s and made its flotation in 1971 a huge success with profits soaring. Next he wanted his whisky to conquer the American market and the Ryder Cup would be his vehicle for brand awareness. Snape was offered the chance to meet Miquel, but originally thought that making the 500-mile trip up to Perth in Scotland was another wild goose chase. That thought could not have been further from the truth. Snape says the Bell's deal for £300,000 for the 1983 and 1985 matches was a remarkable figure.

But it nearly collapsed before it got off the ground because a year before the event, the PGA of America detected a problem: there were restrictions about alcohol brands advertising on site at a sports event in America. However, after Snape told them "if we couldn't swing a sponsor, then the Ryder Cup was on its way out", a compromise was found with Bell's agreeing to limited branding on the course along with providing some hospitality. Despite the glitch, the Bell's sponsorship cash had a significant effect on the match itself because the European team just happened to have found a man – new captain Tony Jacklin – who knew how to spend this kind of money to turn his team into winners. The former Open and US Open champion had not been on the best of terms with the Ryder Cup or the British PGA for a while, but he undoubtedly was the main catalyst to produce the much-needed change of attitude, expectation and performance from the European team. Jacklin insisted on the Europeans being treated like the Americans in terms of how they were cared for before the first tee shot was hit; it was an attitude that ran in parallel with the new sponsor. This meant nothing but the best in clothing, equipment, accommodation and transport. The team members were even allowed their own caddies as money was lavished on the players like never before. Cashmere, Concorde and First-Class all the way – that was the Jacklin philosophy and, for the first time since the matches began, the American team had been upstaged. Not only that, but Bell's liked the way Jacklin upgraded the attitude and the image of the European team. Then the sponsor was soon able to wallow in the reflected glory of a victory by Team Europe.

Snape remembers how the Bell's money led to other commercial doors opening. "Once one sponsor came on board, we could do other deals as well. For instance, we got to fly on Concorde at a cost of just £30,000 when the real price was over a quarter of a million because the players wanted first class travel, but Bell's also wanted the kudos of flying supersonic. The money from Raymond [Miquel] meant we were off and running, from all sorts of viewpoints – especially a commercial one. It meant that 1983 match, plus the next two, were the key moments for the Ryder Cup, without a doubt. The teams were competitive, so we suddenly had a real commercial property to sell where the result wasn't known before it started."

Although Europe narrowly lost in Florida, the first win in 28 years followed two years later in 1985, the first match to be called the Bell's Scotch Whisky Ryder Cup. This new competitiveness was like catnip to the world of commerce on both sides of the Atlantic, with ever increasing numbers of sponsors and hospitality suites. In fact, this moment at The Belfry was the turning point for hospitality, an industry that began to grow exponentially from the middle of the 1980s and particularly at sporting events. Double decker hospitality suites and private lounges with their champagne-drinking guests were at The Belfry in their thousands for the first time because the commercial atmosphere had altered and also the venue was a perfect setting for the kind of infrastructure that was needed.

Growing interest from television, in particular, and the media in general also prompted more income and, by 1993, the match was titled 'The Ryder Cup by Johnnie Walker', a move that placed the sponsor's name in a less prominent, below-the-title position. This was significant because European Ryder Cup organisers were now gaining the upper hand – demand was matching or even outstripping supply, so it was time for another sponsorship strategy upgrade.

"One brand being associated with the Ryder Cup was not the way forward," said Richard Hills, Ryder Cup Director for the European Tour. "We admired what the International Olympic Committee did with 'The Olympic Programme' (TOP), which was established to maximise opportunities for the generation of sponsorship revenue for the IOC, and we also observed with interest the evolution of the multi-sponsor strategy of the Champions League. We felt these structures were compatible with the way we wanted the Ryder Cup to progress, and it has been the case that this system has worked well." The corporate sponsor list for Gleneagles, for example, had five major names: BMW, Rolex, Johnnie Walker, Ernst & Young and Standard Life Investments. The next significant move will be global sponsors rather than separate ones for the Europe and American matches.

In addition to the high profile top sponsors, there is also an even longer list of official suppliers (at Gleneagles, that ranged from Xirrus for the on-course wifi network to Highland Spring for bottled water) where income for the Ryder Cup may involve cash, but will also be indirect through free product. This kind of event support cannot be underestimated in terms of its advantage to the bottom line of the match's accounts, while product awareness for the sponsor is good value, especially if no cash is exchanged.

All that being said, the amount of sponsorship money (direct or indirect) coming into the Ryder Cup's bank account from the corporate list and the official suppliers is one of the looser estimates, but can be put in the range of £10 million mark in Europe or $15 million in America, that is, approximately the same on both sides of the Atlantic. But, although this figure seems healthy compared to the early days of Ryder Cup when sponsorship was non-existent, it lags well behind other mainstream sports and events. For example, the London Olympic Games in 2012 generated over £800 million of income from sponsors for three weeks of sporting action with just one top level contributor (known as a tier one sponsor) chipping in £80 million.

Separating sponsorship income from hospitality revenue can be something of an exercise in dexterity by the company accountant, but there are some reasonable numbers worth considering. For example, at Medinah in 2012, there were as many as 350 corporate names, including American Express, Pepsi and Daimler AG, that bought sponsorship packages with hospitality included. It was reported that 70 brands each paid around $250,000 to entertain 50 clients per day and another two companies shelled out $1 million to bring 300 guests to the match. Basically, there are far more corporate firms buying hospitality than paying for sponsorship.

Therefore, the gross profit numbers from hospitality packages are much bigger than those directly from sponsors. It is estimated that hospitality income reaches more than $20 million at the American matches and £15 million in Europe, but these figures are also slightly deceptive because to service all those corporate guests requires considerable expenditure by the organisers and that means the net income is much lower. There is the building of the hospitality suites and their decoration; the supplying of food and drink; the security and hostess staff; and even the provision of a daily ticket and car parking pass. When a company buys hospitality, all these factors are included in the price, but it means for organiser's net profit figure is much smaller than the gross. Industry experts say that of the total hospitality cost to a client, as much as half the amount will be spent on support and infrastructure. But if that means the Ryder Cup's net profit from hospitality is only $10 million in America or £8 million in Europe then it is still one of the most successful income areas for the matches in the last 30 years and it continues to grow with each match.

The prize of merchandise

The most recent and fastest-growing stream of income for the Ryder Cup has been merchandising. Up until the Walton Heath match in 1981, any merchandising at the matches was rudimentary and usually organised by the club and their own professional. The PGAs began clothing their own players in team colours and supplying special golf bags during the 1950s, but there was no indication that many fans wanted to wear the same clothing as the pros and no understanding of how the Cup's logo could be used to sell branded souvenirs.

However, all this changed in the 1980s with the arrival of Jacklin and his desire for everything to be first-class for his team. At this time, Team Europe was able to sign supplier deals with clothing companies and golf manufacturers for the players and, from there, it was a small step for more gear to be manufactured to sell at the match. For the 1985 match – the first at The Belfry – Ryder Cup clothing, in particular, became a must-have item for the fans. They could wear their team's colours – things like a replica golf shirt, a sweater, a cap or a sun visor – and then buy a souvenir with the Ryder Cup logo on, anything from a tee peg to a tea mug. The Americans followed suit so that modern-day crowds began to look like they were attending a football match, often wearing red (the USA team's official colour) or blue (showing an allegiance to Europe).

There has been an increasing appetite for Ryder Cup merchandise ever since and items are sold before and after the event as well as during it, generating huge amounts of cash for the organisers and their licensed partners who continually come up with even more innovative items on which to put a Ryder Cup logo. In 2014, that meant a Ryder Cup tartan for kilts and bowties.

Industry sources estimate the modern-day merchandise tent at a Ryder Cup course sells between £1.2 and £1.5 million on each of the six days. Increasingly important is the pre-sale period of at least a year that allows worldwide sales via the internet. Industry estimates put the gross merchandise income at over £10 million for a European match and $15 million in America.

A complicated and profitable business

Delving into the profits and losses of the Ryder Cup is a strange and complicated business. The deals between the match operators and all their commercial partners (from host clubs to TV companies, sponsors and even the public who buy the tickets) have changed wildly over the nine decades of the Cup's history. Originally, the two PGAs were the Cup's sole owners and operators (Samuel Ryder merely helped produce the deed of trust that provided the rules of engagement between the teams) and it was a hand-to-mouth existence for each of them with regard to the matches – keep the costs down of the home event and hope there was enough profit to fund participation in the corresponding fixture two years later. For decades, that was the strategy: avoid losing any money rather than think about making any.

Then there was the commercial seachange of the matches in the 1980s and, as the Ryder Cup moved into the 21st century and the money involved stretched beyond tens of millions, information about the event's income and expenditure became much more sensitive and less accessible.

Nevertheless, the European-based matches are run nowadays through limited companies, so some of the key financial figures are a matter of public record. Originally, the ownership of matches in Europe solely belonged to the British PGA, but the European Tour was handed a 50% share in the 1991 and the two bodies formed a joint-venture company, Ryder Cup Ltd. Then the Tour became managing partner in 2004 and Ryder Cup Europe, LLP (limited liability partnership) was created. By now the Tour had a 60% ownership stake; the British PGA – a non-profit organisation – was acknowledged as the founding partner and owner of the trophy along with 20% of the LLP; and the PGAs of Europe – also non-profit – was given the other 20%.

The European matches became significant income accumulators after 1985 at The Belfry. That was the first contest on this side of the Atlantic to gross over £1 million in revenue, although there was still only enough money to pay all the PGA's bills over the following three years. Then came the two changes in ownership. Nowadays, the overall income and profitability of the matches are enormous.

The gross revenues have reached around £65 million in Europe, a figure estimated to be made up of TV fees, ticket sales, direct sponsorship, hospitality and merchandising. Following the 2006 match at the K Club, Ryder Cup Europe LLP announced a gross profit of £15 million. In 2010 at Celtic Manor in Wales, the figure was down slightly to £13.5 million; and the estimated final number from Gleneagles in Scotland was set to be £17 million.

These profits are spent by the stakeholders who now include a third partner, the PGAs of Europe. Firstly, there is a three-year build-up to every European-based Ryder Cup. The costs include such full-time staff, a large number of meetings and promotional events plus expenses for the captain. But there are still millions of pounds and euros to distribute. The Tour has the widest remit to distribute the money and not only benefits countries in Europe but also many across the globe. The Tour acknowledges as many international players as possible who compete in their events as well as the tournaments themselves which are often long-term partners on the Tour's International Schedule.

Several major golf development projects have been started through the Ryder Cup Trust Fund (for example, every child in Scotland from the age of nine to 16 is guaranteed a free golf lesson before the 2014 match at Gleneagles). Other initiatives include charities donating over €2.5 million worth from the 2006 and 2010 matches alone; golf courses being built in far-off places; and other tournaments being staged or supported, like the Seve Trophy and many Challenge Tour events. The British PGA uses its share of any surplus to fund areas like training its members, to promote golf to the next generation of players and also some to support tournaments like the

PGA Cup (the club pros' version of the Ryder Cup). The PGAs of Europe use their money in countries from Iceland to Hungary, primarily for grass roots projects. Where once the Ryder Cup organisers had empty pockets, nowadays they are experienced commercial managers whose most important role is to spend the profits wisely.

The income numbers for the PGA of America look broadly the same with gross income now estimated to be reaching somewhere between $90 and $100 million. This figure is constructed in the same was as for the European matches, from TV rights, sponsorship, hospitality, ticket sales and merchandising. A larger amount from broadcasters is the main difference compared to Europe's numbers and that is simply because the American TV market is livelier with more high-spending commercial broadcasters (NBC, CBS, ABC, Fox and ESPN) wishing to bid for the rights.

When it comes to the question of ownership of the Cup, the American situation is much simpler with the PGA of America retaining 100% of the rights to the matches based in their country. However, there is a slight nod to the PGA Tour whose commissioner (currently Tim Finchem) sits on the main board – known as the Official Party for the US Ryder Cup Team – alongside the PGA of America's own president, vice-president, CEO and honorary president. From there, profits of around $25-£30 million are distributed and the PGA of America spend its Cup surplus much like its European counterparts, mainly on golf development and charitable donations (almost $20 million alone from 1999 to 2012), but it also has to file and pay tax returns like any other business.

All in all, the finances and the ownership of the Ryder Cup have changed beyond all recognition over nine decades and the commercial success of the matches in recent years is largely due to a more sophisticated operational structure and not just the competitiveness between the teams. Whereas the matches started out with no money, few spectators and just a little hope, now there is plenty of cash, an abundance of fans and vast amounts of certainty for the future of the Cup.

5

Conflict & Controversy

On the day the two planes hit New York's twin towers, the staff at The Belfry were fine-tuning their preparations for the 34th Ryder Cup, due to start in just over a fortnight's time. The resort's Brabazon course, situated north east of Britain's second city of Birmingham, looked immaculate and was already closed to the public to protect its condition. The tented village and numerous grandstands were under construction; hotel bedrooms had been allocated to the various players and officials; and there was very much an air of excitement about the place.

The Belfry's general manager Mike Maloney was in his office when he found out about the terrorist attack 3,000 miles away. He was preparing to welcome the first officials from the PGA of America's advance party who were due to arrive in a couple of days time. "It was a Tuesday and one of my managers rang me from the golf bar to tell me to get to a television. I knew immediately there would be an impact on the Ryder Cup."

Once airports in America were closed and the true horror of the deaths in the towers and the planes was apparent, the cancellation of the Ryder Cup was a minor news item compared with the global search for the perpetrators and the series of political decisions by world leaders that led to wars in Afghanistan and Iraq, military actions that are still reverberating over a decade later.

This was not the first time the Ryder Cup had been disrupted by war (matches were also postponed during World War II), but this delay was tinged with extra significance because it came at a time when the event itself was ensnared in a conflict of its own making.

Two recent matches – at Kiawah Island in 1991 and The Country Club of Brookline in 1999 – had been anything but gentlemanly contests, far removed from the dreams of Samuel Ryder who wanted the matches to be bridges of friendship. Golfers who would normally take pride in displaying respect for opponents and upholding perfect etiquette had become furious soldiers in a no-holds-barred war. The Cup had always been a contest fought between players with more than a dash of extra passion and temper, but these two matches in the 1990s were wildly out of synch with tradition. The 1991 contest had been dubbed "The War By The Shore"; then in Massachusetts eight years later "The Battle of Brookline" took place. Both discredited the Ryder Cup and some of the players who took part. In a strange way, the terrorist acts of 9/11 helped resolve the wounds opened up by those two Ryder Cup matches.

The opening salvo

The Ocean Course at Kiawah Island in South Carolina was a breathtaking site in 1991, set on a shoreline buffeted by unforgiving Atlantic waves and featuring merciless winds that created an extreme test even for the world's best golfers. The Pete Dye design was only officially opened a few months before the match, so all the players were nervous of the massive, dune-filled layout. Professional golfers vehemently dislike – even sometimes fear – playing a links that could make them look foolish and, in the Ryder Cup where every single shot is captured on camera and analysed, the Ocean Course certainly offered that very prospect.

Tensions between the teams had never been higher and it was not just the fault of the Kiawah course. Continental European players had been part of the Ryder Cup for 12 years and the long-time invincibility of the Americans was now consigned to history. Europe had held the trophy since 1985 and the US players were angry about their own performances. "The Europeans had been better than us, and they weren't shy about reminding us. The British media especially weren't bashful about letting us know about that," Paul Azinger told *Golf Digest*. An antagonistic tone was set at the Wednesday evening pre-tournament dinner when a video history of the Ryder Cup was played that contained everything about American victories, but nothing about any wins by Europe. The visitors found the film insulting and several wanted to walk out. "Unbelievable" was Nick Faldo's reported comment and he later added: "The disappointing thing is that even though we'd [kept the trophy] on the last three occasions, the Americans won't recognise we're No.1."

Then on the eve of the match, a local radio station in Charleston had the bright idea of encouraging its American fans to make middle-of-the-night phone calls to the hotel where the European team was staying, something they crudely entitled "Wake Up The Enemy".

The difficult course, the string of American defeats, the European feelings of being disrespected, the fervour of the fans – it felt like a blue touchpaper had been lit and that the Kiawah match was ready to explode. Of course, the mood of increased US patriotism at this match was palpable as a result of the recently fought first Gulf War.

The media – both American and European – reported that there was an atmosphere of xenophobia at Kiawah that was not helped when a fighter jet fly-past and Marines' guard of honour for the players at the opening ceremony was climaxed by a group of local cadets from a South Carolina military college performing a 10-minute close order drill that would not have looked out of place in Red Square. This might have been billed as another celebration of the Gulf War victory, but it did not feel appropriate to many of the non-American onlookers. One renowned American journalist (John Garrity of *Sports Illustrated*) wrote afterwards: "Sam Ryder's homely little trophy is turning into a blood prize".

Once the matches began, an estimated 25,000 fans per day poured into Kiawah (easily a record for the US at the time) and the course was covered with people wearing the Stars and Stripes on their clothing or holding an American flag. One senior member of the US team, Hale Irwin, believed the home fans went too far: "At Kiawah, you're in a part of the world with a lot of military installations, and the environment was just charged up. The good ol' boys down there got that rebel-yell thing going, and the whoopin' and hollerin' wasn't exactly reserved. It went beyond a golf competition."

Then there was the controversy over Steve Pate's injury. Although making his debut, the likeable Californian was one of the US team's hottest players in practice that week. But on his way to the tournament dinner, he suffered bad bruising to his chest when a line of limousines crashed into each other. Pate was thrown to the floor of his vehicle and the edge of a car seat dug into his side just below the ribs. The initial concern was that he might not be fit to play at all, but after a CAT scan it was felt he should stay on the team. Anyway, no reserve was on site and any player called in would have been at a severe disadvantage. Pate was ruled unfit for opening day action, but then given a chance in a fourball match on the Saturday and lost. The question was soon raised about whether he could play the next day in the singles.

By the final day of the match, Pate's condition was just one of many rumbling disputes between the teams. The wearing of army-style camouflage-coloured baseball caps had annoyed the Europeans and there had been a huge row between Spaniards Seve Ballesteros and Jose Maria

Olazabal and Americans Paul Azinger and Chip Beck over the use of golf balls with different compressions. Then when Pate was a late withdrawal from the singles (it happened actually after the draw had been made; he was due to play Ballesteros), the European captain Bernard Gallacher smelled a rat. With the scores after day two level at 8-8, the way Pate had been withdrawn favoured the Americans. Gallacher knew that the rules stated that if Pate had not played at all in the pairs matches and then immediately been removed from the singles, Europe would have been awarded a full point. But a late withdrawal through injury meant both teams received half a point each. Englishman David Gilford was sacrificed as the singles matches were adjusted and many Europeans wondered why Pate had been fit enough on Saturday, but not on Sunday.

In the end, the final day of singles was full of the highest drama: Europe won the opening two points and then the US team struck back. When the last match on the course between Irwin and Germany's Bernhard Langer reached the very final green, the tension was almost unbearable. With both players wilting under the pressure, Langer lined up a six-foot putt to win his singles game, a full point for his team and tie the overall match at 14-14, thus allowing the Europeans to retain the trophy. The German thought he had hit the perfect putt, but the ball failed to drop and the Americans had won 14½-13½.

The whoops of joy from the US team and their supporters were long and loud as a wave of relief swept over them all. The Europeans were dumbstruck. Any antipathy soon dissolved, but some observers believed a tie might have resulted in a different post-match atmosphere. "I swear to God, if Langer had holed that putt," said BBC commentator and former Ryder Cup player Peter Alliss much later, "there would have been fisticuffs." Luckily for the Cup and golf in general, no such thing happened. The teams and supporters seemed to re-discover their regard for each other and shook hands instead. In fact, many Europeans partied so hard that anyone unaware of the result might have thought they had won.

However, the niggle between the teams was only covered by a thin veneer. The normally-anonymous Beck summed up the attitude of the American team: "For us to come through redeems our Tour a little bit. [The Europeans] have been ungracious winners the last couple of years. They've criticised us and degraded us, and it's been hard to take." If a professional golfer who would give up the game to sell insurance (as Beck did almost a decade later) was so roused by events in 1991 then the level of rancour must have been almost off the scale.

Relative calm before the storm

The Kiawah win in 1991 was followed by another US victory in the 30th Ryder Cup at The Belfry in England two years later, this time under the calmer captaincy of Tom Watson, and there were still undercurrents of ill-feeling. Watson himself was not averse to a little pre-match gamesmanship. In fact, the US captain sent a message of intent to the Europeans in the tournament dinner on the Wednesday evening when he instructed Payne Stewart not to sign a menu for Sam Torrance. This friendly tradition of autograph swapping was curtailed by Watson to remind his players that the Europeans were not their friends during this week of battle. But if the American thought he was adept at keeping the tension at boiling point between the two teams, then he could take lessons from a certain Mr Ballesteros.

The Spaniard had a dazzling effect on one of four European rookies in the 1993 team, the 25-year-old Peter Baker, a Shropshire lad with a cheery smile and down-to-earth manner, but a relative newcomer to playing against Americans (he had only ever played in two majors, neither of them in the States). Baker was a rising star of European golf; two wins earlier that year had secured his Ryder Cup place and he felt that he had all the necessary mental fortitude and desire for the contest ahead. But his first team meeting at The Belfry left him in shock. "I came back to my room and my wife asked me if I was ok. I said 'I thought that I was motivated and driven, but these guys…well, it's unbelievable.' I couldn't quite fathom what I'd seen and heard in the team room. It was so intense, incredible. It rubbed off on me and meant I wanted to prove a point. Seve (Ballesteros) and (Bernhard) Langer were so desperate to win. They weren't derogatory about the Americans, but what they said was just rallying us. This was our chance to prove we were the best players in the world. We were fed up of being told their tour was better than ours."

Perhaps because of what happened at Kiawah, the two sets of players were largely respectful but not overly friendly before the match took place. Europe led by a point after day one and Baker was then to play in the morning foursomes on day two with fellow rookie Barry Lane. The team's biggest star promptly gave them a sense of the kind of gamesmanship they could expect.

"We were having breakfast," says Baker, "when Seve appeared; you always sat up when he was around. He joined us and you could see there was something he wanted to tell us. 'Your opponents (Ray Floyd and Payne Stewart), they are good players,' he said. 'Floyd is a very tough man to beat. Somewhere along the line he will do something to put you off: rip his golf glove off; rattle his clubs or something.' Me and Laney looked at each other and we said: 'You mean, like you do, Seve?' – we couldn't help ourselves. 'Oh no, not like me… well, maybe,' Seve said."

But despite teasing their illustrious teammate, Baker and Lane were now ready for a Ryder Cup battle Seve-style. Sure enough, Baker recalls that on the 15th green with the match on the line, the wily Floyd walked all over his line before he had a chance to putt to win the hole. "He [Floyd] did it at the right time and the right place which I didn't really appreciate." But was that really deliberate? A man who had won four major championships and was in his eighth Ryder Cup? "It was 100% deliberate," according to Baker.

Baker and Lane lost their match on the next hole. They had learned that the Ryder Cup was a different level of competitiveness, an event where players stretch the boundaries of etiquette and even the rules of the games to gain an advantage. "There are certain things that you can do to impose yourself on the other guy in matchplay," says Baker, "maybe calling whose shot it is or something like that, dominating the pairings. But the niggles do go on in these matches and all the players know it. Even if the fans might not notice these little moments, they are there. You see, Seve was right."

Europe were eventually beaten in 1993 by the middle of Sunday afternoon. Ballesteros, who won only two points out of a possible five, was distraught. "Seve was absolutely balling his eyes out after we lost," remembers Baker. "He wasn't alone either, but his desire to win was incredible. His emotion was unbelievable."

The Spaniard was again in floods of tears after the matches in 1995 and 1997, but each time they were tears of joy as the Europeans pulled off two dramatic victories: firstly, after a final-day surge at Oak Hill Country Club, New York, and two years later in Valderrama, Spain, where Captain Ballesteros in his ubiquitous golf buggy urged his men on with so much advice on almost every hole that some of his players had to tell him – not very politely – to leave them alone.

The US team was embarrassed by the defeats, particularly the one at home at Oak Hill – it was only their second loss in America – and the boisterous, flag-waving celebrations by the Europeans on the final green on both occasions did not help their mood. When the match came back to America in 1999, the stakes would be extremely high.

The inevitable nadir

So the 33rd Ryder Cup match at The Country Club of Brookline, Massachusetts, had all the makings of being another difficult match for both teams. Yet again, the press was stirring up the match into a war-like confrontation: the Europeans had won the previous two matches and a third consecutive defeat for the Americans would be unprecedented. Plus, although this was the first match since 1983 without Ballesteros as either player or captain, the controversial (in America, anyway) Spanish contingent had a new recruit, Sergio Garcia, and a new villain for the US fans. The country's new 19-year-old sensation had created headlines a few weeks earlier in that year's PGA Championship at Medinah with some on-course histrionics.

Both sets of players were caught in an emotional vice with massive crowds now in attendance, millions more watching on TV and their own reputations under a very bright spotlight. Some observers believed that it was the American team and their fans who were most likely to crack under the pressure and this seemed likely after the visitors shot 10-6 ahead at the end of day two. That evening, US captain Ben Crenshaw fired his team up to the point of tears and the result the next day was an over-hyped atmosphere in which the mood among the US fans – many who were said to be at their first golf event – was uncomfortably tribal. There were vicious undertones in their cheering and loud remarks, often fuelled by plenty of beer and very hot conditions. For two days, there had been playful joking between the home crowd and a couple of thousand supporters from Europe, but the Sunday's environment was unpleasant and the banter mostly disappeared.

That day of Sunday singles turned out to be the noisiest, most disruptive and obnoxious day in Ryder Cup history. Whether the fans fed off the US team's energy or the other way around is unclear, but Brookline proved to be a low point for both crowd and player behaviour.

There were early reports of verbal abuse of some of the European players (Colin Montgomerie was the main target); deliberate noises coming from the crowd during the backswing of several European players; and Ryder Cup rookie Andrew Coltart's golf ball suspiciously went missing when it landed just off the fairway during his match with Tiger Woods. Perhaps the most unpleasant moment came when one wife of a European player claimed she was spat at by a drunken American fan. But these might have been passed off as isolated incidents if the match between Justin Leonard and Jose Maria Olazabal had ended in a less controversial manner.

Leonard had been four holes behind against Olazabal at one point, but then his putter got hot and he pulled level at the 16th. The US team now needed only a half point from the Texan or his teammate Payne Stewart (playing behind him in the last match of the day against Montgomerie) to regain the cup. A huge crowd gathered on the 17th green as the American studied an uphill, double-breaking 45-foot putt while Olazabal was also on the green in two shots, but considerably closer. There was silence as Leonard tapped his putt forward and then bedlam as he holed for a highly improbable birdie. A spontaneous mass stampede across the green then took place involving his teammates, various caddies and even some wives who believed the putt guaranteed the half-point the US team needed to win the Cup. Such wild, mass celebrations were becoming common in Ryder Cups, but two things made this one highly inappropriate: firstly, this singles match was still alive (the Spaniard actually had a putt to halve the hole) and, secondly, stampeding feet trampled all over the green and, allegedly, over Olazabal's line.

It took several minutes for order to be restored and then the somewhat shaken Spaniard attempted his putt, but almost inevitably he missed. This indeed meant that America were guaranteed the necessary 14½ winning points for their win, but after all the pressure of nearly three days of fierce competition and the abuse that the visiting players had suffered from the home fans on the Sunday, the restraint of some of the Europeans snapped. Vice-captain Sam Torrance fumed: "It's about the most disgusting thing I've seen in my life. This is not sour grapes. The whole American team and spectators ran right across the green over Olly's line." The words might have slightly exaggerated the incident, but his sentiments were real and felt by his whole team. Torrance singled out Tom Lehman who ran 50 yards down the 17th fairway after Leonard's putt to fist-pump the crowd. "It was disgusting and Tom Lehman calls himself a man of God," Torrance said with words that were heard by television audiences around the world. Lehman admitted a little later that day when things calmed down that he wished the response of the Americans had been different, but he defended the invasion of the green as something that happened in the heat of the moment. "That was over-exuberance, no question about it. It was not a good thing, but what is done is done. I wish we had contained ourselves. Sometimes you get carried away."

The subsequent name-calling, at least in some elements of the press, was a little childish: the British saw "the ugly American" caricature at Brookline and branded the US skipper as "mental Ben" Crenshaw rather than his normal nickname of "gentle Ben". The US defenders of the incident called the Euros "whiney" and some called the visitors sore losers. Davis Love III commented: "We didn't cry when we lost two in a row."

It could be argued that the reaction happened because of events that dated back not just to Kiawah in 1991 but to the many controversial incidents that had occurred during the previous 70 years of competition: the seething resentments, hidden jealousies, angry confrontations and thinly-veiled antagonism that could no longer be contained. The Battle of Brookline saw the result of a perfect storm of emotions that had been building up for all those years. In other words, the sad scenes of boorishness were an inevitable climax that should not have surprised anyone.

Brookline will always remain a scar on the Ryder Cup's image and hardly a match goes by without a reference to the worst of the incidents, usually with the caveat that this should never happen again. Then, a tragic perspective on the matter was delivered the following month with the death of one of the US team, Payne Stewart.

He was the one American who embodied the spirit of the Ryder Cup, according to all the Europeans. Stewart always insisted that both teams should celebrate and commiserate together after each match and he was not proud of the behaviour of some of his counterparts at Brookline. He was playing Montgomerie in the final singles match just behind Leonard and Olazabal and the insulting words that he had heard directed at the Scot left him deeply unhappy. Soon after the Leonard-Olazabal contest ended, Stewart conceded his match to Montgomerie to put an end to the possibility of any more trouble on the course.

The 42-year-old with a taste for wearing flamboyantly-coloured plus-fours on the course had won his third major title earlier that year and was at the top of his game. His death came when a private jet carrying him and three other passengers to Texas was thought to have suffered a cabin leak that caused a fatal loss of air pressure. Everyone on board, including both pilots, was rendered unconscious. The jet eventually crashed, everyone on board was killed and the sport was rocked. It was fitting that the PGA Tour created an award the following year under Payne Stewart's name. The recipient is lauded for charity work as well as for upholding the traditions of golf, something that Stewart tried to do even in the poisonous atmosphere of the Brookline Ryder Cup.

Recovering the respect

Although the chatter after the events at the Country Club at Brookline rumbled on for many months, there was a strong consensus that no such incidents could take place at the next Ryder Cup, planned for The Belfry, England, in September 2001. It would be a severe test for the captains – Torrance and Curtis Strange (friends for years and sensible men) – and the whole of the sport was behind their determination to tone down the players' celebrations and urge the fans to adopt greater decorum. More practical steps such as extra security in the crowd and the swift removal of any offenders would also help.

Then with just a couple of weeks before tee off, matters were taken out of the captains' hands when almost 3,000 people died in the 9/11 terrorist attacks on America. Almost overnight, any enmity between teams in an international golf match seemed irrelevant and, five days after the attacks, the match was officially postponed for 12 months. The Belfry grandstands were immediately de-constructed, advertising hoardings garaged and thousands of boxes of merchandise sent into storage while nearly 100,000 match programmes were pulped. General manager Mike Maloney and his staff faced the task of re-selling all the hotel bedrooms, function rooms, golf-course tee times and everything else that had been booked over the week of the Ryder Cup in order to prove to their insurance brokers that every effort had been made to minimise the commercial damage. "We hit the phones as soon as everything was official. By the time the match was due to start, we had achieved 65% occupancy of the tee times, bedrooms, function rooms and all other hotel facilities. Then we had to let our insurers and the PGA's insurers sort out the rest."

Postponement for a full year rather than just a few days or weeks pleased everyone. It allowed the officials plenty of time to set about the difficult task of re-scheduling every aspect of the Cup, including the future dates of all the other team events on the golfing calendar – the Presidents Cup, Seve Trophy and Solheim Cup. Odd-year Ryder Cups were no more.

Captains Torrance and Strange used the delay to ensure that the atmosphere – especially among their players – was more appropriate than it had been at Brookline. Torrance told *Golf Today*: "I was actually delighted it was going to be played the next year. Every other Ryder Cup captain in history has had three or four weeks after the team has been announced [to prepare]. I had over a year. And I made the most of it. I used that time to try to put the Ryder Cup in perspective after the terrible events in New York. And also after the way the match had got out of hand in 1999."

As it turned out, The Belfry in 2002 was another remarkable match and mutual respect was renewed. Both captains had worked hard for this match to be the antithesis of Brookline and even former players were relieved. Irishman Eamon Darcy had played the last of his Ryder Cups in 1987 when there was real competitiveness between the teams. "[The intensity] needed to be pulled back. It was getting a bit out of control and 9/11 changed everything and brought everything into proportion. When people start clapping and cheering balls going into water, it's time to stop all that."

Hal Sutton was a member of the American team that was due to fly to England in 2001 and had been a winner in Brookline two years earlier, but he also saw the need for a lowering of the pressure level. "Those planes going into the Twin Towers put things into perspective for everybody that this was just a competition and life goes on. The intensity was different afterwards."

The delay caused by the 9/11 terrorism was an unwanted surprise for the Ryder Cup organisers, but there was also an upside – any worries about the Cup atmosphere boiling over again any time soon were dismissed in September 2002. "There wasn't one negative comment about what happened," said Strange afterwards. "People got it (that their behaviour had to be impeccable)." Everyone at The Belfry that year was connected to the tragedy of 9/11 as much as to the golf match and neither the word 'war' nor 'battle' was ever mentioned.

Just getting started

Conflict and controversy have been part and parcel of Ryder Cup matches ever since the inaugural contest. Opponents have clashed and captains argued;

teammates have been known to butt heads; and ex-captains and players often heard giving an opinion, wanted or not. Compared with normal strokeplay events that now make up the vast majority of the golfing calendar, the Ryder Cup has always been in a league of its own in terms of debates, disputes and disagreements. Often times and with two years between each match, a media that is increasingly hungry for stories of turmoil and tumult will fan the flames with even the smallest comment from a prospective player, ex-captain or almost anyone with an opinion.

In one sense, of course, this sort of behaviour is inevitable because the relationships between people in the world of men's professional golf are just a microcosm of those in every other kind of small community. Not every golfer is going to be pleasant all the time to every one of his rivals, and personalities will clash almost as often as friendships are made. Usually, the more high-profile the personality, the bigger the quarrel. While some rows are never even made public – they are settled instead in the privacy of the locker room – others create major headlines.

Even before the inaugural Ryder Cup started in 1927, there was a disagreement between the two sides: the PGA of America wrote to their British counterparts demanding the eight singles matches take place on day one and the four foursomes on day two. When it was pointed out by the British that the result might be settled on the opening day if that format was agreed, the US administrators changed their minds. It was the Irish playwright George Bernard Shaw who summed up the relationship between the UK and US as two countries divided by a common language and this incident perhaps proved that the phrase was true even of golf and the Ryder Cup.

Prior to this and in the wider, social sense, there had been a close but complex relationship between the two countries for decades. At times, there were feelings of antagonism, especially politically because of a history of antipathy that dated back a couple of centuries to the revolutionary war between Britain and America (with a little French involvement thrown in). With every emerging decade of the 20th century, it seemed like competition between the two countries became more intense, so sporting battles were very attractive and the Ryder Cup became an obvious opportunity for either the British Limey and American Yank to establish bragging rights. When the US team delivered victory on home soil in the inaugural match (remember, the GB team had easily won the two previous unofficial contests), it was the best possible result because it made certain that another match would happen – how else could the British recapture their honour? Certainly, one's honour and reputation was the kind of thing that young Henry Cotton was keen to maintain.

The Cheshire-born sporting prodigy was only 22 when the US Ryder Cup team came to Britain in 1929 to make the first ever defence of the trophy.

That second match at Moortown in Yorkshire began Cotton's controversial relationship with the competition.

Some golfers are absorbed into the whole team ethos, they subsume themselves into the group; they try their best and play their role, win or lose. Cotton, however, could not help himself – he *had* to stand out from the crowd. Even as the youngest man on the 1929 team, he sensed that the Ryder Cup was an opportunity for his own personal glory. He noted that the British amateurs had already made a habit of losing the Walker Cup to the Americans (five amateur contests, five GB losses to date), so the professionals of Britain held the nation's golfing reputation in their hands and Cotton was primed to play a key role. In front of 10,000 spectators in Yorkshire, the dapper Cotton holed the putt that brought Samuel Ryder's trophy home and his legend was established. Yet this was the only highlight in Cotton's Ryder Cup career; the rest was one struggle or skirmish after another.

It was not a shock to Cotton himself that his Cup career was bumpy because he was a man who always pushed back against authority. In fact, it was the reason he became a golfer. As a teenager, he was a fine cricketer at his school in Dulwich, south London, but a row with other, more senior players led him to write an insubordinate letter of complaint for which his headmaster wanted to have him caned. Cotton refused the punishment and swapped his cricket bat for golf clubs as a further insult to his school. He then practiced so hard from the age of 13 that his strong hands (which he always believed were one of his main attributes) would bleed, yet his talent was obvious and he became the youngest ever British club professional at the age of only 19. Three years later, he was a Ryder Cup golfer and the British press were enamoured with their new star, with his fine clothes and smooth swing.

For the 1931 match, Cotton became embroiled in a rather complex dispute that began when the PGA team selection committee named 24 players who were in line to play in Ohio in the 3rd Ryder Cup match. Cotton felt he was good enough to be on the team sheet without such preliminaries, but was prepared to play the selectors' game until a new directive was announced: the entire British team had to return from the Cup together directly after the match rather than stay in America for the US Open in Ohio just a week later. The GB players had been allowed to play in the same major championship in 1927, so this was a surprising change of policy and Cotton objected. The PGA insisted, claiming that this ruling was better for morale and for anyone to break ranks was unpatriotic. Cotton was desperate to test himself in the US Open, so he offered to pay for his own return trip and even moaned about the situation in *Golf Illustrated* magazine, gaining much sympathy with many readers. However, the PGA's stance was as intransigent as Cotton's and the association asked for a letter of apology. Unsurprisingly, no such letter was sent.

Instead, the 24-year-old Cotton took the initiative and booked a private tour of golf clubs in the States thereby thwarting an eleventh-hour compromise request from the association that the player remain under the PGA's control while abroad. The sorry tale left Cotton out of the team along with two other banned prospective players, Percy Allis and Aubrey Boomer (ineligible because they lived and worked in continental Europe, Alliss in Berlin and Boomer in Paris). Both joined Cotton on his US tour schedule.

In his autobiography, *This Game Of Golf*, Cotton explains that he had already visited America in 1928, so to remain in the country for the chance to win a major seemed obvious. Of his dispute with the association, he rather graciously wrote that he had "a difference with the PGA committee over the right to remain in the States after the match that I insisted upon and they refused to grant. (So) I stood down from the side".

The row was actually as much cultural as practical. There was a rather Victorian view in British golfing circles that the professionals should all be thankful of a "free trip" to the States and that this was a gift from the PGA who could ask for almost anything in return. The idea of a free-spirited golfer like Cotton spending endless time away from his job at a golf club was frowned upon. Given the perspective of the 21st century, Cotton's position seems both reasonable and obvious while it appears odd that the PGA did not encourage *all* the Great Britain Ryder Cup players to contest the US Open because, if one of them had happened to win the title, it would have provided a huge fillip to the sport back home.

An editorial in *Golf Monthly* sided with the PGA, pointing out that all the other 23 originally-nominated members of the squad agreed to the conditions and Cotton had left the association with no choice.

Sadly, there were no winners from the affair: the GB team lost the Ryder Cup match 9-3; neither Cotton, Alliss nor Boomer won the US Open; and Cotton himself was struck down by illness and forced to return home early.

Before the next match, as if to further spite the PGA, Cotton moved to Belgium to take a club job at the Royal Waterloo Golf Club where he was essentially a touring pro, relieved of most of the normal duties of his contemporaries in Britain such as giving lessons and being around for competitions at weekends. Like Alliss and Boomer before him, Cotton was now banned from the Ryder Cup team because he lived abroad. Cotton's move to continental Europe worked wonders for his game because in 1934 he won the first of his three Open Championships. Sadly for the Ryder Cup, he would miss both the 1933 and 1935 matches.

Cotton was back for the 1937 contest, but by this time the Americans had the upper hand, even though six of the US team that year rather daringly brought their wives with them to Southport & Ainsdale (esteemed British journalist Henry Longhurst reckoned that "women on these trips are an encumbrance equivalent roughly to conceding two shots per round"). Despite this, the Brits lost and their only compensation was that Cotton beat all 12 US team members when he won the 1937 Open title at Carnoustie the following week.

The outbreak of World War II meant a 10-year absence for the matches and, when they returned in 1947, the urbane Cotton was 40-years-old and made captain of the GB team. However, he could not resist causing another controversial moment.

The penniless British PGA had agreed to doubling the journey distance for their team because Oregon fruit-packing millionaire Robert A. Hudson footed the entire bill for the Cup that year (all three previous American matches had been staged on or near the east coast to cut down travel time and expense). So the GB captain and his players were probably ready for a bit of a fight after their exhausting 6,000-mile journey to the north-west corner of America. Once there, Cotton levelled a protest almost immediately, claiming that the clubs used by the American team were illegal. The GB skipper noticed the enormous amount of backspin that American players managed with their irons (particularly their pitching wedges) and it seemed slightly unbelievable to him.

The claim was either hopeful or mischievous and explained simply by the fact that American golf equipment companies had made several improvements to clubs and balls during the last decade, while Cotton and his teammates were using almost second-hand gear by comparison. Nevertheless, on the very eve of the foursomes matches on day one, Cotton called for a full-scale inspection of the American players' clubs. The Americans – most of whom also enjoyed the advantage of playing throughout World War II on the PGA Tour – blamed jealousy for the Englishman's actions.

As it turned out, the Americans' clubs were found to be legal and the US team went on to retain the Cup with an 11-1 win. Obviously embarrassed by the whole affair, the two PGAs (and also the captains and their players) said nothing of the protest to the media at the time; Cotton's allegation only emerged afterwards. However, such Cup controversies are not forgotten easily and Cotton's counterpart as captain that year, Ben Hogan, had a long memory.

An intense man and former caddie, Hogan won his first two major titles a year later in 1948 (he would go on to win a total of nine) and he was soon announced as captain once again for the following year's match at Ganton Golf Club in Yorkshire. Still only 37-years-old, Bantam Ben's reputation as one of the truly great players of all time was still being built when he suffered a near-fatal car crash in the February of Ryder Cup year. Both he and his wife nearly died and Hogan's fast recovery made him a folk hero.

Hogan's injuries reduced him to the role of non-playing captain in 1949 and, although his rival skipper would be Charles Whitcombe rather than Cotton, the Wee Man was determined to exact revenge for the earlier British equipment allegations.

On the eve of the Ganton match, Hogan claimed that the clubs belonging to the GB team were illegal and should be examined. These were the days when the face of a wedge was not necessarily covered in lines of grooves as they are today. Some wedges featured a series of dotted holes instead and at least one British pro was said to have used a drill to make the dots deeper in order to get more spin, so perhaps Hogan's claims were not without substance. Nevertheless, the move took Whitcombe by surprise because the West Countryman had not been involved in 1947 and, at 54 years of age, was from a slightly more restrained generation of golfers.

This time the story broke in the media and any notion that the Ryder Cup was an event without controversy was lost forever. Hogan was, of course, the toughest of professionals and knew exactly what he was doing by sending flustered British PGA administrators into a panic. First, they called in two manufacturers to examine the clubs, but they could not agree on the question of legality, so then a mad dash was made to the nearby town of Scarborough where the chairman of the Royal & Ancient's Rules of Golf committee – and famous journalist – Bernard Darwin was reportedly enjoying a fine dinner. Darwin agreed with Hogan and ordered that the faulty clubs should be made legal again. The phrase "nothing that a little filing will not put right" was allegedly both his decision and his instruction to the GB team. The Ganton professional Jock Ballantine then carried out the work on the clubs overnight so that everything would be ready on the opening day.

Was Hogan really worried about the clubs and any advantage they could give the home side or was he just setting the record straight while also delivering a psychological blow to his opponents? Well, it was probably a bit of both, but it is unlikely that the incident did anything to bring the two teams together in terms of respect and affection. Hogan was the kind of professional who sought every advantage he could within the rules.

Despite the dispute, GB actually led after the first day of foursomes – they won three and lost just one – but Hogan's team fought back on day two and had retained the Cup with only four of the eight singles completed. The final score was a 7-5 win for the visitors and the Americans had won the psychological battle as well as the one on the golf course. This had been the most controversial match of the eight played so far and, for better or for worse, the Ryder Cup had grown up. From now on, the trophy would be fought over tooth and nail with no quarter given or asked and the days of extreme etiquette were over.

Waiting for a spark

The eleven Ryder Cups from 1947 to 1967 produced only a single GB victory (Lindrick in 1957). American wins in Britain were usually close affairs, but the reverse fixture was always a US walkover. The players, captains, British PGA, press, fans… everyone had an opinion on why the Americans were able to hold on the trophy so tightly: bad putting by the British; superior practice facilities in the US; better conditioning of the American players, both physically and mentally; or the greater number of high-pressure tournaments on the PGA Tour where more money was at stake.

Star British players like Brian Huggett raged about the imbalance between the teams. The pocket-battleship Welshman (he stood just 5ft 6in tall) always had a fiery temper, but playing against some Americans with what he felt was their sneering arrogance was too much for him to stomach. "The American players tried to make you feel inferior and we were. They loved to give us a whacking. They were very tough about the matches even in those days. They never took it easy. And they were bloody arrogant. I played in six Ryder Cups and got 12 points and I enjoyed every one of those buggers."

In 1969, the PGA appointed a captain with a new philosophy to international competition, a man who actually confessed to hating "the Yanks" and was not slow to tell them. Eric Brown's captaincy meant the GB team would go down fighting more fiercely than ever before and he told his players that not only *could* they win, but they *must* win. He shouted and cursed his way into their heads because he wanted his toughness to become theirs. Brown's personality may have invigorated some of his players and unsettled others, but the balding Scot achieved one thing even before the match began – he convinced the Americans that they had a fight on their hands. "He was not a good captain for me," confesses Brian Barnes, a leading member of the 1969 team. "I was embarrassed by his win-at-all-costs attitude." Yet, with Brown's opposite number Sam Snead also known for his brusque manner, the atmosphere at Royal Birkdale that year was always going to be highly charged.

The most controversial incident started on the first morning in a foursomes match featuring Bernard Gallacher and Maurice Bembridge, representing GB, against Lee Trevino and Ken Still. Four birdies in the first five holes from the Americans should have laid the foundations for a comfortable win, yet by the 8th hole, the match was level and nerves were starting to jangle. Bembridge and Still then stared each other down on the 13th tee when the Englishman asked his opponent to move out of his line of sight. A surprised Still tried to embarrass Bembridge by melodramatically making everyone else on the tee – players, caddies and officials – move as well. Then on the 13th green, Still's bunker shot appeared to hit him – which should have meant automatic loss of the hole – only the American failed to acknowledge it. When Trevino, the senior partner in the pairing, promptly conceded the hole, Still was mortified. It was the turning point in the match that Bembridge and Gallacher won 2&1.

Still and Gallacher were then involved in another bad-tempered match on day two, a fourball with partners Dave Hill and Brian Huggett respectively. On the very first green, Still was again accused of being in his opponents' line of sight (this time by Huggett). On the second green, the childish behaviour continued when Still shouted out to his caddie as Gallacher was preparing to putt and throughout the match Huggett felt both Americans stood too close to him on the greens. Tension was at breaking point on the 7th when Hill missed a putt and then immediately tapped his ball into the hole. Unlike normal strokeplay, the rules of matchplay require the ball to be marked and the player wait his turn for the tap-in putt. The feisty Gallacher was not slow to tell Hill that he had putted out of turn, in effect, breaking the rules. "You can have the hole and the goddam Cup," blurted Hill as he conceded and stormed off the 8th tee.

Perhaps unsurprisingly on the next fairway, Huggett and Still found themselves shouting at each other about what had just happened and then the fans began to jeer the Americans, something totally out of character for Royal Birkdale's normally super-polite golf galleries. When one fan apparently had to be restrained from throwing a bottle, it was clear that things were getting out of hand. At this point, both captains joined up with the match along with British PGA president Lord Derby and even a couple of policemen to cool things down. However, that was not before some rather blue language was exchanged on the 8th green when the canny Gallacher (perfectly within the rules) conceded a Ken Still putt that was on the same line as Dave Hill's longer attempt. The concession prevented Still from putting and therefore showing his partner the line. "If looks could kill, Still would have been on quite a few murder charges," Huggett said afterwards. Only one of the three players kept his golf game together – Dave Hill was inspired throughout the shenanigans and his outstanding play gave his pairing a 2&1 win, although the American refused to shake the referee's hand afterwards.

The poisonous atmosphere at Birkdale was even felt among Hill's teammates. Frank Beard admitted years later in his 1992 book *Making The Turn* that "Dave and I had a few words over something, I don't remember what. Feelings ran so high that players were getting into arguments with their own teammates."

However, all the incidents were submerged by the very last moments of the overall match – a 16-16 tie was delivered via the iconic moment now known as The Concession. When America's greatest player Jack Nicklaus refused to let his friend and fellow major champion Tony Jacklin attempt a final-green, two-foot putt, thereby ensuring the tie, the Ryder Cup had delivered one of the greatest ever examples of sportsmanship. The two champions walked off the green with their arms over each other's shoulders, the applause rang out and the gentlemanly nature of golf returned. Nicklaus's magnanimous gesture covered over all the spitefulness that had gone before. Then, at the post-match banquet, it was agreed that the Cup would stay in Britain for 12 months before being shipped back to the Americans who had, after all, retained the trophy with a draw.

The tie felt almost as good as a win for the success-hungry British and Eric Brown's explosive passion contributed enormously to a much-improved home team performance. Yet, the GB captain's wide-eyed craving to beat the Americans also brought about some crucial mistakes that unwittingly prevented victory.

The Sunday singles in 1969 were split into morning and afternoon sessions and both Brian Barnes and Neil Coles were sent out twice in very unhelpful circumstances. "I'd just lost my morning match," remembers Barnes, "when Eric told me I was lead-off man in the afternoon. I literally had 10 minutes to get a bite to eat and I was off again." Meanwhile, Coles was totally exhausted from having played all the previous five sessions. "Eric originally said he wouldn't play me twice on the last day, but then he changed his mind. In the afternoon, I played Dan Sikes and was out in 42, yet I was only 2 down. There were people like Bernard Hunt who were as fresh as a daisy, but didn't play at all in the singles. Anyone could've beaten Sikes that day."

Hero or villain, Eric Brown was unlike any previous GB captain in terms of the fury that he brought to the match, raising the question of whether the British would be better off always playing with some extra emotion against their opponents. Perhaps the answer was delivered two years later in St. Louis, Missouri when, under Brown's captaincy for a second time, the British were again soundly beaten.

The captaincy conundrum

Over the years, the selection of the best Ryder Cup captain has appeared to be more of an instinctive feeling than a science. The committees that have made the various appointments will always come under fire from someone in the sport who believes they made the wrong decision. In fact, the captain probably provides as much pre-match controversy as any single person apart from their own picks for the team.

For almost two years, the captain is the figurehead of the build-up, continually asked about tactics, wildcards, course set-ups and the rest. Some skippers perform their tasks in similar ways while others revolutionise the job and, in the incestuous world of golf, a single decision by a captain can set off a series of shock waves that can be felt many years later. Sometimes the interweaving of all these strong characters and their selection along with their thoughts and actions (some of them highly controversial) feels like a soap opera with plot lines linking across episodes over many decades. One of the best examples is the connection between the 1997 match in Valderrama and the Gleneagles contest staged a full 17 years later.

Back when the Ryder Cup came to Spain, Team Europe had been operating for almost two decades and seemed, to the outside world anyway, a close-knit operation whose winning formula was based on togetherness. Europe's 'Big Six' major winners of the last few years – Seve Ballesteros, Bernhard Langer, Nick Faldo, Ian Woosnam, Sandy Lyle and Jose Maria Olazabal – had helped bring about three wins and a tie in the last six matches. At Valderrama, Ballesteros was the first to take the skipper's role, but surely all the others would eventually get their turn. However, of the remaining five, Lyle's candidacy looked quite weak, mostly because he had been the first to stop playing in the Cup, in 1989, after he had suffered a sharp dip in form.

But Lyle also had another disadvantage: he had never been regarded as the deepest thinker about the game and was seen by some as too mild-mannered and naïve for the rigours of the increasingly arduous Ryder Cup captain's duties, someone who might struggle with the media demands and the various formalities. As the Ryder Cups of the new millennium came and went, Lyle would be the odd man out in the captaincy stakes: Ballesteros's appointment was followed by Langer (2004), Woosnam (2006) and Faldo (2008). The closest Lyle got was as a vice-captain in 2006 while Olazabal was still considered too young.

Immediately after Faldo's failure to win the trophy in 2008, the conversation about Lyle becoming captain began for Celtic Manor in 2010. It seemed an obvious move, at least to many of the golf press and those on the outside of the European Tour's think-tank. Among those supporting the two-time major winner was fellow Scot Colin Montgomerie. "It'd be a shame if it wasn't Sandy. There's no other outstanding candidate," Monty declared in September 2008 and added that he himself was targeting Gleneagles in 2014 when he would be 51 and likely to be too old to make the team. It all seemed to make perfect sense.

What then happened as the crucial selection meeting of the European Tour committee approached was a wild change of views. Not only that, but as the cast of characters grew – willingly or not – the scheming behind the Ryder Cup captaincy selection was exposed in all its glory.

Firstly, support for Lyle as Celtic Manor captain suddenly began to evaporate, but no one was openly saying why. One reason postulated in the media was that Lyle offended too many people when he had walked off the course at the Open Championship at Royal Birkdale six months earlier. The

Scot said the extremely bad weather conditions gave him no option. "For the first few holes, I wasn't too bad," he had said, "and then the rain came and got my timing and I got out of position and I couldn't make a golf swing. I was all over the place. I lost momentum, I couldn't really hit the ball hardly at all and it was total meltdown to be honest."

Lyle was not the only person to exit Royal Birkdale on that first day (former PGA champion Rich Beem threw in the towel after nine holes), yet it was the kind of PR miss-step that the Scot could ill afford if he was to lead a Ryder Cup team. "Unacceptable," said BBC commentator Mark Roe of Lyle's withdrawal. Privately, some senior members of the R&A and the European Tour agreed. As a past champion, it was felt Lyle treated the oldest golf championship in the world with disdain.

So, in January 2009, when the Ryder Cup Committee unexpectedly announced the name of Colin Montgomerie as the next Ryder Cup captain, Lyle's Open walk-off was assumed to be the reason his own captaincy bid failed. Lyle had simply shot down his chances by his own actions and the matter would be put to rest. But, no, that's not how the captaincy selection always works because the desire for the job can be extraordinary; also golf pros have notoriously long memories.

Lyle said very little when Montgomerie was selected for Celtic Manor, even though the choice suffered from a sizeable flaw: Monty was still a top player (he had finished 12th on the European money list as recently as 2007), so it was not an outrageous prediction that he might automatically qualify to play on his own team or even warrant a captain's pick given his record in the event, even though he would be 47 by that time. However, Lyle chose another reason to question the decision and waited a few months before he finally dropped his bombshell.

In a newspaper interview, just before the 2009 Open Championship, Lyle was asked again if he had lost the Ryder Cup captain's job because he walked out of the Open. The still-smarting Scot decided to put his walk-off into context and compared it to a controversial incident back in 2005 when Montgomerie was accused by some of taking a deliberately incorrect drop on the slope of a bunker after a rain delay at the Indonesian Open. "Monty dropped the ball badly and that is a form of cheating," Lyle told the media. It was not the classiest thing to say, but it summed up how badly Lyle had been hurt. Just to rub more salt into the wound, Lyle also called Monty "aloof" and claimed that he had been turned down by his countryman for an assistant's role at Celtic Manor. "What [Monty] did was far worse [than me walking off after 10 holes of the 2008 Open]."

Almost before the story hit the presses, Lyle realised he had made another mistake. There then followed a series of apologies and further statements. Firstly, Lyle said he was sorry to have brought up the Indonesian incident and that he was not at war with Monty. Then Montgomerie – who had said his drop in the Asian tournament was "an unwitting error" – dismissed Lyle's comments by saying: "It's a rather strange apology to be honest." And, finally, European Tour boss George O'Grady put a full stop on the story: "The Tour fully understands Sandy Lyle's disappointment at not being elected captain, but deeply regrets his comments which are considered wholly inappropriate and ill-timed."

This whole affair summed up the conflicting opinions among golf's elite when it comes to a Ryder Cup captain and who is the best man for the job. Some of the players in the Lyle drama had already found the spotlight themselves over similar captaincy controversies.

The man in charge of the European Tour committee that selected Montgomerie was the chairman Thomas Bjorn who backed Monty despite being one of the players who spoke out loudest against the Scot's actions in Indonesia. The Great Dane's relationship with Ryder Cup captains had been in the news before this – back in 2006 he raged against Ian Woosnam because he was not made a captain's pick by the Welshman. Bjorn particularly hated the fact that he had not been told personally before the announcement and heavily criticised Woosie's ability to communicate either to him or to his team. "Pathetic," was how Bjorn described Woosnam's captaincy and he also said that he had "totally lost any respect" for the Welshman, a remark which prompted the Tour to fine him heavily.

This web of connected captaincy controversies became more complicated when Woosnam raised a complaint of his own and his surprising target was the normally whiter-than-white Bernhard Langer. It was reported that the German – who led the 2004 European team to a famous victory – had provided Woosie's opposing captain Tom Lehman with some Ryder Cup advice. "It seems strange to me that Tom Lehman has asked Bernhard for advice and that [Langer] has complied," said Woosnam, who found out about the advice-sharing just weeks before the teams did battle at The K Club. The Welshman (a former vice captain himself) said he had asked two former European captains for help, but not Langer and definitely not any Americans.

This was probably the first time that a Ryder Cup build-up had included such counter-intelligence claims, but Langer admitted surprise that Woosnam had not approached him. The German also claimed to have "held a little back" in terms of guidance for Lehman who had long been a friend within the Christian community on the PGA Tour. Still, it was another moment of myth-shattering about European team unity.

Langer's own captaincy had been relatively short of disputes, especially when his contentious captain's pick – Colin Montgomerie – worked out perfectly: the Scot had suffered a rather ordinary season by his own standards, yet holed the winning Ryder Cup putt. Theirs was a great friendship, but what would the German have advised if, nearly a decade later, Monty had asked him about making a bid for a second Ryder Cup captaincy in 2014?

The predictions for selection of the Gleneagles captaincy had seemed similar to those of 2010: whereas it was supposedly Sandy Lyle's turn back then, it was obviously Paul McGinley's job in 2014 with only fellow Irishman Darren Clarke even close to being in the frame. It was argued that McGinley had served his time as a team member (three appearances, all victories) and had twice led a successful Seve Trophy team. Clarke's captaincy could easily wait two years.

However, when the Ryder Cup is at stake, nothing is straightforward. The fun began when the name of Colin Montgomerie was thrown into the mix as if from nowhere. A Scot should lead the team in Scotland was the thinking and Monty had, after all, originally targeted Gleneagles rather than Celtic Manor for his captaincy. There were raised eyebrows among the media and many of the top European Tour players when the eight-time Ryder Cupper quickly jumped on his own bandwagon. "Obviously, it would be a dream come true if I could be seen to be captain at home in Scotland," he said. "It will be a great honour. It seemed to be between Darren and Paul and now my name seems to be mentioned an awful lot, so we will see."

Just days before the 15-man European Tour committee were to vote, it seemed McGinley had slumped from being a sure thing to an unlucky near-miss. A number of players, including Rory McIlroy, sent messages on social media supporting the Irishman and reminding everyone that the captaincy had most recently become a one-time-only affair. Yet, despite this, there was a story on the Sky Sports News channel on the eve of the vote that forecast Monty would get the job.

Despite all the modern media outlets and various ways of expressing himself about his seeming demise, McGinley refused to join the debate at all and, as it turned out, keeping his counsel was the best move he could have made as the Tour committee eventually voted him captain for 2014. "I read and followed every word that went down… and watched with interest. Like a yo-yo, my chances seemed to go up and down and up and down," the relieved McGinley said afterwards. So the Irishman won the day, although of course, Montgomerie's supporters would simply re-iterate that a Scotsman should really have captained the team in Scotland.

For Monty, however, there was also another, more subtle reason why he threw his hat into the Ryder Cup captaincy ring again – a reason that went unmentioned at the time. Montgomerie was a key member of Seve Ballesteros's team that triumphed in the Spaniard's homeland in 1997 at Valderrama and the Scot had not forgotten the kudos the whole of Spain handed to its heroic countrymen. Perhaps it was inappropriate for Monty to try for the 2014 captaincy, maybe it was controversial, but what better way to ensure your golfing legacy than to mirror the achievements of Europe's greatest player. For sure, it underlines that the Ryder Cup captaincy selections are often connected and only one thing can guaranteed – an element of controversy.

Quarrels that won't die quietly

With a Ryder Cup taking place only once every two years, non-golf fans might believe that the matches would make few media headlines during the intervening period. But this assumption could not be more wrong, especially in recent times. One of the most controversial mid-match stories that kept the media happy began just after the 2004 match that Europe won in Oakland Hills, Michigan. The victory had been the third one by Team Europe in America and, much to the delight of all concerned, there was no repeat of the scenes at Brookline. Those wounds seemed to have healed, especially after the US captain Hal Sutton spoke out before the contest began. "Look, y'all have been kind of like a bad marriage partner. We've apologised for five years for what happened in 1999. So y'all need to forget about that. No more apologies or anything else." The fact that Europe went on to pummel Sutton's team 18½-9½ without any suggestion of ungracious behaviour by American players or fans seemed to have put the ugly issues of the past to bed.

However, a few weeks after Team Europe arrived home, one of the conquering heroes, England's Paul Casey, was interviewed by *The Sunday Times* newspaper. A 2004 Ryder Cup rookie, Casey was one of a new crop of Englishmen who were starting to make a mark on the Cup; another three also made their debuts at Oakland Hills. A man not short of self-confidence, Casey felt like puffing out his chest and revealing his views on the opposition – he said in the article that he had learned to "properly hate" the Americans at the recent match. He followed that up with his opinion about the US crowds who he described as "bloody annoying" and then tried to sound worldly by stating that American people did not really know what was happening outside their own borders. Casey's comments initially caused no reaction until a follow-up story was printed in the British tabloid newspaper, the *Daily Mirror*, which ran its own version of the player's comments. Under the headline *Stupid Americans: I Hate Them*, Casey suddenly got plenty of attention even though the word 'stupid' never appeared in the original article.

The word "hate" was the spark and, though it had been a feeling referred to before within the context of the Cup (as far back as Eric Brown when he was captain in 1969), this time the internet spread the Casey story like wildfire. The Englishman immediately received what he described as "nasty emails" and tried to douse the flames by claiming the hate reference was a tongue-in-cheek way of explaining Europe's Ryder Cup motivation methods.

"(The American fans) do have a tendency to wind people up when they are chanting 'USA'... it just makes you want to beat them even more. That's the point I was trying to get across. They probably fail to realise it really sort of riles us and the rest of the world."

Considering Casey played mostly on the PGA Tour at the time of his interview, had a home in America, an American girlfriend (who later became his wife, though they are now divorced), an American coach and was a graduate of Arizona State University, his words were somewhat surprising.

US Ryder Cupper Scott Verplank said what most of his fellow countrymen were probably thinking. "If Casey's really that uncomfortable or that annoyed, I don't think anybody would miss him if he went back to England. I wouldn't think this is the smartest thing to do if you're going to stay over in the United States. How can you say derogatory things towards a group of people and not expect some guys to take it personally?"

Verplank was not the only one to express his views and Casey became so distraught that he skipped the next two US tournaments on his schedule and even sought trauma counseling. "The hurt I've caused will live with me as a huge source of regret for the rest of my life. [My words have] made people angry, which I fully understand... the word 'hate' was my error. I shouldn't have used it," he said.

However, if Casey's views had not been linked to the Ryder Cup, then they would almost certainly have been ignored by Britain's tabloid press and the furore would never have erupted. A star from another sport saying the same thing might have been described as slightly naïve or innocent. Instead, the reaction to his comments proved that the Ryder Cup is always a tinderbox for controversy.

But the headlines over Casey's comments did not stop there. Rather than lie low for a while, Casey then found himself in the middle of another spat just a few weeks later, this one about the next match in the series in Ireland in 2006. This time the Englishman criticised the appointment of Tom Lehman as captain of the American team, saying he had been a ringleader in the antics of the US in the 1999 match at Brookline.

Casey's sarcasm levels were sky high when he said Lehman's appointment "would go down well in Europe", adding that the US captain would not be on the Christmas card list of many Europeans who witnessed his Brookline antics. "His appointment could affect the atmosphere of the [2006] match. I don't think people on this side of the Atlantic want to see him as captain... I think people are afraid that [his captaincy] might bring up a Brookline-type situation at the K Club."

Casey spoke out while taking part in the 2004 World Cup and, although his teammate, the more cerebral Luke Donald did defend him ("I think people who are *not* Americans can get upset with Americans quite easily.

They do seem to be very insular," he told the media), these kinds of quarrels have a longer life because of he Ryder Cup. Casey's "hate debate" has followed him around for over a decade.

In 2013, the "hate" word to be addressed again, but this time by the eloquent Tom Watson after he had been made captain for the Gleneagles match of 2014. The media-savvy Watson showed Casey how to manage the word and turn it into a positive for his team. At the American's first press conference after taking the captain's job, the mild-mannered man from Missouri put a 21st century spin on hatred that he said was nowadays directed towards the fear of the wrong result rather than the individual opponent. "We're tired of losing [the Ryder Cup]," he said, "and I have learned to win by hating to lose. It's about time to start winning again for our team. That's the attitude I hope my players have. It's time to stop losing. Tiger [Woods] hates to lose just like I hate to lose, and we're partners in that."

Watson's speech was aimed at forming a bond between him and his players, but sometimes neither words nor deeds can stop a captain and his team running smack into conflict and controversy.

In 1979 when the first Team Europe was to face the US in West Virginia, the visiting captain John Jacobs was not only expected an exemplary performance from his players, but also the same level of behaviour. So, when Mark James turned up at Heathrow Airport in what Jacobs described as "a terrible state", dressed scruffily and not in team uniform, the team skipper was livid. The mercurial James then proceeded to miss a team meeting along with his good friend Ken Brown. Together, they seemed at odds with the rest of the squad.

Then they declared that they only really wanted to be paired with each other during the match. This was not an impossible request for Jacobs to accept, but James was plainly suffering from a chest injury during the pair's first match together on the opening morning and could not play in the afternoon foursome. When Europe's captain then put a rather sullen Brown with the likeable Irishman Des Smyth, it proved to be a disaster that even their opponents could not help but notice. "It was obvious there was no rapport between them," said Hale Irwin, who gladly won the match 7&6 in harness with Tom Kite. "There was not even the slightest bit of idle conversation. Smyth didn't play very well and Brown played like he didn't care." After Team Europe's inevitable defeat that week, Smyth was declared the innocent party and absolved of any blame, but Brown was banned for a year from international team golf and both he and James were heavily fined.

However, this was not the first time that a British player had fallen out with this team and his captain. Two decades earlier, an even more contentious incident occurred, this time during the match at Lindrick Golf Club when the home team was under the captaincy of Welshman Dai Rees. The British had suffered seven consecutive defeats by the time this contest took place, but there were several indications that this match might be more competitive. "We made [the course] very English," team member Max Faulkner recalled later. "We didn't water the greens for three days [before the matches] and we left the grass around the green an inch and a half long." The British felt happier about playing greenside shots from this kind of rough than the Americans and, during one practice session, Faulkner smiled to himself when he saw one US player stabbing unsuccessfully from the rough. "He grabbed the club too tightly," Faulkner explained of his opponent. "We saw we had an advantage." The home side also benefitted by insisting that both teams use of the smaller British standard golf ball, 1.62 inches diameter rather than the 1.68 inches which was the norm on the PGA Tour. A surprise win for the British was perhaps possible.

However, when Team GB lost the opening days foursomes 3-1, their prospects dimmed and, to make matters worse, Rees found himself in the middle of an almighty row. With just eight singles matches to play on day two, the British captain had no room for error in selecting the most in-form players from his team of 10. But rather than pick the two players he believed should be left out (after all, Rees himself had been on the course playing in the foursomes rather than watching the rest of this team), the skipper asked his teammates what they thought. Max Faulkner soon spoke up that his form had been "rubbish" and he volunteered to stand down. His foursome partner on day one, Harry Weetman, promptly said he felt the same way and the whole matter seemed settled.

But the captain's relief at seemingly settling a difficult situation was soon turned into despair when Weetman– who was considered one of the team's most consummate matchplay golfers – spoke to the press immediately afterwards and revealed his abject disappointment about not playing in the singles. Not only that, he said he would never play another Ryder Cup match under Rees. The captain had been badly undermined and subsequently had to work until past midnight to soothe the issue, explaining to the press what had actually happened.

Strangely and despite all the fuss, the next day the GB team was inspired and won 6½ of the 8 points available to take the trophy for the first time since 1933. Rees was carried shoulder high from the course by celebrating fans while Weetman faced a British PGA inquiry. Although the investigation blamed Weetman's friends and family rather than the golfer himself for the mess, the Shropshire golfer was given a year-long suspension from PGA-sponsored tournaments. "Inexcusable," said the editorial in *Golf Monthly*, yet the magazine admitted that the incident may have unintentionally helped the team to win. "The recent evidence is that our professionals tend to play better, as a team, when someone has ruffled their feathers," stated an editorial.

A few months later, at the behest of Rees, Weetman's suspension was reduced and by 1959 the two men played together in the 13th Ryder Cup in California, although they could not conjure up another surprise; the US team were comfortable victors.

The One-Man Controversy

In the history of the Ryder Cup, one player has unwittingly dragged controversy along with him whether he played or even if he did not. Tiger Woods has been such a phenomenon among golf fans and media worldwide since he emerged as a professional in 1996 that whenever there is nothing much happening in the sport, everyone turns to see what Woods is getting up to.

His relationship with the Ryder Cup has always been portrayed as a mixture of love and hate and that in itself has prompted a controversial question: why does the man, regarded by many as the greatest player of all time, have such a poor record in the competition? Before the Gleneagles match, Woods had a worse Ryder Cup record than any of the iconic European players of the last 25 years. His 43.94 winning percentage over the seven matches he played in before 2014 ranked below Lee Westwood's mark of 56.76% and Sergio Garcia's 64.29% as well as former greats from Seve Ballesteros (60.81%) to Nick Faldo (54.35%). Even Tony Jacklin, who played against some of the greatest US teams in the history of the competition, managed a winning percentage of 48.57.

Although it is also true that Woods is not alone among American Ryder Cup players of the modern era in having a poor winning record – see Phil Mickelson at 44.74%, Davis Love III 44.23%, Jim Furyk 36.67% and Steve Stricker 31.82% – the numbers make no sense for someone with such a great matchplay record, firstly as an amateur (three-time US Amateur champion) and then as a pro (Woods has won a trio of World Match Play Championships). The media, the fans, even Woods' own teammates, have constantly been drawn to this question about the Californian's poor Cup performances which are offered as a key reason why the American team has won so infrequently over the past 17 years.

To discuss Woods' Ryder Cup career is like focusing on a different golfer than the one who is still a reasonable bet to beat Jack Nicklaus's record of 18 major titles. The raw power of Woods changed the game like no other golfer in history – courses were made longer because of him, prize money grew exponentially, millions more TV fans tune in when he plays, and the impossible can seem mundane when he hits his very best form.

Yet there were no stories of derring-do by Woods in his first seven

Ryder Cup matches up to 2012. In fact, even if Woods won a full five points in each of his next three Cup appearances (from 2014 to 2018, by which time he would be an elder statesman in the team at 42-years-old), his winning percentage would only be 61.45, still short of Ballesteros and far behind Arnold Palmer (71.88), Tom Watson (70.50) and Jack Nicklaus (66.07). Perhaps most astonishingly, Ian Poulter's win percentage in his first four Ryder Cup appearances was over 80%.

One theory is that Woods feels psychologically uncomfortable in the Ryder Cup environment every two years. Like the rest of the world's top golfers, he is nowadays used to playing for the benefit of himself, his family and his bank balance, but for the week of the Cup he is thrust into a team situation where there are extra demands on his normal routines. He has to concern himself with the needs of others, the results of matches that do not even involve him and the instructions of his captain.

Woods himself will never reveal his inner most thoughts on the matter because to do so – in his mind – would give his opponents an advantage, certainly during the week of the team event, but perhaps also in regular strokeplay tournaments afterwards. After all, his 11 teammates in the Ryder Cup are his rivals during every other tournament. Woods either cannot or will not adapt or change for the few days he wears a US Ryder Cup shirt.

Some observers point to Woods' demeanour in the team setting; classically, he is the player who has the fewest inspiring words at the pre-match press conferences ("It's going to be fun" is about as close as Woods gets to showing an emotion). Woods is the first to walk back to the clubhouse on the group practice days when his teammates all wait for the final fourball to finish and he seems the most dis-engaged at the various ceremonial events. Sympathetic insiders say he plays ping pong with his teammates and is generally well-liked, especially by the younger players, but it often appears in public that Woods merely puts on a brave face at the matches when 'team' appears to be Woods' least favourite word.

Renowned golf psychologist Karl Morris believes that the regular routine of stroke-play events takes some professional players so far away from the team concept that they find it very difficult to return to it. "The Ryder Cup really is a unique environment for one week every two years and some people like Ian Poulter get fired up and it helps them focus, but others find the whole thing too intense. And if you've been starved of the feeling of a team or if it's just not for you, then it's a difficult place to be."

To fully understand Tiger's psychology at the Ryder Cup is tantamount to guesswork because his small coterie of close friends are not even certain of how he thinks sometimes. The former basketball star Charles Barkley believed he was inside 'Team Woods' at one time, but later told the media he was "baffled by Tiger being closed off and keeping [him] at a distance".

And the sex scandal that broke up Woods' marriage in 2009 was allegedly a complete surprise to the player's caddie Steve Williams who was not just the best man at the Woods wedding, but also spent thousands of hours with him on the range and on the golf course. Even his long-time coach Hank Haney was puzzled by Woods' lack of openness. In his book *The Big Miss*, Haney said: "I realise now that as hard as I tried to understand Tiger, he tried just as hard not to let me."

The conflict between being a great individual player and a poor teammate has never been spotlighted more intensely than by Tiger Woods, but how does such an attitude actually play in the Ryder Cup? Perhaps a contrast with Europe's talisman Ian Poulter is worthwhile.

The passionate Englishman has been a Team Europe leader on his every appearance in the Cup, while Woods – the man who should be the touchstone for the Americans – has appeared unable to inspire those around him, even his playing partners. The answer might be in their respective golfing backgrounds that are so totally different even though the two men were born just 11 days apart on 30 December 1975 (Woods) and 10 January 1976 (Poulter).

While the Englishman was selling Mars bars and tee pegs as an assistant pro in Hertfordshire in 1996, Woods was signing a $40 million sponsorship deal with Nike as he joined the US PGA Tour. When the American was winning his first major championship and making his debut in the Ryder Cup in 1997, Poulter was still two years away from even playing full-time on the European Tour (he tried and failed four times at the Qualifying School before achieving his Tour Card in 1999) and it would be seven more years (2004) until the Englishman actually lined up as a Ryder Cup player.

Poulter's original sporting dreams involved playing a team sport, football, for which he had some teenage ability, while golf only took over his life later on when he realised a career as a professional footballer was not possible. Woods, by contrast, was a golfing prodigy aged only two when he appeared on American television showing off his incredible golf skills. Playing golf on his own (or perhaps with his father) was Tiger's childhood.

In addition, Poulter had to scrap to reach the top echelon of the sport, slogging for five years as an assistant pro (where his jobs included cleaning members' golf shoes) and remaining grounded to the realities of normal life. For Woods, a normal life meant being cosseted and controlled by other people, including his long-time closest confidante, agent Mark Steinberg. Whereas Poulter had to wear garish clothing to get noticed and is happy to frolic around the golf course with his young family, Woods has tried to proceed through his life (especially off the course) unnoticed, moving from final green surrounded by security guards and driving in cars with tinted windows like a wraith, stopping for no one who is not a sponsor or a member of his family or his inner circle. While, Poulter is a magnet to fans, media and Ryder Cup supporters offering constant opinions and information about himself (particularly via social media), Woods is guarded and single-minded about his own game and his own life to the exclusion of almost everyone else.

Poulter's self-confidence can appear at first to be a man-made facade, but it is totally natural. He boasts that he does not need a psychologist because he already understands that he is a great golfer and why pay someone to tell him what he already knows. Woods' idea of an insight into his soul is to confess his 2009 infidelities with a lame rehearsed speech in front of an invited audience and no questions from anyone, especially not the media.

So while the extrovert Poulter is inspired by the team competition, the reticent Woods is diminished by it and, not surprisingly when they first met, their characters clashed on more than one occasion. It is reported that after a practice round a few weeks before the US Open in 2007, the 'cheeky chappie' Brit (who had only played in one Ryder Cup at this stage and was having a relatively poor season) turned to Tiger and asked him "How are we getting home?" This clearly intimated that he wouldn't have minded a lift home on Woods' private jet to Orlando where they both lived. Even though Woods never extended an invitation, Poulter turned up at the airport anyway and talked his way on board. The tale is told in Hank Haney's book which includes the words of the text that an angry Woods sent to his swing coach: "Can you believe how this dick mooched a ride on my plane?"

More recently, the two men have warmed to each other, but their team golf stories have remained polar opposites. Only in the more relaxed atmosphere of the Presidents Cup does Woods seem relaxed. When the heat is turned up at the Ryder Cup, then strange things happen to his game: the best example is his duck-hooked opening tee shot in 2006 into water when he was only using a 5-wood. If that error is to remain as Woods' Ryder Cup legacy, then Poulter's will be the five straight birdies he managed on day two in Medinah in 2012 to win his fourball match, in partnership with McIlroy, and galvanise his whole team to an unlikely victory the next day.

The last word

So, the conflict and controversy that hangs around every Ryder Cup match is managed in different ways by different players. Some do so effectively, others less so. In their diverse ways, both Woods and Poulter are controversial Ryder Cup characters: in strokeplay, one of them reigns supreme while the other has conquered the world's most competitive team tournament.

Coming up with a successful strategy to effectively operate your team with 'Tiger Woods, World No 1' in a Ryder Cup uniform has usually been the biggest question-mark hanging over recent American captains. Coming up with a way to get the best out of 'Ian Poulter, Ryder Cup phenom', has been a matter of just picking him for the team.

For some commentators, Poulter and Woods seem to sum up the state of the two sides over the last decade or more: the Americans full of uncertainty in the team situation and the Europeans motivated by it. Perhaps the key question is what kind of personality is the more effective in the Ryder Cup team room: a mischievous Englishman or a calculating American? And maybe the answer is found in that mysterious place known as the team room.

First adopted by Europe's captain Tony Jacklin in the 1980s, the team room is a place about which the players speak in hushed, reverent tones and it is where magical things seem to happen. The most passionate speeches are delivered in this private space and the most tears are often shed there too. A code of silence usually protects all team room activities and anything said inside those walls is mostly rumour and supposition.

However, very occasionally, the rule is breached like when Peter Hanson told a Swedish Golf Federation website about the motivational phone call received by the 2010 European team from Seve Ballesteros who was too ill to attend the event because he was suffering from brain cancer. "Go get them [the Americans] so hard that they will all be caddies in the future," said the heroic Spaniard, according to Hanson. Rousing words like these are exactly the kind that coaches yell at their football teams before sending them onto the pitch and, given he is a big football fan, it is likely that Poulter has had similar words of encouragement in the European Ryder Cup team room. However, no American player has ever suggested that Woods utters anything similar.

Woods could learn something from Paul Azinger, one of America's most battle-hardened players as well as a hugely successful captain who valued the team concept above everything when it came to the Ryder Cup. In fact, Azinger even made teams within his team when he was skipper in 2008. He created three 'pods' of the four players who would practice together and then play alongside each other in the pairs matches on the two opening days. He had watched a TV documentary on how the US Navy turn raw recruits into SEALs, the special operations combatants who are feared around the world. "Those guys eat, sleep, and train together until they know what the others are thinking. Every man knows what his fellow SEAL is going to do before he does it. They bond with each other in a way you can't understand if you've never been there," explained Azinger when asked about his unusual team golf strategy before the match. "PGA Tour players are hardwired to beat the guys next to them, then one week a year we think they should go against their nature and become a championship team. But maybe if you want to bring the Ryder Cup team together, maybe you have to break it apart." With their captain's permission, the players ended up picking their pod teammates and loved the whole idea. When the US team won for the first time in nine years, Azinger's plan was headline news. And his side won without an injured Tiger Woods.

Azinger also promoted bonding in the team room where many of his sharpest memories of Cup matches come from. He knew that this room was extraordinary and where his teammates could be open with one another in a profound and inspirational way. His own experience as a player was proof enough.

In an interview with ESPN.com before the 2012 match in Medinah, Azinger was asked about his favourite memories from when he was a player. One particularly poignant one came from the US victory at The Belfry in 1993. "Chip Beck…made a comment I'll never forget. He and John Cook beat Monty [Colin Montgomerie] and Nick Faldo [in Saturday afternoon fourball, 2-up]. They were supposed to get beat, [they] had no business winning. Chip's comment after they beat those guys on 18, I'll never forget it as long as I live. We were in the team room that night. And he said, 'I just want everyone in here to know that the will to win can overcome a mechanical breakdown like I had out there today.' And we just busted out laughing."

Azinger's opposing captain in 2008 had different experiences in the team room. Nick Faldo was described as aloof and remote when he was a skipper, perhaps a product of his belief that as a player he never needed anyone to tell him to get excited about the Ryder Cup. Years after he led Europe to defeat at Valhalla, Faldo tried to explain his captaincy ordeal to the Daily Mail: "So you need someone to tell you to be passionate to play well in the Ryder Cup? I have to say I didn't need a battery inside me to go and play…I'd have walked barefoot to the first tee to play if that was what was asked. If the Ryder Cup doesn't inspire you and give you passion, I don't know what would."

But as Captain Faldo, that attitude may well have been the cause of his problems – he was heavily criticised for leading a team room that was apparently "passionless", according to some sources. "I don't know what more I could have done to address that issue. On the first day I stood up in the team room and said if anyone sees me looking through them, they have my permission to kick my backside. I thought I had broken down that barrier of what I am supposed to be like." The words 'looking through them' were Faldo's attempt to explain his tendency to internalise; he may have highlighted his weakness, but it is doubtful that he fully avoided it.

The team room atmosphere is highly sensitive to the personality of both captains and players and, somehow, Faldo failed to connect with everyone in the way that his predecessors had managed. "A captain can't have a significant effect on you winning a Ryder Cup but they can have a significant effect on you losing it," offered a cryptic Lee Westwood who had never missed a session in his five previous Cup appearances but was controversially dropped by Faldo for a foursomes session in 2008.

So while Faldo struggled on the team bonding front, Azinger flourished both as a player and a captain. Azinger's story about Chip Beck back in 1993 may have been treated as comical, but more crucially it was also motivational, the words coming directly from the heart and the laughter merely breaking the tension of the moment. Beck encapsulated the reality of the Ryder Cup during what is a surreal week of intense competition and Azinger fully understood that, incorporating that feeling into his attitude as a player and then as a captain.

A speech from the heart is easy for Ian Poulter as well; for him it would be as normal as breathing. For Tiger Woods, showing that level of vulnerability in front of his teammates would be nigh on impossible. But if Tiger ever found a way to achieve such a connection with golf's greatest team event, then one of the Ryder Cup's greatest mysteries might come to an end.

6

Power & Politics

Politics in all its many colours has operated in the shadows of every Ryder Cup contest and backroom power games have regularly shaped the outcome of matches. Captains, players, selectors, administrators and even presidents and princes have all been involved in different kinds of behind-the-scenes politicking, some consciously trying to gain an advantage over the opposition and some unconsciously making a difference to the tone of the tournament. Meanwhile, real-life politics, various developments in the societies of Britain, Europe and America, have also shaped the attitudes of the golfers through the years and even influenced the spectators.

Dave Stockton was never accused of being a wily political operator within golf's corridors of power, but he won himself the 1991 captain's job at a very delicate and also crucial time for the US Ryder Cup team. The Californian took the post amidst much anxiety among the grandees of the PGA of America whose teams had not won any of the previous three matches (two losses and one tie). The string of poor results had come as rather a shock and Stockton was the next man up in terms of leading the team. He was an interesting choice because, although he had the correct golfing credentials (two PGA Championships), he was also known as the King of the Corporate Outings and perhaps not everyone's first choice for a potential crisis situation because another defeat in America was almost unimaginable for everyone connected with golf in the US. Once he had turned 40 in 1981, Stockton earned a healthy income from golf clinics, as many as 90 per year. Now, as a consequence, Stockton's critics pointed out that spending so much time with corporate America had hardly kept the new Ryder Cup captain fully in touch with the latest players coming through on tour. This was underlined when he made 49-year-old Raymond Floyd one of his captain's picks on a team that was already full of players over the age of 30. Floyd's inclusion (he had just played the role of Ryder Cup skipper himself in 1989) raised many eyebrows.

Stockton's style of captaincy would be one of consensus. His team at Kiawah Island, South Carolina, included many strong characters – Floyd, Hale Irwin and Paul Azinger to name just three – and the captain was not the kind of man to run roughshod over everyone's views. So when some players – including debutants Corey Pavin and Steve Pate – wanted to wear combat-style baseball caps (rather than normal team headgear) in honour of the American solders who had fought in the first Gulf War six months earlier, Stockton said OK. After all, the PGA of America had already set the tone by showing a video in one of the pre-match dinners called War By The Shore, so with Stockton's decision on top of that, political correctness was waved goodbye.

When the matches got under way, the intensity levels soared and ill-feeling soon emerged between both players and spectators. After all, for the US team and their supporters, there was even a slight feeling of desperation – surely, they could not let the European team take the trophy for the fourth successive time. Chants of "USA, USA, USA" were heard loudly and constantly for the first time and matched by equally raucous calls of "Europe. Europe" as the fans added to an unusual and ultimately unwelcome atmosphere.

To make matters worse, the Ocean Course on Kiawah Island was brutal. No professional golfer wants to look foolish and, with the world watching every shot, there was every chance that a few goats would be found this week. No one seemed to totally like the course set-up and jocular Northern Irishman David Feherty complained that from the very back tees, his drives were not even making some of the fairways. Players became snarly with each other as they battled the course, the conditions (the wind off the Atlantic caused all kinds of issues) and their matchplay opponents. Minor issues about the rules turned into fierce arguments; sometimes attitudes became objectionable or even downright rude. Sandy Jones, the future chief executive of the British PGA, was a mere observer at Kiawah and regretted what he saw. "It was the first time I thought that if Samuel Ryder had seen what was going on, he'd take his cup back."

By day three, even the high quality of the golf and the sizzling drama of the singles matches could not hide an atmosphere that was on the edge of ugly even though the camouflage-style headgear had been put away. In previous matches, there had been fans on both sides occasionally and quietly cheering a missed putt, but there was more jeering than cheering at Kiawah. This time there was regular taunting and on a much larger scale, both crude and unruly. Irwin who eventually brought home the winning half point for the American team, felt there was too much patriotism drifting into the Ryder Cup and this was not a good thing; golf should not be war. "The fierceness had increased and the military side of life had definitely made Americans more aware of their country, but boorish behaviour doesn't have a place in our game. Now you might say it's all in good fun, but if that behaviour is at the expense of someone else's self esteem then I'm against that. I think we should applaud great shots from all players."

After the European team lost following a missed 6ft putt by Bernhard Langer on the 18th green in his match against Irwin, Dave Stockton was thrown into the ocean in celebration as Stars and Stripes flags were waved incessantly. The visiting team cried almost to a man. The balloon of tension had burst for both sides and the so-called war by the shore was over.

Perhaps the most remarkable thing to happen in 1991 was that, despite all the angry words and the finger-pointing, the two sets of players – and also many spectators – celebrated and commiserated together. The largest after-match party in a huge tent in the resort was led by Ian Woosnam dancing on tables while many of the 3,000 travelling European fans sang until their throats were sore. Onlooking US fans wondered if the Europeans could have partied any harder if they had won the match. "The Europeans were gracious in defeat, much more gracious then we would have been," said Stockton, who returned to his corporate gigs prior to cleaning up on the seniors' tour and becoming a renowned putting guru.

For the next three contests, it was important that the respective PGAs calmed the match atmosphere down and that was achieved in 1993 (a second consecutive American win) and in 1995 and 1997 (two European victories). But again in 1999 another American captain made a decision away from the course that would damage the image of the Ryder Cup.

Ben Crenshaw has always been a proud American, but his team was losing badly at the The Country Club of Brookline in Massachusetts. They were 10-6 down after two days and he was feeling the pressure of widespread criticism about his leadership skills. Gentle Ben, as he was known, was not the kind of man to play political games off the course; he had been a player much loved and admired by his fellow pros on the PGA Tour, a man who broke down in tears on the final green after his second Masters victory because of the recent death of his coach and mentor, the revered Harvey Penick. However, the Ryder Cup can do strange things to people and Crenshaw chose an unusual person to address his team on the evening before the final day's singles. Fellow Texan and the governor of his home state, George W. Bush (the future 41st President of the USA), gave a speech to the American players that created an even worse situation than Dave Stockton's decision to allow battle fatigue caps on the course eight years earlier.

Little known outside Texas at the time, Governor Bush wanted to inspire the US team by reading a letter to them that was written by a soldier who expected to die at the Alamo in 1836. The political jingoism of Bush's words reached their peak when he read: "I have sustained a continual bombardment and cannonade for 24 hours and have not lost a man. The enemy has demanded a surrender at discretion. I have answered the demand with a cannon shot and our flag still waves proudly from the walls. I shall never surrender or retreat. Victory or death. P.S. The Lord is on our side." Were such words appropriate? On reflection years later, the answer would almost certainly be "No". One wonders what Lee Trevino (a former captain himself and a Mexican-American) would have made of the speech had he been in the room because the words conjured up memories of a Mexican army siege.

Despite the misgivings of hindsight, the speech left some players in tears and produced a battlefield mentality the next day; the US team suddenly saw themselves as troops in a golfing war zone. Adding fist-pumping, yelling actions of hyped-up players to an initially anxious and later raucous crowd (many fans had been drinking for hours) brought about a final-day atmosphere that has lived on in ignominy.

For players like the rather sensitive David Duval, who was making his Ryder Cup debut, there later came an admission that the team felt like they had to go out and kill their opponents. Mission accomplished, according to Ben Crenshaw. "The governor's speech hit 'em pretty good," he said afterwards.

The two teams had been playing in an atmosphere of subdued tension for several years, but the Brookline behaviour – US players whooping and hollering like banshees; insisting on more noise from the crowd; individual fans baiting the European team; not to mention the infamous invasion of the green in the crucial Justin Leonard-Jose Maria Olazabal match – was widely regarded as unacceptable. The relationship between the teams had become poisonous and, immediately afterwards, some commentators wondered if the matches were worth scenes that were so out of context with the traditional spirit of the game.

All those involved in the match eventually had their say. Many Americans felt any bad behaviour from the crowds was just unfortunate and any breaking of etiquette was unintentional. However, the majority of the Europeans (whose previous defeats had always been accepted so graciously) were raw with anger at the US fans and players who, they claimed, seemed to wind each other up into an unnecessary frenzy. Needless to say, there was little joint-partying by the teams this time.

Nevertheless, tempers cooled, especially when Payne Stewart – a Ryder Cup captain of the future, for sure, and perhaps the only American player at Brookline who maintained his dignity when he conceded his singles match to Colin Montgomerie – was killed in a plane accident four weeks later. The two captains for the next match, Sam Torrance for Europe and Curtis Strange for the US, were determined that their teams would not repeat the ugly scenes from 1999. But then an act of political terrorism put golf's troubles into a different perspective.

Across a clear, blue New York skyline on 11 September 2001, just 17 days before the players were due to face each other in the 34th match at The Belfry, two planes flew into the twin towers of the World Trade Centre and changed the course of history as well as the standing of the greatest single international team competition of the age.

There was no appetite for the Ryder Cup immediately after 9/11 let alone any desire by people to travel by air; American airspace was not reopened for more than a week due to fears of more bombs on planes. It was soon agreed to postpone the match until 2002 and, when it was eventually played, there were no backroom power plays by either captain; the crowds were still noisy, but definitely respectful; the players pumped their fists, but made sure to shake hands afterwards.

Captains Torrance and Strange had been at pains to have the match played in the best of spirits. As Strange said: "People understood that Sam and I were trying to get out this message of 'Let's be civil and respectful'... [that Ryder Cup] was the best week of my life... it really does become more than just winning or losing." Although there were a few awkward moments (for example, Sergio Garcia's final afternoon sprint down the 18th fairway – once the match had been won – followed by a mock collapse in exhaustion annoyed the US players), the teams toasted a successful week for golf and the disappointments of Brookline became things of the past.

Team politics

One of the recurring themes of successful Ryder Cup teams is the strong relationship between teammates and their captain. A good captain is supposed to know how each of his players needs to be treated (a comforting word for some, a sharp instruction for another) and also which players will perform best together in the various pairings. Perhaps even more important is the knowledge of which players he should *not* pair together. Leading a happy team is one of the skipper's most fundamental jobs.

However, for decades, many captains spent a minimal amount of time fussing over their players. The skipper would chat informally with the team when they all gathered about who was on form and maybe ask for suggested pairings, but pep talks on the morning of the matches were not formal affairs, they were simply done in the corner of the locker-room. Starting with the Tony Jacklin and Jack Nicklaus in 1983, it was much clearer that choosing the foursome and fourball pairings as well as the order of players for the final-day singles was a skill that each captain had to get right. Egos had to be massaged and tempers soothed when certain choices were made. The job of the captain and the politics of the teams were now hot topics.

Then, at The Belfry in 1985, the concept of team rooms emerged along with the idea of official vice-captains. As the spotlight on the Ryder Cup became more intense, so the job of the captain grew to be much more pressured and there was constant media speculation during the match about every decision, especially about which players were omitted on days one and two and the singles line-up on day three.

On every first day at the Ryder Cup, the choice of his pairings is particularly crucial. It was not Jacklin's exclusive idea that friends playing together worked best, but it certainly became a more obvious tactic in the era of Team Europe because of the number of different nationalities. A Scot with a Scot had been one ploy some of Jacklin's predecessors had recognised, but partnering two Spaniards together (able to speak their own language and fully comprehend the nature of their particular brand of golf) seemed to be a stroke of genius and delivered even better results. The Seve Ballesteros-Jose Maria Olazabal combination in the pairs matches would be held up as the ultimate example of good captaincy. Find pairings like this – two friends with the same cultural sensibilities and complementary golfing brains – and victory was yours.

However, when the very top players are involved, individual temperaments need to be handled sensitively if the team is to benefit and not every captain has managed this feat. In 2004, it had long been an open secret that Phil Mickelson and Tiger Woods did not send each other Christmas cards, yet US skipper that year Hal Sutton chose to make them his lead fourball pairing on the opening morning of the match. In fact, it was virtually his first decision and a "big dog" pairing matched the character of the captain, a bold Texan who stood on the first tee alongside his players wearing a gigantic, black cowboy hat. When the experienced European pairing of two Celts, Colin Montgomerie and Padraig Harrington, went two up after the first two holes against the Mickelson-Woods combination, the writing was on the wall for the Americans. By the time the US pair lost that morning fourball match, Sutton had already paired them again in the afternoon foursomes. For a second time in just a few short hours, the world's top two ranked players failed to gel, Mickelson slicing his drive on the final hole so badly that Woods was forced to take a drop. These two golfing greats had lost two points and, not surprisingly, the whole US team suffered from a crisis of confidence. Halfway through the singles matches, it was confirmed Sutton's team had been defeated at home for only the third time.

"History demands it" was how Sutton had explained his Woods-Mickelson decision, but he should have thought a little harder about what might happen if the world's No.1 and No.2 golfers stood on the same tee together in a Ryder Cup. Back in 1999 Woods was asked to form a partnership with his then-nearest threat in the world rankings, David Duval and their one outing together that year in a day two fourball match resulted in defeat.

This kind of unfortunate clash of characters between great American players had also happened decades earlier. Sam Snead and Ben Hogan were the fiercest of rivals for over two decades, but were never paired together in a Ryder Cup match. In fact, they were deliberately kept apart. Their era was one of the playing captain – Hogan was Snead's skipper in 1947 and 1949, with Snead having the Texan in his team in 1951 – but what Hal Sutton did not understand about Woods and Mickelson, these two latter-day greats knew about each other. A description of their relationship during their playing days was somewhere between lukewarm and icy cold most of the time.

Snead was raised in hillbilly country in the mountains of Virginia, the youngest of six. He had clawed his way out of poverty barefoot and his experiences left him with a sharp temper. Hogan was a tough Texan with a taciturn nature and a work ethic that was mythical. Although they knew each other well, Snead resented Hogan's perceived position as everyone's favourite golfer of the era and, even though Slammin' Sammy won more tournaments, it was Hogan who won more majors. The 1950 season was the last straw for Snead. He won the money list, the Vardon Trophy for the lowest scoring average on the PGA Tour and eight official titles while Hogan collected only the US Open title and was promptly named golfer of the year. It could easily be argued that Hogan's acclaim at this moment was based on romantic reasons more than golfing ones because he had fought back so bravely from a near-fatal car crash the year before. In any case, Snead was desperately disappointed. "Hell, I damn near wanted to throw up and hang it up," commented Snead years later about that season. Somehow they were successful Ryder Cup colleagues for the third and final time the following year and kept their dislike for each other at bay.

However, perhaps Hogan was more successful than Snead as a teammate. His 1947 captaincy was marked by a rather lurid affair. In the James Dodson biography *Ben Hogan: An American Life*, the author writes about how, on the eve of the match, Hogan gave teammate Herman Keiser $1,000 to pay off a young woman who was said to be ready to go to the newspapers over a little liaison they shared. It is debatable whether the fiery Snead would have acted in such a demure way because the matter never made the newspapers at the time. But despite Hogan managing to hush up the story and keep his team on track to victory, Keiser got his comeuppance – the US team won by a record margin that year, 11-1, but the philanderer was the one American player to lose.

Lack of love between teammates is not solely the domain of the

Americans. Nick Faldo was often famously unresponsive to some of his partners and fell out with the great (Ian Woosnam) and the good (David Gilford) during various matches. Debutant in 1991, Gilford was particularly unfortunate to partner Faldo, a man who his second wife Gill labeled as "socially, a 24-handicapper". Perhaps the quietest, most unassuming man ever to play in these contests, Gilford's balding pate and his unfashionable golfing heritage – he was born in the northern industrial town of Crewe in Cheshire – seemed incongruous against Faldo's tall, dashing good looks and softer southern accent. Gilford was hardly offered a single word of advice or encouragement by his illustrious partner in their foursome match at Kiawah Island and the experimental pairing lost 7&6.

Perhaps the tone had been set a few weeks earlier when Gilford and Faldo exchanged scorecards at the end of a round at a European Tour tournament. At the time, Gilford noticed that Faldo had made "10 or 12 mistakes on my card and that's no exaggeration". The Cheshire man told *The Guardian* later: "I don't know what (Faldo) was trying to say or do, but I've never had that before with anybody. I am a big fan of what he has achieved, but he's not a wonderful man."

Contrast Gilford's 'Faldo experience' in 1991 with his partnership with Seve Ballesteros four years later. The Spaniard was jabbering in Gilford's ear throughout their opening afternoon fourball match and they triumphed 4&3, the only European winners in that session. The Englishman then won two more points over the next two days and was one of the successes of the tournament.

Meanwhile, the more often Faldo played in the Ryder Cup (he represented first GB&I and then Europe 11 times) the less he was forgiven for his surliness. A Ryder Cup team room proved not to be his milieu. Bernard Gallacher – three times his Ryder Cup captain for Europe – made Faldo his captain's pick on two occasions, but the skipper admitted there was one reason only for the Englishman's selection. "Faldo brings you points," he would tell the media. "Is that it?" asked the press, expecting some extra clarification. "Yes," stated Gallacher, clearly unimpressed by the player's team bonding qualities.

Of course, Faldo can answer accusations about any lack of team mindfulness with the fact that he virtually won the Cup for Gallacher in 1995 at Oak Hill. The Englishman's crucial singles victory over Curtis Strange was one of grittiest examples of matchplay golf ever seen and his tearful reaction on the green that afternoon showed genuine emotion.

When Faldo eventually took the captain's role in 2008, there were plenty of ex-players either cool or indifferent about his appointment, while the media was savage in its predictions of his downfall. The six-time major champion was his usual spiky self in his press interviews and then made a rather inappropriate speech at the opening ceremony that focused as much on the achievements of his children as on his team. When Faldo's men lost, it brought pleasure to his critics who claimed they were right about the captain's lack of understanding about team politics.

In more modern times with players surrounded by their entourages – from wives to swing coaches – the problems of managing the team are not always about the golfers themselves. Prior to arriving in Spain for the 1997 match, Earl Woods – father of Tiger who was making his debut in the event – announced his unhappiness at not being part of the official party allowed to travel on a specially-chartered Concorde flight from JFK Airport in New York. Woods Sr. declared that he had done more for his son's career and, therefore, the team than "all the wives and girlfriends combined". But the PGA of America saw things differently and, when the WAGs took their seats on the jet next to their beloved players, Woods Jr. sat alone while Woods Sr. was at home. US team captain for Valderrama, Tom Kite had none other than President Bill Clinton providing words of inspiration for his golfers before departure. But Earl Woods probably undermined the whole process of team-building as his son managed 1½ points out of a possible five in an American defeat.

For any captain, perhaps the most pressurised situation is to deliver victory in front of the home fans and there is no better example than the 1997 match at Valderrama that belonged to Ballesteros. He was the main reason the event went to Spain in the first place and was, inevitably, made captain, so to lose in front of his countrymen was not an option. However, even before a ball was struck, Ballesteros arguably overstepped the mark with an imperious attitude as to who should make up his dream team. In doing so, he squashed the dreams of a fellow Spaniard.

During the qualifying period, Miguel Angel Martin had been a surprise success. The compact player, a handsome man and native of Heulva in southwest Spain, was enjoying a banner season and had already secured enough points to guarantee his place on the team for the first time when he unluckily injured his wrist in July. Martin faced a dilemma – play on with the injury and risk it getting worse by the time of the Ryder Cup or undergo summertime surgery and hope to recover in time for the contest. Martin chose the knife and insisted he would be back to full fitness by late September. Ballesteros, however, was not convinced and, anyway, he really wanted his long-time pal and experienced Ryder Cupper Jose Maria Olazabal to play. The problem was that Olazabal was returning from injury himself and would not qualify automatically for the team. Neither could Ballesteros justify using him as a captain's pick over Faldo and the in-form Jesper Parnevik, both of whom were based in America and unable to earn Ryder Cup points in Europe. The captain himself had a dilemma, but he also had a solution, albeit a far from unanimous one among his peers.

After a series of meetings, Ballesteros insisted that Martin's wrist should be tested just one month after surgery. When the player refused, the selection committee had a problem because two years earlier in a similar situation, Olazabal himself had been given extra time to prove his fitness. There was a good deal of sympathy for Martin among the European Tour rank and file, but Ballesteros's opinions prevailed and Martin was replaced on the team by Olazabal. Murmurings of heavy-handedness were heard, but no one rocked the boat because the team was being skippered by the genius that was Seve Ballesteros. Only when Martin withdrew from a regular tournament in mid-September because of his original injury did the Olazabal decision seem to have been the correct one. Ballesteros's friend then brought home 2½ points for his team to help secure victory in the first match on continental Europe. Ballesteros achieved his dream as hero of the Ryder Cup and the Spanish golfing public. Miguel Angel Martin never qualified for the Cup again.

Choosing the captain

The choice of a Ryder Cup captain has always been undertaken in a committee room and quite often after much debate. The media may lead the cheering for a particular candidate, but many times, the most obvious candidates have been chosen.

From the American perspective, Walter Hagen's six captaincies from 1927 to 1937 were a mark of the man's role in helping get the Ryder Cup started, while after World War II, the country's greatest players like Ben Hogan, Sam Snead and Byron Nelson took their turns as the captaincy evolved into a non-playing role more suited to an elder statesman. Arnold Palmer's selection in 1963 at the age of 34 made him the last to perform the dual role of player and captain on either side.

By the time the US began facing the full golfing might of Europe in 1979, the American captain's criteria seemed set: a major champion – ideally a PGA Championship winner – who had come to the end of his playing career on the main tour and (unless you were Jack Nicklaus who was skipper on two occasions) would be given one chance only. Even as Europe began to win more often, this American strategy for captains continued. Some men with impeccable qualifications, like Hale Irwin and Craig Stadler, missed out yet although conspiracy theorists might postulate that these champions were not adept enough at the political game with "the blazers" of their own association, the real reason might be that there were simply too many candidates and not room for everyone. However, the 2012 defeat at Medinah helped end this 30-year-old system of captaincy selection.

The appointment of Tom Watson for the Gleneagles match in 2014 was not only a surprise, but it bore no relation to another supposedly key criteria for a captain – to be young enough to have some playing connection with the current team members. Watson would be 65 at the time of the match and, although he still turned out in the occasional major, he had been playing on the Champions Tour (not the regular PGA Tour) for 15 years.

Win or lose, the Watson appointment opened up the debate about the American Ryder Cup captaincy in a way that had not happened for decades. Some players, like two-time Ryder Cupper Brad Faxon, had even more radical thoughts about the captaincy. "We are running out of captains in the way that they were previously selected – 47-50-years-old, a major champion who [had] played Ryder Cup," said the eloquent Faxon. "I spoke to the PGA of America about how there are a lot of players who don't fit that bill, but who would make great captains. Someone at the association then asked me what I thought about captain selection and, instead of answering, I asked *them* a question: 'Do you really want to win?' and they found that quite shocking. But take this out of the golf context and there is no business in the world that would appoint a new guy at the head of it every two years. I said 'You're not doing it this way because you want to win' so it will be very interesting to see what happens next time." Faxon's idea of a long-term captain has not been the American way since Ben Hogan held the post two years consecutively in 1947 and 1949. In fact, Bernard Gallacher's three captaincies between 1991 and 1995 for Europe were the last sequence of that kind and it seems unlikely ever to be repeated.

From a British and European perspective, appointing a Ryder Cup captain has seemed as mysterious as the system that identifies a new pope. In the beginning, a committee of the most illustrious names in golf – the likes of Harry Vardon, J.H .Taylor and James Braid – sat down to decide who should receive the honour. Then in the post-war period, it was accepted practice that potential captains should "make it known" to the PGA Ryder Cup committee members that they would be prepared to do the job. Still, even with this system in place, outstanding candidates like Peter Alliss, Max Faulkner (one of Britain's few Open champions) and Christy O'Connor Sr. were never made captain. Was it jealousy, favoritism or a personality clash? Impossible to know, but certainly some players were better able to "manage up" to the committee than others. A few long-term Cup players, like Neil Coles, just objected to all the politicking and did not want the post. However, sometimes the selection committee got the decision right by default.

"You could have knocked me over with a feather," says Tony Jacklin about his selection as skipper for the 1983 match. The two-time major champion had fallen out with the PGA and the European Tour about several things including not being chosen to play in the 1981 contest. "I was teed off with officialdom. They offered me a blazer and a badge to come to Walton Heath in 1981 as an official and I told them to sod off. They were a shower. I still don't know what made them come to me and I don't think I'll ever know."

The former Open and US Open champion had fallen out of love with the Ryder Cup to the extent that in a 1979 authorised biography he admitted: "Quite frankly, I don't like team golf because nine times out of 10, we're going home (from the Ryder Cup) with our tails between our legs... I don't think golf is a team game. There's too much selfishness – you have to be your own man and do your own thing." It has to be remembered that by this time, six of Jacklin's seven Ryder Cup appearances had ended in significant losses with only the famous tie of 1969 to offer any solace. Britain's only great player of that era recognised that the Cup was on its deathbed during his playing days. "I think it was a great concession on the part of the Americans to keep the Cup going under the new format (with Europeans). I thought there was a danger of it being scrapped altogether."

What the selectors and Jacklin got right with his appointment was that the captain really should lead the team in all manner of ways. Firstly, Jacklin wanted to cut through the sport's red tape and ensure that his players were treated like superstars not also-rans. "I kept asking for things and they kept saying yes," said the Englishman and that simple change in the attitude to Team Europe bore immediate fruit. Jacklin's men lost only by a single point at the PGA National course in Florida in 1983 – the best result ever on foreign soil by a GB or European team. "We are not afraid of them anymore," said Jacklin at the time, whose drive for perfection led to victory at The Belfry two years later, the first GB or European win in almost three decades.

Jacklin captained four straight European teams and one of his closest lieutenants, Bernard Gallacher, took over for the next three matches. Since then the job has been a one-and-out appointment partly because there has been a queue of candidates, but also due to the fact that the workload of the captain has increased and there is the lure of the lucrative Seniors Tour in America. How times have changed.

Finding the format

If finding the right captain has sometimes been a struggle over the years, then it is nothing compared to the many attempts to find the most effective format for the Ryder Cup matches. Even in this domain the teams have sometimes played politics, wanting a particular change to give their team an advantage. Nowadays, the format of the Ryder Cup seems perfect – 12-man teams playing foursomes, fourballs and singles matches over three days with 28 points to play for. Since it was adopted in 1979, most of the matches have been very closely contested with the final day singles providing some of the most thrilling climaxes in international sport. But it has not always been that way and there was often a fierce fight to "win the rules".

From the 1st Ryder Cup to the 13th (1927-1959), the format of the contests remained the same. It was a two-day event with all matches played to a maximum of 36 holes. Day one consisted of 4 foursomes (alternate shot) with 8 singles matches on the second day. Each match was worth a single point and a total of 12 points were available, so 6½ points were required to win the Cup. This format mimicked the Walker Cup that had started in 1922 and, for a while, it seemed to work. Foursomes was the most traditional pairs format, while matchplay singles was how all professionals cut their teeth in the game.

There were no changes over the next three decades, but there then followed several years of fiddling with the format to help make the contests more competitive. The US had been so dominant (10 wins out of 13 matches) that the match format was one of many things that took the blame. So in 1961 at Lytham came the first major alteration – 18-hole matches replacing 36 holes so that separate morning and afternoon series could be played. The faster format, it was thought, might give the weaker British players a better chance and it would also mean more golf for the spectators. The Lancashire coast golf fans saw four foursomes in both the morning and afternoon on day one and then eight singles either side of lunch on day two. The teams were now playing for a total of 24 points. However, the result was another solid American win.

The two PGAs then tweaked the format again for Atlanta in 1963 – fourballs were introduced and this meant that two-day matches were a thing of the past: the contest would now last for three days. A total of eight foursomes took place on day one (four in the morning and four in the afternoon), eight fourballs on day two (again, split either side of lunch) and then eight singles in the day three morning and another eight in the afternoon. There were now 32 points on offer and, once again, the reasoning was that fans and also sponsors would be happier. Yet no one acknowledged the needs or views of the players – a common theme in years to come.

The high temperature and humidity in Atlanta – especially in the afternoons – were totally alien to the visitors and, out of a possible 16 points from all the afternoon matches, the GB team managed just two halves. The exhausted British team lost 23-9, but the format was still tried again in 1965 in the more temperate climate of Royal Birkdale. However, the US team recorded a resounding win, this time 19½-12½.

The three-day, 32-point arrangement remained the same through another five matches, up to and including the 21st Ryder Cup in 1975, with one slight amendment. That happened in 1971 when – much to the delight of all the players – foursomes and fourballs alternated on each of the first two days. Having the two shorter foursomes together on one day and the two longer fourballs on the next had never made much sense. However, despite a 16-16 tie in 1969, the 32-point system only brought more record US victories, by as many as 14 points on two occasions (1963 and 1967).

Before the 22nd match in 1977, debate about the very future of the Cup was taking place because of these consistently heavy losses by the GB&I team. So another format change was made: fewer matches and just 20 points to play for. The teams agreed to five foursomes on day one, five fourballs on day two and 10 singles on day three. New idea, same result. The US won 12½-7½ at Royal Lytham with the visitors' victory confirmed while five singles matches were still out on the course.

Then came the news that the GB and Ireland players would be joined by continental European stars in 1979, for the 23rd match. This change finally brought with it the format that is so successful to this day – eight foursomes, eight fourballs and 12 singles. Whether days one and two begin with foursomes or fourballs is the choice of the home captain and the only time the format variation came in that very first match for Europe in 1979 when the singles were split into six morning matches and six afternoon games. So, since 1981 both sides have been in total agreement about the format, a situation that had only taken 24 matches and over half a century to achieve.

The politics of selection

In the early years of the Ryder Cup, the most controversial topic for political infighting among the game's administrators and the match selectors centred on who should actually play for each of the teams. It was all about a player's place of birth and also their residence. Being a "home-bred" American player was an issue that troubled the sport in the US for several decades.

The problem was that the genesis of golf in America had a very British flavour to it. The first records of golf equipment coming to the former British colony showed the recipient to be expatriate Scots who had settled in South Carolina in 1743. Adventuresome young pros from Britain then set sail for America over the next century to make their lives in a new country where their skills would be better rewarded. And then, as the 19th century waned, so professional golf in the US became more formalised. The best players were mostly ex-pat Scots and Englishmen. Some of them had become naturalised Americans, but others had chosen to remain loyal to the old country.

The question of whether you were an ex-pat or home-bred golfer only became an issue as the prominence of the sport increased. When 20-year-old Massachusetts-born Francis Ouimet won the 1913 US Open, he was lauded as an all-American boy and the whole country was enraptured with his story. Prior to Ouimet's win, the title of the best player in America was the domain of ex-pat players and even the young amateur's win proved an exception to the rule for almost another decade.

Over a decade later, the Ryder Cup actually provided the PGA of

America with a perfect platform to make a statement about the future of professional golf in the country. The association wanted American-born players for the matches and not ex-pats. So the deed of trust that was agreed between the two teams for the inaugural 1927 encounter stated that players could only be selected if they were resident in the country of their birth. This meant that even naturalised ex-pats were not eligible, something that caused a stir among this group which had done so much to raise the standard of American golf. Caught in the politics were players like Tommy Armour (born in Edinburgh, but a US citizen since 1920 and a great friend of Walter Hagen's) who would never play in a Ryder Cup.

The home-bred decision was just one of the political games that have been played over the decades in the name of fair selection of the two Ryder Cup teams. Another controversy in more recent times has come from the PGA of America's own rather peculiar rules. The most obvious example was the need for Ryder Cup players to have been a PGA member for five years. Initially, this seemed like a sound idea and promoted the men who were experienced enough to undertake the contest and had also served their organisation well over a number of years. The rule, however, did not account for superstars who burst suddenly into the golfing firmament, like Arnold Palmer and Jack Nicklaus. Bizarrely, both men were major champions before they were actually qualified to play in a Ryder Cup and Palmer, in particular, was deeply hurt. The PGA of America's intransigence over this matter probably led to Palmer and Nicklaus supporting the move to separate the tournament professionals (via the PGA Tour) from the association in 1968.

Other selection rules have hit other great players. Snead played in seven matches, but it would have been eight except for the fact that after telling the PGA of America he was taking a short holiday in England just before the match in 1961, he then, at the last minute, agreed to play in a pro-am championship in Cincinnati. Snead considered the small-time tournament nothing more than "a glorified exhibition" and never even considered asking his association brethren or their sponsors for approval.

However, it turned out that Snead had broken a serious rule by playing in an unsanctioned pro-am while a PGA tournament in Portland was taking place at the same time. Without permission Snead had to accept a $500 fine and six-month suspension, while Doug Ford (twice a major winner) was the next man on the points list to take Snead's place. The cynics would comment that, luckily for the PGA of America, the two men happened to be the same size, so no new blazer and trousers had to be ordered.

In Britain, the Great Triumvirate of Vardon, Taylor and Braid made up a three-man committee to choose the first team in 1927, but after that the personnel of the selection committee often changed with new criteria being put in place each time: in 1931, there were three trial matches to help the committee make its decision; then the British Matchplay champion was given an automatic place in 1947; starting in 1955, the GB team (which had also begun selecting players from the south of Ireland as well as the north) was chosen via the PGA's order of merit points system; while in 1959 this was complicated by three of the 10 players chosen by a ballot among other team members and a PGA sub-committee. Nonetheless, even the most complicated process failed to find a winning team.

During the 1960s, a few more selection ideas were tried (for example, players had to compete in seven of nine eligible tournaments for the 1961 team) and then in 1969 the teams on each side were increased to 12 players with the captain being non-playing. More changes, of course, were inevitable as the GB&I team and then the Europeans (from 1979) searched for a magic winning formula. This included certain players being "invited to play" by a committee chaired by the captain, an idea now known as the captain's picks which was formalised in 1985 by Tony Jacklin. However, even this innovation looked flawed because Jacklin's first three picks (Nick Faldo, Jose Rivero and Ken Brown) all lost on the crucial last day in the singles that year. The US team adopted the same captain's pick principle for the 1989 match and Floyd's team managed a 14-14 draw with his two picks, Tom Watson and Lanny Wadkins, both winning crucial final-day points. That was enough to cement the tactic of captain's choices forever and nowadays only the number of picks changes rather than the principle. The most recent significant team selection change, though, has unearthed another sub-plot: the contrasting fortunes and future of the two tours in America and Europe.

In 2010, half the European team was chosen via the world rankings and half from the tour money list. It was a new idea to adopt the world rankings, but it was also an obvious one – Europe wanted the best team and the best players will be the highest ranked in the world. However, such a move only came about because the PGA Tour in America had become the base for the cream of European talent. The likes of Luke Donald, Justin Rose, Graeme McDowell and Ian Poulter were already based in America in 2010 and other European Ryder Cup players were set to follow.

This, though, raised a question about whether this system would damage the famous camaraderie of the European team. Players from diverse European nations had somehow gelled during Ryder Cup week, it was said, because the European Tour helped bond them week after week. They travelled in the same planes, stayed in the same hotels, ate in the same restaurants, and generally mixed in a way that the American players – with their private jets and hotel room service – failed to do on their own Tour. Now the Europeans based in America had essentially become tour colleagues of the US team – they played the majority of their golf at the same tournaments, therefore they would share more of the same golfing highs and lows. So, whereas the Ryder

Cup often seemed like the PGA Tour vs the European Tour, that division had become much less clear. Seve Ballesteros – one of the guardians of the European Tour – spoke out about it in his official biography *Seve* in 2004. "If (the young players of the next generation) play in the United States... the European Tour will be weakened."

The European players of today find themselves speaking differently about their tour allegiances. Lee Westwood moved his family to Florida in 2013 and has even won a place on the PGA Tour's player advisory council, but has resolved to see the Ryder Cup simply as a battle between two continents. "I'll always consider myself European and the Ryder Cup is about Europeans playing Americans," he said. However, Paul Lawrie (a Scotsman intent on playing mostly in Europe) believes the Cup is still a contest between the two tours. "Personally, I feel like I represent the European Tour. The Cup is important to our tour, it makes a lot of money for us and we rely on it to a certain extent."

Critics of the world rankings argue that it might cause a potential schism in Team Europe between the American-based and European-based players. So many captains and players of the past have spoken of the European's team spirit as being the deciding factor in the matches, but how can that Euro advantage be maintained. The Jacklin, Gallacher and Langer eras were all marked by long and rowdy celebrations by all the European team even on the plane journeys home – if those moments were not a unique chance for player bonding to help win future matches, then nothing was.

The nightmare of non-selection

While playing on a Ryder Cup team is a special moment in the career of any player, spare a thought for those who miss out by the slimmest of margins or because of a controversial selection made either by the captain or a committee. These non-picks can be based on many non-scientific reasons: the personal relationship between selector and golfer; past performance on the host course; how the player's personality fits with the rest of the team; or just a hunch that another guy might play better. The only certainty is that every two years, at least one very good player misses out on making the team and feels aggrieved. And with good reason. Tommy Horton's story is as illuminating as any.

It began in 1967 when the 26-year-old, newly-married Horton was coming into his prime. He had begun winning tournaments and over the next few years his place in the top 10 British or Irish players in the money list was commonplace. Yet the man who spent his golfing childhood in Jersey (just a few hundred yards from where Harry Vardon also fell in love with the game) was not selected for any of the Ryder Cups between 1967 and 1973. During those six years, Horton was golden, so something was obviously amiss. True, the Jerseyman suffered a couple of injuries in that time and no one is always on his very top form, but Horton felt that not making any of those four teams was too much of a coincidence. The press asked the question and the normal blandishments were offered as reasons by the selectors, but it was Horton who found out the real answer.

"Eric Brown was the captain twice during that time and he just didn't like me," Horton says now. The story goes that the two men clashed at a meeting at which Eric (who enjoyed a drink) was rather the worse for wear. "I said (to those at the meeting) that my old boss always told me not to listen to a member who slurred his speech with a glass of whisky in his hand (i.e. Eric Brown). When Eric was captain of the Ryder Cup team, I had no chance. We were different personalities."

The hard-driving Brown was not the only one to disappoint Horton during his six years of Ryder Cup isolation. After not being selected yet again in 1971, Horton spoke separately to the three selectors for the GB&I team: Brown (the captain that year), Dai Rees (skipper in 1967) and Christy O'Connor Sr. (who played in all four matches that Horton missed).

"I played in an exhibition one day and Dai came up to me and said he was a great believer in my golf, but one vote against two doesn't count to get me selected for the team. A little later, I'm with Christy and he says the same thing to me. I thought 'One of them has got to be lying'. Then Eric Brown saw me in a lift at a tournament soon afterwards and said how he felt sympathy for me (not being selected) and said he was sorry because he liked the way I played. So I said to him 'Now I know you're all bloody liars because you've all apologised to me'. Knowing they lied to me hurt more than not getting in the team." Years later after a long and successful career, including Ryder Cup appearances in 1975 and 1977, Horton is reflective rather than enraged. "It's bound to happen, it's human nature. I was very passionate about wanting to play, that's all."

In 2010, Edoardo Molinari happened to win the Scottish Open, the final qualifying tournament, in front of Ryder Cup skipper Colin Montgomerie who then preferred the ebullient Italian to English stars Paul Casey and Justin Rose who were currently both in the world top 10. Certainly, Molinari was hot at the time, but the selection was definitely contentious. However, the Italian contributed a key half point to Monty's winning team so any vestige of controversy has been conveniently erased.

These days very few players openly criticise each other, especially while they are still actively on tour. Feuds are less attractive when you might meet your nemesis on the 1st tee at a tournament. However, that did not stop Peter Hanson from revealing his displeasure at playing only one match in the first two days of the 2012 contest at Medinah. Hanson had been in great form just before the event, yet was beaten 5&4 in his fourball with partner Paul Lawrie on the opening afternoon. The Swede expected another outing the following afternoon – even playing a few practice holes in preparation and marking the pin positions on each green in his notes – but he was told by skipper Jose Maria Olazabal 20 minutes before the tee-off time that his services were not required. "I played really well during the practice rounds, but when I didn't get to play more than 14 holes in the first two days, that really got to me and I was very disappointed. [Being told so late on was] probably why I got so upset. I was already in game mode." Hanson fled to the locker room and stayed there for a couple of hours while his teammates battled on. "I didn't take it very well, but I took it for myself. I didn't let it go out over anyone else. I didn't damage the team, and that was the main thing."

It took several weeks before Hanson was able to discuss the incident with Olazabal and shake hands. "There are no hard feelings whatsoever," the Swede said a month after Medinah. "You know, you just go up and say sorry for what happened." Yet, whether it is being left out of one fourball contest or the team itself, the pain will diminish over time, but it is still real.

"I regret not playing more [Ryder Cups] because I thought I warranted it," says Tommy Horton today. "If you were a Ryder Cup player back then, you had made it. I had won championships, but some Ryder Cup players had never won a single tournament, so being in the team was a big deal for them. [Not being selected] doesn't hurt anymore, but I believe in facts and am never frightened to tell the truth. I deserved to have been in before 1975. I should have played four or even five times, not just two. It hurt me back then that I wasn't selected, but once I got in the team, I thought 'It's over, I've done it'. There was no more hurt after that."

Being left out of the team can cause all kinds of hullabaloo. In 1947, when Vic Ghezzi – a major champion himself – did not make the Ryder Cup squad, he wrote a letter accusing the great Ben Hogan (captain of the team that year) of deliberately adjusting a newly implemented points system in such a way that he was left out of the team. The PGA of America never acted on the letter, but it left a sour taste in many people's mouths.

Actually, Hogan was not averse to throwing his captain's weight around to make sure his players knew who was the boss. Most famously in 1967 at the age of 55, Bantam Ben was skippering the US team for the third and final time when he had an interesting little spat with Arnold Palmer. The 38-year-old Palmer had won eight majors by this time (one fewer than Hogan) and had even captained the team himself four years earlier, so he understood the captain's need to deal sensitively with all the various egos. But that did not stop a pair of great champions from clashing.

Palmer had always claimed that Hogan never called him by his first name, preferring to say "Hi, fella" as a greeting, so it was no surprise a contretemps occurred during a pre-match conversation. It had been decided that both teams would play the smaller, British standard golf ball during the match and Palmer is reputed to have said to Hogan: "Supposing I haven't got any small golf balls." To which the US Ryder Cup captain delivered a caustic put-down: "Who said you're playing, Palmer?" An ice-cold relationship between two of America's best ever players had long been in place and even the Ryder Cup could not melt it.

Disagreements over non-selection can occur even when a player or captain has retired from the Ryder Cup; there are still power games to be played. One of the most striking within European team history centres on Tony Jacklin's outrage at Bernhard Langer not making Mark James's 1999 team for Brookline. Jacklin even said James was lucky to get the job as captain and poured scorn on his team of seven rookies.

"Lambs to the slaughter" is how Jacklin predicted Europe's fate. "As captain, I wanted the strongest possible team. I would have put Langer in." At this point, the German had played in nine Cup campaigns and had only just missed out on an automatic slot for Brookline. Jacklin's temper got the better of him because Langer's place was taken by debutant Andrew Coltart. Although a fine player, the Scot was said to be a "hunch pick" by James who then proceeded to play Coltart only in the last day singles when he was easily beaten by Tiger Woods.

The phlegmatic James ignored Jacklin's protestations, but then did his captaincy reputation no favours by later revealing in his book *Into The Bearpit*, published after Brookline, that he gleefully tore up a good luck card from Nick Faldo and threw it into a waste bin. James would later reason that the card incident followed Faldo's disingenuousness because the multiple major winner had also been critical of the Yorkshireman's captaincy. Selecting and non-selecting players has always caused unwanted headlines, but this sequence of events was hardly a highpoint in relations between senior European players.

However, maybe the saddest story of a player's non-selection came in 1981 when Calvin Peete, one of the first black golfers ever to make a mark on the PGA Tour, was barred from the team because of a PGA of America regulation that stated all full members must have a high school diploma. This requirement had passed unnoticed until Peete's stellar play in the build-up put him into a qualifying position. But without the certificate, the team left for Britain without him. The good news is that Peete – helped by his wife – studied hard over the next two years, passed the necessary exams and qualified for the team in both 1983 and 1985.

From servant to celebrity

The story of becoming a Ryder Cup player is also a tale about how society has treated the professional golfer over the years. From being a person not even allowed into the clubhouse of a golf club in Britain until the Open of 1925, the professional golfer's status in the world has matured over the decades and, the more prestigious the Ryder Cup has become, so has grown the reputation and standing of all pro players.

Back in 1927 when the first official Ryder Cup took place, the match was between pro golfers from the best (and probably only) two nations of the golfing world, Britain and America. But the significance of international sporting competition was not fully appreciated by the world at large in those days. Yes, the newspapers and newsreels provided details of the winners and losers, but there was no wall-to-wall coverage of the event as there is today.

In fact, playing any kind of international sporting contest was rare in the 1920s. Teams of pro golfers from England had played their counterparts in Scotland since 1903 and Americans would take on Canadians occasionally, but the cost of travel and the time it took precluded much competition on foreign soil. Pro golfers in the early part of the 20th century were not used to playing under the flag of their country; they were individuals trying to win enough money to make a decent living. Probably the first man to break the mould and be internationally heralded as a celebrity golfer was Harry Vardon. This remarkable Channel Islander, who won seven major championships, started the trend of one-man barnstorming tours of America in 1900. He played more than 80 matches in America that year, returned twice more and inspired at least one generation of US players. Vardon was treated like a star in America, much more so than he was in Britain, and by the 1920s (a time when Vardon's best days were behind him), sportsmen in general and golfers in particular were becoming far more recognised and respected. But it would be one of Vardon's late-career rivals, Walter Hagen, who did most to enact social and political change within the golfing world.

Hagen was the first professional golfer to challenge the status quo. He was not an overtly political animal, but his actions during a longstanding career could hardly be seen in any other way. Certainly, his determination to help create an international team match between America and Britain was a large part of his strategy. By the early 1920s, Hagen – born of German stock, but American through and through – was the sport's unofficial world champion and a man who could win in any country. The chance to play in foreign lands was of immense interest to Hagen because it was a question of both power and politics.

In terms of power, Hagen, with his rather rounded figure and slicked-back hairstyle, felt he needed to conquer Britain in order to achieve absolute domination of the sport. After all, the home of golf was in Britain – more especially, Scotland – and the only reason the sport existed in America was because of the passion that the ex-pat Scots and English had for the game. Hagen won the US Open in 1914 and 1919, but that was not enough. He became a regular visitor to Europe and was behind the unofficial challenge match between American and British pros in 1921, the first precursor of the Ryder Cup. In Hagen's mind, such a competition was crucial to his strategy; it would help him in his individual quest to be seen as the best player of the era when America became the No.1 golf nation.

In terms of politics, Hagen represented the coming of the new age, both in golf and within American and British society. The man known as The Haig hated the fact that the golf pro of his era was a servant to a golf club, a place where the upper class amateur player was able to become a member, but the working class pro was only an employee. In order to force a change, Hagen made a number of overt political acts to embarrass high society Britain. For example, the self-titled "Sir" Walter was aghast when he was not allowed into the clubhouse at Royal Cinque Ports on arrival at the 1920 Open Championship, but rather than kowtow to the outdated rules of the Kent club, he hired a Rolls Royce that he parked in the club car park and used as a mobile changing room. In 1923 at Royal Troon, Hagen's reaction to being denied clubhouse entry to collect his runners-up prize was to set up a picnic on the front lawn of the club where he carried out his own celebration.

Here was a man earning a reputed $300,000 a year, the kind of money that most pro sportsmen at the time, along with most of the golf club members he encountered, could only dream of. Hagen had been raised in a golf industry that relied professionals as caddies, greenkeepers, clubmakers and repairers while amateurs controlled the championships, the clubs, the money and the sport's future. Support for the pro outside of his menial club tasks was minimal; the upper classes, particularly in Britain, would rather help their own, hence the support for the Walker Cup in 1922 and not the professional attempt at an international team match a year earlier. The state of the game in Britain was reflected in the pages of *Golf Monthly* where regular features in the 1920s and 1930s were about fashionable automobiles on offer or the latest plane. News about university golf was common along with pictures of tuxedoed men and their beautifully dressed wives at a summer ball or Christmas celebration. The magazines were aimed at the amateur club golfer, not the professional player.

Meanwhile, in America, golf was also mainly for the well-to-do until the early decades of the 20th century when the sport saw huge expansion and the egalitarian nature of US society meant that attitudes changed more quickly than in Britain. For example, Hagen did not work as a normal golf pro but was attached to Oakland Hills Golf Club near Detroit, Michigan, where members actually encouraged his tournament play; he became a 'touring professional' who publicised his home club and brought it prestige. However, The Haig could still find himself sidetracked by the rich and the powerful. In fact, he was the US captain of 1933 who was chatting to the Prince of Wales (an avid golfer and president of the R&A) in the Southport & Ainsdale clubhouse when many of his teammates thought he should have been with Denny Shute who proceded to three-putt the 18th green and hand the trophy to the British.

The idea of a British pro acting as a touring professional for his club was almost non-existent in Britain at this time; Samuel Ryder's patronage of Abe Mitchell was an exception. The pros of the pre-World War II era were still calling members "Sir" (a practice that would actually continue for several more decades) and having to ask permission to take part in any kind of tournament.

So, the advent of the Ryder Cup – pros playing for king and country or the grand old flag – helped change the status of the golf professional. Becoming a Ryder Cup player was one of the ultimate accolades for a British or American pro golfer and, as the 1930s progressed and it became clear that pros were the best players in the world (well ahead of any amateurs, now that the great Bobby Jones had retired) then a professional golfer became a man of even greater substance in his community. Pros were becoming heroes, winning fortunes, gathering admirers and respect where once they were seen as hucksters and men of marginal importance or ability. Another tale about Hagen emphasises the point.

"Sir"Walter sat down to lunch at Royal St George's in Kent one afternoon in 1928 with his friend Gene Sarazen and the then Prince of Wales. When staff at the club questions the legitimacy of the pros in the dining room, the prince set the record straight once and for all: "You stop this nonsense or I'll take the 'Royal' out of 'St George's'."

The power game

Although every professional golfer rejoiced at the creation of the Ryder Cup, there was still a political pecking order within the contests and there have been no better operators of that power game than the American captains. The first exponent was the superbly confident Hagen. In 1931 on the first tee of his singles match against GB captain Charles Whitcombe at Scioto Country Club, Columbus, Ohio, the American icon was served with a cocktail by his valet. Not only this a sight to see, but typical of the multi-major winner, "Sir"Walter proceeded to send his opening drive straight down the middle of the fairway. Whitcombe, by contrast, was a fine example of the reserved Englishman, a man who was so modest that when he was captain in 1935 he actually dropped himself for the singles despite being part of the only winning partnership in the previous day's foursomes. He was unfussy in both his golf game and his life, so Hagen's tricks unnerved both him and his team. The comments among the British team who either saw or heard of Whitcombe's first tee treatment would have been both priceless and, almost certainly, unprintable – a cause for feelings of real antagonism against all Americans.

In fact, relations between the people of the two nations were changing. In Hagen's era, those among the British golf community showed deep respect for American talent. *Golf Monthly* magazine made this plea to fans at the Open as early as 1926: "The golfers of America are paying the British championship the compliment of sending their greatest players to compete and it is our duty to give those worthy emissaries from our sporting neighbours not only a cordial and generous welcome, but also to provide them a fair field."

However, World War II caused – or more likely merely confirmed – the shift in perspective between people of the two nations. British respect seemed to be replaced by jealousy, while any possible humble attitude from Americans appeared to have morphed into cockiness. The soldiers of the two allied armies were the main source of these feelings. The so-called "damned Yanks" had all the money and took all the girls, while the British Tommy earned less, was dressed less sharply and lacked the Americans' confidence. Ironically, the post-war British Ryder Cup teams complained about lacking money, good clothing and confidence as well.

The average British male had few friendly post-war words for Americans. There were feelings of resentment that the British war effort had virtually bankrupted the country while America had profited and now led the world both economically and politically. Even in golf, the feeling was the same, especially as the PGA Tour had played on during the conflict while British golf was frozen in time from 1939 to 1945. Pros from both sides of the Atlantic had fought bravely (the 1946 US Open was won by Lloyd Mangrum who was wounded in the Battle of the Bulge), but whereas politicians like Winston Churchill talked about the special relationship between Britain and America, it wasn't evident in the Ryder Cup. Both societies had changed because of and during the war – sport had become the new battlefield.

There were post-war feelings of despair about all British sport, not just golf. For example, the 1948 Olympic Games in London was dominated by Americans (84 medals compared to GB's 23); tennis stars from the United States won five of the first six Wimbledon titles after 1946; and even the US football team managed to beat England at the 1950 World Cup in Brazil, one of the tournament's biggest ever shocks.

The chances of winning back the Ryder Cup any time soon after the war (the British lost in both 1935 and 1937) seemed remote. US golfers were now superior because they not only played like major champions, but most of them *were* major champions. They had been winning tournaments and raising their level of competition while the game in Britain lay devastated. Plus, the American professional game simply had a larger pool of players to pick from. Although British pros in the late 1940s and early 1950s were honest men of ability, there was a kind of institutional weariness about them in comparison to the more lively, more exuberant Americans. British golf felt grey in the immediate years after World War II, a reflection of British society's continuing tendency to make-do-and-mend, to accept years more rationing (it did not end until 1954 and was briefly reintroduced in 1956 during the Suez Crisis) and to feel generally exhausted from such a destructive conflict. By contrast, American society was enjoying a golden age with a growing middle class who lived with a vibrancy that overwhelmed anything the former colonists could offer. And in golf, American pros played for big prize money, had access to the best equipment and played on superbly maintained courses all year long. This disparity would last for decades.

The very fact that the British team's trip to the first post-war Ryder Cup match of 1947 in Portland, Oregon, was paid for by American businessman Robert A. Hudson was humiliating enough, but what happened two years later confirmed that only one team led in the power game.

For the match at Ganton, Yorkshire, in 1949, the American team brought with them a huge amount of food, including 600 steaks, twelve sides of beef, a dozen large hams and twelve boxes of bacon – these were treasures beyond belief for the British where managing food rations was most family's weekly priority. The US team went to great lengths to bring the steaks through customs, applying for a special exemption from the authorities because the meat was unlicensed.

The media noted the contrast between the American food strategy and that of the touring Australian cricket team of 1948. The Australians had shown empathy with their English hosts by enjoying whatever food was placed before them. If the British had to suffer from a lack of home comforts, then the visiting Australians would suffer as well. The approach created more of a brotherhood between the teams.

The guileless Americans might argue that they did eventually agree to share their bounty with the home players, but the pride of the home side (and also the British media) was more hurt than any feelings of gratitude for the belated largesse. Faulkner, the young English star of the GB team, joked that the Americans only wanted to share their food after the final day of competition, once the GB team had lost.

Various American captains would continue to play heavily on his country's feeling of superiority. In 1967, US skipper Ben Hogan listened to the polite applause for the GB team as they were introduced one by one at the gala dinner before the match began in Houston, Texas, each with a short explanation of who they were and what they had achieved in golf. When it was his turn to introduce the American team, Hogan pulled a masterstroke. Each US golfer was asked to stand up as he was named, but nothing else was said until they were all on their feet. Only at that point, did the man known as Hogan utter the words: "Ladies and gentlemen, the United States Ryder Cup team, the finest golfers in the world." Peter Alliss remembered in his autobiography that what followed Hogan's statement was a "storm of applause and the British were 10 down before a ball had been hit".

What the British team lacked was swagger. A British player even of the quality of Neil Coles found it hard to combat such a difference. While Americans were well travelled (at least within their own country) and joined a Ryder Cup team expecting to win, Coles walked into his first match in 1961 relatively unsophisticated in top-level international competition. He also found the atmosphere between the two teams maintained America's upper hand. "There was no mixing with the Americans. We had a lot of dinners in those days – a welcoming dinner, a victory dinner, maybe another, but the Ryder Cup was my first experience of playing with Americans since almost none of them travelled here to the Open and I didn't know any of my opponents."

This lack of knowledge about the opposition worked more to the advantage of the Americans who wanted to maintain an imperious attitude and, of course, also their winning ways. Even the Anglophile Arnold Palmer was imperious at times and managed a particularly hurtful put-down in a post-match interview in 1963 after another GB team had performed poorly, losing 23-9. "I think our boys work harder. Whenever our players were not on the course, they were practicing, while the British stayed around the clubhouse." As a power play to keep the British in their place, it was a masterstroke. For the GB players in general, however, it felt like a slap in the face and was unlikely to cause an outbreak of mutual love between the teams.

But perhaps the ultimate political strike by an American captain involved controlling his own team. Tom Watson was captain for the first time in 1993 and knew his golfing history and how the sport had enjoyed long-term support from the country's presidents from William Taft and Franklin D. Roosevelt (both keen players) through Dwight D. Eisenhower (who hit golf balls on the White House lawn every afternoon) and on to John F. Kennedy and George H. W. Bush. However, Captain Watson received some objections from his players about taking a trip to Washington to see the then President Bill Clinton before hopping on to Concorde and flying to Britain. It is well known that top US golfers tend to be fiercely Republican, but Watson was stone-faced when his team objected to making the effort to see their Democratic leader. The man from Missouri told his team: "We're representing the United States and he's the president. We go and we show him the respect he deserves. Period." No player wanted to upset Watson, so the entire team met their president and, just over a week later, brought the trophy back to America.

PGA politics

A different kind of sports politics would affect the Ryder Cup in the 1970s when the landscape of European golf began to change. Golfers in Great Britain and Ireland were simply not good enough to challenge the Americans for the Cup at this time, the losses were constant and by ever larger numbers. With some reluctance, there was a growing realization among the grandees at the British PGA and the leading players that either the Cup format was adapted or the contest would die.

Any revolution had to start with the European Tour pros themselves and their tournament calendar, so just 11 days after the 1971 match, John Jacobs (then a highly respected ex-pro and golf teacher) was made Tournament Director-General within the British PGA. This was a brand new job, but it was crucial because it meant the tournament pros had their own advocate in the PGA's corridors of power. Jacobs acted quickly and, for the 1972 season, he and a team of four executives organised a 20-tournament tour – 13 events in Britain and Ireland and a further seven on the European continent. The tour players now had the undivided attention of sponsors and tournament organisers, while Jacobs and his team wanted to increase prize money and television coverage as well as the quality of the golf courses that the pros would be playing on. In effect, they wanted to match what the Americans had been able to do since the PGA Tour first took shape in 1929 and later broke completely free from the PGA of America in 1968.

The only slightly strange decision by the European tournament pros in hindsight was that they left the ownership and responsibility for the Ryder Cup with the PGA because at that time, the matches were a financial burden and more likely to be scrapped altogether than ever make a massive profit. Instead, the tournament pros took the PGA Championship, a strokeplay event that they considered to be the highlight of their annual tournament calendar.

Coles became chairman of the PGA European Tour board of directors in 1977 and saw the changes first hand. "There was a group of us playing in the tournaments who had wanted our own section within the PGA for a long time; it was building for a while beforehand. We wanted to employ our own people, hire and fire our own people, improve our golf tournaments and improve our situation. John Jacobs came in as the man to look after this and was the only full-time employee for a while. There were not very many guys – myself, Dai Rees, Bernard Hunt, Peter Alliss, a few others like Brian Huggett – who made a living playing tournaments; most pros were still club professionals with a connection to their clubs. This all followed what was going on in America. We never had conversations with the Americans, but we knew what they were doing and so we did it ourselves. We had dozens of pros who were tournament pros, whereas they had hundreds who could play all year." Ken Schofield, who became executive director of the Tour in 1975, said his organisation's focus was to build tournaments at that time, not worry about the Ryder Cup. "There were only 17 weeks of events [in the early 1970s], so we were concentrating on filling the calendar for our members."

Then, shortly after continental European players joined the Ryder Cup in 1979, the commercial tide began to turn for the event and the tournament players soon realised that they had let a diamond slip through their fingers. Talks about ownership of the event soon took place and were progressing steadily (although without resolution) when Sandy Jones was appointed chief executive of the PGA. The quietly-spoken Scot was friendly with many of the top players of the day and also Schofield, his countryman. Jones understood that his association had battled through the bad times with the Ryder Cup, but he also recognised that the European Tour was in a much stronger position to operate the matches, especially given their relationship with TV companies and almost weekly experience of staging huge tournaments. The same evening that Jones was confirmed in his new job at the PGA in December 1991, he received a congratulatory phone call from Schofield who raised the topic of the Ryder Cup. "I told Ken we should make the Ryder Cup a 50-50 partnership that night. I think you've got to be fair in life and say that, when two parties are making a contribution, both parties need to benefit from it and the financial benefit was important to both sides."

The quick decision avoided any confrontation between the players and the PGA and, with the European Tour using its own workforce to manage the matches, even more money began rolling in from the Cup. Then in 2004, a further revision was made to the ownership of Europe's half of the Cup: the European Tour was given a 60% share and became managing partner; the British PGA was handed 20% and recognised as the founding partner; and the PGAs of Europe organisation was provided with the final 20% as recognition that continental Europeans were a hugely important part of the event. Jones was a prime mover in this change as well, accepting the PGA's new position. "I knew it was the right answer for the match and I also knew that if the [Ryder Cup] grew, the tour was going to grow and the PGA was going to grow [as well]." Nowadays, a full-time Ryder Cup staff based at the European Tour offices at Wentworth in Surrey reports regularly to a Ryder Cup committee – including many senior current players – that operates with a 60-20-20 voting rights split.

By contrast, the PGA of America has retained full ownership of the Ryder Cup, a situation that has led to several disagreements with the PGA Tour pros over the years (most notably over a lack of appearance money in 1999). Although these confrontations ended with a compromise and brought more openness in terms of how the modern-day profits are used, the senior figures on the PGA Tour envy how their European counterparts now control their side of the Ryder Cup. PGA Tour commissioner Tim Finchem sits on the US Ryder Cup committee these days, but his counterpart at the PGA of America – the association's president – is an electable officer who stands down after two years, so having long-term one-to-one talks to deliver any ownership change (as happened in Europe) is difficult and the chances of any change is pure speculation.

An unusually united Europe

It was the 23rd Ryder Cup match in 1979 at White Sulphur Springs, West Virginia, that marked the arrival of Team Europe. But although the sporting world was full of World Cups by then, the idea of 12 sportsmen representing a single continent was unique. The political irony was that the British – who still controlled the organisation of the Ryder Cup and provided the bulk of the players – had never really felt very European. Great Britain had long looked more to the group of Commonwealth nations for military alliances or economic trading partnerships rather than the countries of Europe albeit that they were geographically closer. In fact, there was once speculation that the GB Ryder Cup team could morph into a Commonwealth squad rather than a European one.

In fact, politically speaking, there were good reasons to deny any sporting link up with continental Europe. The two World Wars of the 20th century had done little to unite the leading nations of Europe, at least from Britain's point of view: France and Germany were Britain's oldest enemies even though their royal families had inter-married on many occasions; Italy, Spain, Holland and Portugal had also been at war with Britain in times past and there were few cultural connections in the modern era; the Nordic countries kept themselves to themselves; and eastern Europe was only just emerging from the Cold War. In golfing terms, though, a union made more sense because the tour was, after all, called the European Tour. However, there was no certainty that a team from many different countries around Europe would bond in a meaningful way against a powerful American team that had such a victorious history in the Ryder Cup. Yet, as luck would have it, the politics of golf were increasingly in favour of the formation of Team Europe.

The late 1970s was a time when great players were emerging from continental Europe; Seve Ballesteros was the first. The darkly handsome Spaniard was charming in many ways, but he also had a notoriously hot temper as well as a number of chips on his shoulder about Americans. Just as many British players of the past had been made unwelcome by the PGA Tour (invitations were few and far between for decades), Ballesteros suffered from the attitude of US protectionism. Actually, Tony Jacklin had been one of the first European pros to point out the resentment from some American players. "Gardner Dickinson and Bob Goalby resented me on the PGA Tour," he said. "They thought I was taking money out of their pockets. Nicklaus and Palmer were different. Their attitude was that if you think you can beat me, come and try." So Jacklin found an ally in the Spaniard who particularly wanted to be Americans *in* America. Ballesteros was a master at taking an innocent comment from an opponent and turning it into a deeply personal slight. When Americans regularly called him "Steve" rather than "Seve" during his early trips to the States, his resentment only grew. Even though many US fans and players loved Ballesteros, his passion for Ryder Cup victories never diminished.

With a Spanish champion as Europe's on-course general, the Ryder Cup was a different kind of golf match from 1979 onwards; two continents were doing battle for the first time in sport. Ballesteros's sense of deep, personal honour filtered through to the rest of the team: if he had been slighted by Americans, then so had the rest of the team; because he fought like a dog, so did every one of his teammates; if the atmosphere between the two teams turned dark, then that was fine if it meant there was more chance of a European victory.

One of his Spanish counterparts Manuel Pinero says: "I think the Americans were scared of Seve, in a way. He was the first player to go there and treat them like they were ordinary golfers. It was the way that some of the Americans were when they first came to Europe; he was a bit arrogant."

Ballesteros helped bond the European nations in a way that was had never happened before in any other sport. "The Ryder Cup became the glue that kept the European Tour together," said Schofield, "and it would eventually become the most successful European entity; it was recognised by politicians, not just sports people. We were very proud of that fact."

There was, however, an element of irony about the new, close relationship between professional golfers throughout Europe because in May 1979, just four months before Ballesteros and Antonio Garrido of Spain became the first continental Europeans to play on a Ryder Cup team, Margaret Thatcher was elected prime minister of the United Kingdom. Not only was Mrs Thatcher the first woman to govern the country, but she was also known as a Euro-sceptic, suspicious of her near neighbours and unwilling to offer an unconditional hand of friendship. The UK and Ireland, along with Denmark, may have joined the European Union in 1973, but Mrs Thatcher's attitude was that countries likes of France and Germany could not be trusted. In fact, the mood in Britain when she took office was one of circumspection about Europe. The UK had even held a national referendum about its membership of the European community and it was known that Mrs Thatcher would have been happy to leave. The feelings of the British government at the time, however, did not cause one significant bump on the road to the integration of Team Europe with Ballesteros as its talisman. However, there were internal problems to solve.

Having made his debut in 1979, the talismanic Spaniard found himself in a row with his own European Tour, and the Americans were indirectly to blame. Ballesteros felt that he was now worthy of appearance money, something that was often paid to attract players over from the US like Tom Watson and Lee Trevino, but it was never paid to members of the European Tour. The issue was a thorny one and Ballesteros had his supporters, while his Ryder Cup captain John Jacobs supported a ban on all appearance money. The wrangling meant Ballesteros only played seven European tournaments in the build-up to the 1981 match (not enough to qualify automatically) and his lack of support for the Tour was resented by many of the top players who were due to play. In the end, Jacobs felt unable to make the Spaniard one of his two captain's picks. "Sheer insanity," said Tony Jacklin who was also omitted. "[Seve] deserved better and was treated awfully." No Ballesteros (or, indeed, Jacklin) meant no chance for the European team at Walton Heath who faced an American team with 11 major champions. The great surprise was that the Americans only won by 18½-9½.

Ironically, Jacklin was then made captain himself for the next match and, immediately after his appointment, the Englishman was told to fix "the Ballesteros situation" so the two great players met for breakfast at the Open Championship in 1983. Jacklin fully understood the Spaniard's point of view about appearance money. "Seve was a proud man with genius. He was very angry and quite rightly when we met at the Prince of Wales hotel in Southport. He was venting and very unhappy. His reasoning was the same as mine, but he really wanted to play against the Americans. I said I could [motivate the team] off the course, but I couldn't play. I needed him."

Ballesteros went back to Spain to think about his answer and two weeks later the prodigal son returned to the Ryder Cup. By doing so, the Spaniard's passion helped unite players from all over the European continent and inspired a long-awaited victory over the Americans in 1985. The fact that the European team carried a logo of the newly-deceased Ballesteros on the golf shirts and golf bags almost 30 years later is testimony to how the Spaniard came to represent the very spirit of the tournament and how solving one of golf's biggest political problems began a renaissance of the matches.

7

The Future

If Samuel Ryder had been asked in 1927 'what will the Ryder Cup look like in a generation's time?', his guesses would have in no way matched the reality. Even if Cup icon Tony Jacklin had been posed the same question when he made his debut as a player in the matches 40 years later, would his forecasts have been any nearer the actual truth? The changes to the Cup – the golfers who take part, the numbers of fans who watch, the money that has poured in over recent years – were not forecast by prior generations of players. History tells us nothing is forever, so the predictions for the future can be as radical as the changes that took place in the past. Or is the Ryder Cup – as many commentators currently say – just perfect the way it is and should stay that way?

Despite all the conjecture, just like any multi-million pound (euro or dollar) international business, the Ryder Cup organisers make plans for the future and, in the 21st century, one of the most common ways of predicting that future would be to carry out a SWOT analysis. This is a basic diagnostic test where the analysis is based on four areas – Strengths, Weaknesses, Opportunities and Threats – with all the relevant facts, issues and discussion points listed beneath each heading. Given the historical knowledge, the extensive research, the on-the-record interviews and the informal briefings with which this book has been constructed, it is appropriate for the final chapter to be a SWOT analysis to predict what might happen to the Ryder Cup by 2050. The examination of the Cup delivered here is honest and independent, while the conclusions range from talking points to likely outcomes. All this is written with the knowledge that predicting the long-term future of the Ryder Cup has, so far, been a loser's game. After all, who could have foreseen even a couple of decades ago that pop stars would be reading poems at the event's opening ceremony (Justin Timberlake, 2012) or that we would all be buying Ryder Cup tartan (Gleneagles, 2014)?

Strengths

After 40 matches across nine different decades, the Ryder Cup organisers have many reasons to celebrate. Here is a list of the 10 most obvious positive aspects of the Cup:

Longevity – Since its launch in 1927, the Ryder Cup has survived one World War, the 9/11 terrorist attacks in 2001 and many moments of crisis, yet the sequence of matches has been maintained and the mythology and the folklore have grown with each meeting of the two teams. The Cup is older than other iconic events both in golf (the Masters was first staged in 1934) and other sports (the inaugural football World Cup took place in 1930). The Cup is strengthened by its history, especially as almost every match is a treasured moment and there are enough written and photographic records as well as modern-day video coverage to contextualise every story. The colorful characters, the dramatic wins and losses, the outrageous swings in fortune, are all well-documented and remarkably varied. The magnificent stories of its own past will continue to help the Cup succeed into the future.

Quality – A vast majority of the best golfers of all time have played in the first 40 contests. Prior to Gleneagles in 2014, a total of 302 different players qualified for the Cup (these include a small handful who never actually played because they either had to withdraw due to injury or were not actually selected to play a match) with 148 from Great Britain, Ireland or Europe and 154 from America. The Ryder Cup may have been slightly too late for The Great Triumvirate of Harry Vardon, James Braid and J. H. Taylor while modern-day greats like Gary Player, Greg Norman and Ernie Els were neither American nor European, but the list of Ryder Cup players still contains most of the greats.

Certainly, every modern-day golfer who qualifies for a Cup knows his name will be linked with the best in the history of the professional game. In addition, to the benefit of view of the fans, the most skillful and talented golfers are on view doing battle in the most intense conditions, so the level of golf is likely to be outstanding. This means that sell-out crowds now line the fairways at each event and many millions of TV viewers tune in as well for a must-watch contest.

Respect – There is a real 'band of brothers' feeling about playing on a Ryder Cup team. An incredible bond always exists between members of every winning team, and even those who only experience losing still treasure the chance to represent their country. The Cup even links opponents because of acts of fellowship like the outpouring of sympathy from all participants in 2006 for the recently bereaved Darren Clarke.

Even one appearance can leave a lasting memory like American John Cook's who only qualified for the 1993 match, but describes it as a very special moment in his career. "For however many weeks of the year, golf is all about yourself. But when we all got on the plane heading for The Belfry back then, it was about 13 guys and you could feel it; it was all shared. Nobody took credit or blame; it was about all of us being together. No one questioned anything because you don't question the coach like in football. The old stories don't come up very often, but Chip Beck and I sometimes say a few words about the match. We were sent out as the sacrificial lambs against (Colin) Montgomerie and (Nick) Faldo and we won. We chuckle about it now and again. That evening, Ian Woosnam came into our team room and had a few beers. Then Sandy Lyle came and for three days this had been hard, but after it's all said and done, the smoke cleared and it was all OK between us. I won't forget Woosie coming over, he's quite a guy." There have been plenty of arguments and disagreements between players since 1927, but the vast majority of players view the Ryder Cup as a treasured memory and the enmity is forgotten.

Structure – The format that has evolved over time now regularly produces the closest of contests. It took until the 24th match in 1981 to settle on 12-man teams playing for 28 points over three days, but that structure is now set in stone. It promotes intrigue (the captain has to bench players for the pairs matches), intensity (every single match is played as if it will deliver the winning point) and drama (since Europe's first win in 1985, nine of the 13 Cups have been won by two points or less).

The first two days of foursomes and fourballs offer the unusual scene of the top golfers playing in pairs and that is followed by the 12 singles on day three that provide a regular climax. This system has become the template for other, similar team golf events like the Solheim Cup, while even the Internationals have been lobbying for the same format in the Presidents Cup. Spectators fully understand it, the players have bought into it and the tight results prove its success.

<u>Glory</u> – The pride and passion that is at stake seems to mean more to the players than money. There has never been prize money on offer for representing your tour, your country or your continent, so there is a purity about the Ryder Cup. You win glory, not dollars, pounds or euros. The number of tears shed – either of joy or despair, during and after each event – are testimony to why this should not change. The joy is a weeping Seve Ballesteros with his arms around an equally-affected Nick Faldo on the green after winning the 1995 match, while the despair is American Hunter Mahan's realisation and admission in 2010 at the post-match press conference that losing his singles match also lost the Ryder Cup for his teammates.

The raw emotion these professional athletes show in the team environment is so unlike their normal week-to-week demeanour at regular tournaments. Sinking a three-footer for the Open Championship claret jug or standing over a right-to-left curler for a $10 million cheque at the climax of the FedEx Cup series can send shivers down a golfer's spine, but playing under the Stars and Stripes or the Union flag causes twitches, shanks, tremors and tension like nothing else. The anthems, the patriotism from the crowds, the unique spotlight on every single shot – there's nowhere to hide and no greater test of a professional golfer's ability to play under pressure and only for the glory of it all.

<u>Global</u> – The global awareness of the Ryder Cup via television, radio, internet, newspapers and magazines is staggering. Considering this is a contest between only two of the world's continents and involves only a seventh of the world's population, it is remarkable how much attention the event commands. The 2014 Ryder Cup was set to be available to a potential audience of 500 million viewers in 183 different countries on each of the three days of competition. Although these potential figures can be misinterpreted (remember, this is not the actual number of viewers), the fact that the matches reach so many countries is still noteworthy, and definitely of interest to worldwide sponsors and advertisers.

<u>Legacy</u> – The organisation of the matches is now so forward-thinking and far-reaching that no stone goes unturned to make things bigger and better every two years. Planning for future events can start a decade in advance and nowadays involves governments as well as local golf federations or associations. To ensure that each match operates seamlessly, the two sets of organisers have gathered teams of operations experts, marketing and sponsorship gurus plus media coordinators that are unrivaled. The most recent venues and those bidding to stage matches in the future are committed to working hard to ensure a long-term golfing legacy as well as a magnificent three-day match. In the end, the reputation and awareness of each host venue has been elevated

to such a degree that when the Ryder Cup is over, the logo on the golf course can attract millions of visitors to the club, the region and the country for years to come.

Branding – The branding of sporting events has become much more sophisticated in recent years and the Ryder Cup has worked hard to protect its brand as one that represents sporting heritage, fairness of competition and legacy to golf. Before the commercial sea change of the 1980s, there was not always total collaboration between the two PGAs, the two Tours or even the venues, but that has changed in recent years. It is questionable whether the Ryder Cup is golf's single most visible event (the Masters and US Open boast bigger viewing audiences in America, for example, while the Open Championship has more history), but it is by far the biggest and best international team golf competition and the Ryder Cup brand is just as strong as that of any tournament in golf. The latest significant branding move was the creation of a single, constant Ryder Cup logo for the 2012 match. This was a simple and effective improvement for the commercial prospects of the Cup, particularly merchandising.

Televisual – Most modern-day sports have benefited from working with television companies in many different ways: rules have been changed, tricks of the broadcasting trade employed and even the sport's own traditional venues altered – all in an effort to bring more excitement to viewers. The invention of limited-overs cricket; cameras everywhere, from a rugby referee's head to the inside of a cricket stump; technology to decide if a tennis ball hits a court line or a gridiron touchdown is scored; the widespread use of the time-out to provide a space for more television advertising; teams dressed in ever more brightly-coloured clothing; sports adopting a tie-break scoring system to resolve otherwise deadlocked matches; the courses of triathalons becoming city-centre based – the list of changes for the benefit of television is endless.

Yet the Ryder Cup needs none of these heavyweight adaptations; it could have been made for television. Every single significant shot can be screened in real time, the rules and the scoring are simple and the tension through the camera lens reaches unheard of levels of intensity without any TV trickery or rule-bending. Yes, the Cup is now screened with more cameras and in high definition as well as 3D, but these are natural broadcasting developments and not technologies made for this event. Instead, the matches in 2014 are in many ways similar to those played in 1927 – pairs and singles matches each worth only a single point with the winning team scoring the most overall and even a tie being a possible result. The payoff for allowing the Ryder Cup to remain natural to its roots is that the number of heavenly television moments

– especially in recent times – has been staggering: the tie at The Belfry in 1989 then Bernhard Langer's missed putt at Kiawah Island two years later followed by astonishing comebacks at Brookline in 1999 and Medinah in 2012. The swings in momentum of every match occur minute-by-minute over all three days with drama at every turn and with storylines almost too incredible to believe. Even the most exciting major championship can barely match the spectacle.

Imitation – If imitation is the sincerest form of flattery, then Ryder Cup organisers should be enjoying the warm glow of adulation because so many new international team golf events have been created in its wake. The Solheim Cup, Presidents Cup, Seve Trophy, Royal Trophy and most recently the EurAsia Cup are now prominent team events for top professionals both male and female. But there has also been an outbreak of amateur imitators. Clubs throughout Britain and even some in the US organise Europe vs America matches among their own members, ideally with teams comprising of players born in the two continents. Everyone wants to experience some of the Ryder Cup magic. And 2014 marked the re-launching of one of the most intriguing imitations, the only other competition that can legitimately be called the Ryder Cup.

The story began back in the 1930s when Samuel Ryder's daughter Marjorie married a Rhodesian farmer named Claisen and moved out to live in Africa, actually in Manicaland in the country's Eastern Districts. Once there, Marjorie discovered that the community – in what is now eastern Zimbabwe – included a number of very keen golfers who competed regularly against each other and soon she asked her father to provide them with a trophy to play for. The venerable seed merchant was always a generous man when it came to his family and particularly to these farmers of Rhodesia who, it is believed, were supplying him seeds for his own business. So the father answered his daughter's request, but not with just a run-of-the-mill trophy. Instead, Samuel sent a close replica of the Ryder Cup itself, made from sterling silver and produced by Mappin and Webb of Birmingham, the same makers of the original gold trophy.

The new Ryder Cup arrived in Africa in July 1933 and, originally, the local farmers named their trophy the Matikas Golf Challenge Cup. However, Marjorie's father gave her permission to adopt the Ryder name before he died in 1936 and so the legend began. The trophy was first played for as an individual event with up to 24 players taking part, although the competition fell away during World War II. Then in 1972, a prominent auctioneer from the area, Binks Holland, persuaded a large sponsor to provide suitable support and commercial farmers from all over the country were invited to play in a fourball betterball format over two days. However, the political changes in the country in the late 1970s and early 1980s that led to Rhodesia becoming Zimbabwe meant the golf matches had to be low-key affairs. Nevertheless, the golf community was given another boost during this time when a second trophy was sent to them by the Ryder family. Known as the Ryder Five-0 trophy, it was presented to mark the 50th anniversary of the original competition.

Ryder's first cup sent to Africa was keenly played for over the years, attracting in the region of 80 to 90 pairs, until 2000 when the sponsor (African Distillers) decided that it was not prudent to be associated with a golf event involving a large number of white commercial farmers whose lands were falling victim to the land reform invasions. So the competition ceased for a few years and Ryder's original trophy actually went missing. It was only recovered after an internet appeal. Then in 2006, British Airways agreed to fund a team match between golfers involving three local clubs and only the difficult Zimbabwe elections in 2013 caused a postponement of the new format. However, a committee of devotees then came up with a plan elevate the Zimbabwe Ryder Cup into an international event and new benefactors were found in time for a 2014 re-launch. Four teams of amateur club players of varying handicaps will now play annually for the trophy with an international team coming mostly from Britain playing against local clubs Leopard Rock/Hillside, Borrowdale Brook and Wingate. Played the weekend before its more famous namesake, the Zimbabwe Ryder Cup is now hoping to establish itself as a regular annual event on the golfing calendar.

Weaknesses

It is worth opening this section with the following caveat: no true golf fan (including this one) actually wants or desires the Ryder Cup to falter or be any less fantastic than it is right now. The thought of watching ever closer and more dramatic encounters thrills everyone involved with the game.

And when it comes to spotting potential weaknesses of the event, European Tour Ryder Cup director Richard Hills is emphatic when he says that no one on the organising committee sits on their laurels. "Everything is done carefully and methodically. It would be very pompous for us to say we are recession proof, for example. We know we aren't." Hills speaks from experience because his Ryder Cup memory includes the best and worst of times. "We were at the top of the Celtic Tiger (the name given to the Irish economic boom of the mid-2000s) at the K Club in 2006," he says, "but it was Black Friday (the moment of the Wall Street collapse of autumn 2008) during Valhalla; that's when the commercial world changed. There were lots of empty hospitality suites at the match in 2008, it was that week when

Lehman Brothers went belly-up. People like the bankers from Barclays just did not attend. They couldn't be seen to be at a golf tournament enjoying themselves."

Commercial peaks and troughs will come and go, but there are two major weaknesses for the current Ryder Cup that are deeply embedded in the culture of the professional sport: firstly, issues over scheduling the Cup in the increasingly busy autumn calendar, and, secondly, the power game that is taking place within the upper echelons of professional golf, a place where the Ryder Cup is not everyone's favourite event.

Scheduling Issues – A recent fly in the Ryder Cup ointment has been scheduling. In the early years, the Cup would be staged in the summer so that players travelling over from the other side of the Atlantic could also take part in other golf tournaments such as the Open Championship or the US Open. Later, when trans-Atlantic travel was faster and the players' time away from home was much shorter, the event found a natural home in the early autumn, giving it a privileged spot in the golfing calendar.

However, the emergence of the two end-of-season playoff competitions on both the PGA Tour in America and the European Tour has meant that autumn no longer belongs to the Ryder Cup and, as a worldwide sport occupying all 12 months, there are bound to be clashes of competition dates. The FedEx Cup series, for example, began in the United States in 2007 and has moved around a little date-wise to try to find its best position (currently late August through September). Meanwhile, The Final Series on the European Tour started only in 2013 and is still bedding itself in between late October and mid-November. Consequently, the space in the golfing calendar for the Ryder Cup has been markedly reduced. The reason is a complex one of political games and thirst for power.

Since the mid-2000s, the Tours in the US and Europe have both been trying to figure out the best way to climax their seasons. They now favour the idea of three prestigious strokeplay events as playoffs leading up to a Tour Championship with an elite field (30 for the PGA Tour and 60 for the European Tour) playing for one enormous pot of prize money. However, they also both want the top players to play in all the playoffs as well as the final and have adjusted their rules to make this happen.

The growing problem is that many of the top players want to compete in both the playoff series and the two finals while every year there is now either a Ryder Cup or a Presidents Cup scheduled in between. The FedEx Cup and The Final Series need eight separate weeks in the global calendar starting at the end of August. That prompts two more issues: the PGA Championship (the traditional fourth major of the year always staged in August) bumps heads with the first of the FedEx Cup playoffs and also there is the World

Golf Championship event in China to fit into the mix. With the team competitions as well, a leading US or European player could face 10-12 weeks of solid tournament golf, a situation that not many of them favour.

And the other issue with such a busy golfing calendar is that the later the Ryder Cup is staged in the autumn (especially in Europe), the more likely it will be weather-affected. The 2012 match at Celtic Manor was the first Ryder Cup ever to need an extra day to be completed, something the organisers were fearful of the moment they were told that the first week in October was their date rather than mid or late September.

The signs of autumn weather problems could already have been spotted because downpours at Walton Heath in 1981 and The K Club in 2006 were almost sufficient to cause severe delays. Although organisers coped with the Monday finish in Wales while TV companies re-scheduled and the players were positive, it was not an ideal scenario because free entry for spectators on the extra day ate into the profits. Ironically, the previous week's weather had been gloriously sunny.

In short, though, cramming the Ryder Cup into such a busy and intense part of the golf calendar leaves players tired and exacerbates any weather problems.

Power Game – Scheduling the Ryder Cup is really a collateral issue of the complex power struggle going on within the sport. At the centre of the struggle is ownership of all the key international tournaments and, therefore, how the Cup relates to the rest of golf's calendar.

Originally, the British PGA was presented with the Ryder Cup under a deed of trust that Samuel Ryder actually had drawn up and paid for. The PGA owned and operated matches on Britain while the PGA of America did the same for contests on their side of the Atlantic. Everything was clear and simple. Then in 1992, the British PGA acknowledged that the professional tournament players of Europe (who now had their own organisation, then known as the PGA European Tour) should be 50/50 partners. This was followed by a further ownership change in 2004: the Tour became managing partner with a 60% share and the British PGA and the PGAs of Europe were each left with 20%. This situation brought harmony in Europe with all three organisations heavily involved, but the same cannot be said in America.

Control of the biggest annual golf events staged in America are spread across four different organisations: The Masters is run by the Augusta National Golf Club; the US Open belongs to the United States Golf Association (USGA); the PGA Championship is the PGA of America's property along with the American Ryder Cup matches; and the PGA Tour (the players' own organisation, the equivalent of the European Tour) boasts the Tour Championship (often referred to as the fifth major), the FedEx Cup (which delivers the largest winner's cheque in the sport) and the Presidents Cup.

The problem is that the PGA Tour does not own America's most prestigious tournaments: that is, any of the three majors nor the Ryder Cup. So the world's most dominant golf Tour is actually on the fringes when it comes to competition cachet and, even though the members and their commissioner, Tim Finchem, put a brave face on it, there are obvious tensions.

For example, in 2013 the PGA Championship came under Commissioner Finchem's gaze because it was using the rather catchy tagline "Glory's Last Shot" as a way of linking it to the other three glorious majors earlier in each season – the Masters, the US Open and the Open Championship. For Finchem and his members, however, the phrase implied that nothing of significance remained in the golf season once the PGA Championship had been won.

Now, the PGA Tour commissioner is nothing if not loyal to his members and sponsors and he felt that winning the FedEx Cup should be regarded as just as glorious as triumphing in the PGA Championship, so he requested that the tagline was dropped. When the PGA of America acceded to Finchem's request and therefore indicated to everyone who holds the power in the biggest golf market in the world, it sent a clear message to all the world's leading golf figures: don't mess with the PGA Tour.

Commissioner Finchem and his Tour showed their muscle prior to this in a move that hurt three consecutive Ryder Cups. In 2008, 2010 and 2012, the FedEx Cup final was played on the Sunday immediately before the start of each of those Ryder Cup weeks at Valhalla, Celtic Manor and Medinah respectively. All the Americans on the team and a handful of Europeans rushed to be at the Cup venue for the Tuesday deadline, giving them less than 48 hours recovery time between their final 18 holes of FedEx Cup golf and the start of golf's biggest team event. By contrast, all players taking part in the 2007, 2009, 2011 and 2013 Presidents Cup were allowed a week off for their preparations; no PGA Tour event was scheduled directly before the international team event controlled by Finchem and his tour.

Now, the foremost golfers in the world are used to tight schedules, but not before one of the most important events of the year. It took a plea from none other than the great Tom Watson, US captain for 2014 team, to ensure that Ryder Cup players were treated the same as the Presidents Cup boys and received a week's rest. The negotiations might be gentlemanly and this result was a win for the Ryder Cup, but the situation was another example of the PGA Tour wanting everyone to know who is the ultimate boss. The fact that the Americans travelled across the Atlantic in 2010 and lost a tight match at Celtic Manor meant the Tour's actions could have been partly to blame. Although no one would dare say such a thing, the story emphasises that the Ryder Cup is not at the top of everyone's biennial agenda.

Not surprisingly, the properties Commissioner Finchem controls with his members are those that he fights hardest for and that is where the friction exists.

With the American half of the Ryder Cup 100% owned by the PGA of America, it is unsurprising that Finchem may favour the Presidents Cup. The commissioner could argue that, like the European Tour, his Tour provides the players for the US Ryder Cup teams and his organisation has plenty of tournament expertise, so why not change the ownership in the way that the Europeans have done?

Some independent observers believe the PGA Tour's lack of direct involvement in the Cup is anachronistic and there has been speculation for many years about if, or when, the PGA of America will hand over at least some of the Ryder Cup reins to Finchem. However, it is not the kind of decision that seems likely from a non-profit organisation whose tag line is 'Experts in the game and business of golf'. In fact, rather than showing signs of relaxing its grip on any of its events, the PGA of America has been extremely bullish about its own tournaments: in 2013, it announced a new Ryder Cup television deal with NBC in America that takes their partnership to 2030, while its president Ted Bishop speculated that the PGA Championship may one day be staged outside America.

Would the Ryder Cup as a whole be more successful with Commissioner Finchem and the PGA Tour fully on board? Well, Finchem has to believe so because his influence in the world of golf would be increased if his organisation was a Ryder Cup managing partner like the European Tour. And he knows the value of such a change because, as chairman of the International Federation of PGA Tours (as well as being the best friend of all TV broadcasters, tournament sponsors, hospitality companies and merchandisers involved in golf), he is the most powerful man in the sport even without a direct role in any of the leading tournaments. His influence, arguably, can deliver better commercial deals and also negotiate any issues more sensitively with his Tour's members who now number plenty of top European players.

Officially, neither the PGA Tour nor the PGA of America acknowledge any discomfort over their Ryder Cup relationship, but the fact remains that the US Ryder Cup team is contest by the PGA Tour's leading members and not any of the 28,000 club professionals across the States who are the responsibility of the PGA of America. The European Tour and the British PGA updated their Ryder Cup relationship over 20 years ago, but their American counterparts, for once, are lagging behind.

Opportunities

In the SWOT method of analysis, strengths are usually obvious, but opportunities are often more difficult to pin down, especially when the subject is as successful as the Ryder Cup. The list of opportunities, therefore, focuses only on certain areas of business that can easily be developed more extensively or pursued more efficiently.

<u>Television and the Internet</u> – For the Ryder Cup to become an even more successful event, it starts with television and awareness. The current figure of 500 million potential viewers in over 180 countries is impressive, but the TV sales team cannot stop there and, with countries such as China and India (with a combined population of over 2.5 billion) still emerging as golfing nations, the viewing numbers over the next decade could easily double, especially after the boost golf is expected to receive in the Olympic Games in 2016. And, with the organisers ensuring that money from extra TV coverage is re-invested back into golf-development projects in places like Asia, even more new players should be attracted to the game and thus become potential viewers. This really is a virtuous circle.

The other good news in the broadcasting world is that not only will TV viewing increase via traditional broadcasting channels and normal television screens, but the ways of watching the Ryder Cup via the internet will increase as well. Already modern televisions are connected to the web, while broadband connections are speeding up sufficiently so that laptops and other mobile devices are now quite acceptable places to watch sport. Plus, the increasingly sophisticated smartphone has a screen on which the younger generation in particular is happy to view events, while the smartwatch will be the next viewing device sensation.

But the revolution in watching video content is not just about the screen and the broadband strength. Instead the conversation is about who sends out the moving pictures. The next generation of 21st century broadcasters could well be internet-based companies like YouTube and Google who have not yet taken full advantage of live sport on their networks. The broadcasters as we know them today – NBC, Sky Sports, The Golf Channel, and the like – will either have to move increasingly into the world of internet broadcasting or face losing the rights to show sports events like the Ryder Cup. Internet-based companies understand the web and its future in a way that traditional TV broadcasters do not. When the Ryder Cup organisers work more closely with 'new media' then the audiences will soar and more money will flow in from rights fees as well as sponsors.

<u>Two Organisations</u> – If the Ryder Cup was being set up in the modern era, there is no way that the current organisational structure would be adopted. Ever since 1927, the US-based matches have been the sole responsibility of the Americans while the British contests (later to become European) have belonged to the other home nation, now the continent. The "away" team just has to arrive in the "home" country and then everything is organised for them, while the "home" organisers keep all the money from their event and negotiate all their deals completely separately.

More recently, the two organising committees and their full-time staff have learned to work closely together on all matters in the realisation that each one needs the other to successfully continue the series of matches. Also, the handover every two years has become seamless, even though the "home" organisers spend two years focusing directly on their match and then only have a passive role for the "away" fixture in two years time. The two organising committees share information, ideas and plans, so operationally the Ryder Cups suffer very little. However, it is not a perfect business model. It is a system that would make the leaders of any other kind of global business shake their heads in despair.

The idea of having a single body of people working full-time on every Ryder Cup would make more sense, particularly from some of the commercial perspectives. With the Cup having become a global attraction, it no longer makes sense to carry out separate talks with TV companies, sponsors and other commercial partners every two years.

A single, central organisation would enjoy more leverage in financial negotiations, especially with sponsors, and be able to avert any awkward clashes between European and American sponsors. For example, the official-timing sponsor was announced as Omega in time for American-staged Ryder Cups of 2012 and 2016, whereas Rolex was (and remains) the preferred partner in Europe and had been for almost two decades. BMW is the car sponsor in Europe while Mercedes-Benz provides the vehicles in America. Sponsors would obviously prefer to be involved in every match rather than every other one and the income from a more constant sponsorship would almost certainly be greater.

In fact, the sponsors are desperately trying to find ways to avoid the two-organisation dilemma themselves. The first worldwide partner – asset-management company Standard Life Investments – was signed up in time for Gleneagles and shows that the Cup's future is about securing global deals. Commercial protectionism does not take place within the FIFA World Cup or the Olympics organisations, so maybe the Ryder Cup will again one day follow these business models.

Threats

For a sporting event of such magnitude and success, the idea of the Ryder Cup being under threat in any way might seem outrageous. Yet the Cup's history teaches us that the pendulum of fortune can swing both ways. Currently the matches are stronger than ever, in terms of credibility, commercial viability and size of audience. But even in recent times, cracks have appeared in the perfect façade and who is to say that some of them might not widen in the years to come?

<u>Payment</u> – One of the most obvious possible future problems for the Ryder Cup may be player payments. For some, it's an old chestnut that's been buried, but if money really is the root of all evil then the issue will emerge again and could be damaging. Again, Ryder Cup history is the key to understanding the issue.

Ryder Cup players know that every professional sportsman and women – even Olympians in the modern era – get paid to turn out for their national team. Golfers in the Ryder Cup have always been the exception: no prize money and no appearance fees. This situation has not changed since the very first events.

However, to believe that the players receive absolutely nothing from the Cup is disingenuous and untrue. Even back in the 1920s and 1930s, when the very first participants were forced to travel across the ocean and back on a month-long sojourn to play in the Cup, the players received enough money to compensate them for lost salary because most of them were on unpaid leave from their pro shop jobs. They may also have received a few free gifts, particularly the Americans (maybe a pair of golf shoes or a blazer), but their main concerns were satisfied – they did not lose money playing in the match and so could enjoy the prestige.

Once global travel speeded up, the players settled for a style of Ryder Cup compensation that included a daily per diem and more gifts. Players also received tickets for family and friends and first class treatment throughout the week, along with the opportunity to enhance their contracts with sponsors and equipment manufacturers and fees for personal appearances.

In more recent times, both committees have made sure the players (and their wives) want for nothing during the week. By the time of the match at The Country Club of Brookline in 1999, the amount a US player received for Ryder Cup week was $5,000 and then there were the extras, special gifts for the players, either from the captain or their own Ryder Cup committee and often seen as more valuable than any cheque for expenses. These items might range from engraved watches, other jewellery and expensive luggage to electronic equipment and exclusive memorabilia (often photographs or artwork). Then there were also gifts for the wives and girlfriends, dresses and on-course outfits as well as many more sponsors' presents. All this would be on top of players' clothing, raingear, golf shoes, golf bags and the rest.

Until 1999, the growing amount of expenses and the gifts plus the honour of the occasion seemed sufficient reward for the golfers. And, anyway, a player who qualified for the Ryder Cup in this era would have earned plenty of money, so surely there should be no issue about a week playing for "free".

But Brookline was the moment the American players suddenly looked more closely at the numbers. They saw how the PGA of America – not the PGA Tour of which they were all members – was about to make a very healthy dollar profit from their efforts in the Cup and they questioned the status quo. Some team members, including Tiger Woods (who had recently signed a record $90 million deal with Nike that would help make him the first billionaire athlete in any sport), wanted to know where all the money was going, as well as why some of it was not finding its way into their own bank accounts. Mark O'Meara acted as spokesman and told journalists at a press conference: "You should come and donate your salary to a charity that week, too. You guys don't mind doing that, do you? Either that or [the PGA of America] shouldn't charge the spectators to come and watch."

There were plenty of critics of the players' stance, particularly in the press, but a few months after the Brookline match, the PGA of America felt obliged to come up with a compromise plan: each golfer agreed to forgo actual payment and accept a total of $200,000 worth of donations in his name to a charity of his choice and, perhaps, a college development programme.

That move cost the PGA of America $2.4 million per Ryder Cup and appeared to put the issue to bed. But they were wrong. The feelings of financial resentment emerged again in September 2002. Woods was asked at a World Golf Championship event in Ireland if the $1million first prize on offer would mean more to him than winning the Ryder Cup that took place the following week. Tiger did not hesitate in choosing the cash and gave a simple explanation. "Why? I can think of a million reasons."

Then in 2008 just before he made his Ryder Cup debut, Hunter Mahan threw more fuel on the fire when he referred to the American team as "slaves" working for nothing during Ryder Cup week. Mahan said: "At some point the players might say, 'You know what? We're not doing this anymore, because this is ridiculous'. Mickelson and Tiger – their time is worth money. Is it an honour to play? Yes, it is. But time is valuable. This is a business." He even went so far as to predict a player strike. "Don't be surprised if it happens [American players refusing to play in the Ryder Cup]. It's just not a fun week like it should be. The Presidents Cup is fun. Jack [Nicklaus, the 2007 American captain] just made it fun. From what I've heard, the Ryder Cup just isn't fun. The fun is sucked right out of it. That's the word I hear a lot."

Even more recently, in 2012 at Medinah, the media again raised the payment issue because almost all the competitors had arrived at the match directly from the Tour Championship the previous Sunday with its $10 million prize. Steve Stricker was the most eloquent on the subject. "One [event] is monetary, the other is pride. The FedEx Cup is playing for your year. You can do a lot of good things and you're playing for a lot of money. Next week you're playing for something totally different. You're playing for your country, with teammates. You have partners. You can see it across every guy's face. You go through the whole gamut of emotions." With the verbal dexterity of a top politician, Stricker refused to choose which event was more important to him, thus leaving the money vs patriotism debate still open.

No European players have ever openly questioned the lack of appearance money and most of the ex-Ryder Cup players – even the Americans – have little time for the idea. Four-time American Ryder Cupper Mark Calcavecchia is able to put things into perspective when he recalls his first appearance in 1987. "I was one of the broke-est guys ever to play in the Ryder Cup. Now there are 24 guys who play and don't need another quarter of a million dollars to play in it. Heck, there's 50 guys who would pay a quarter of a million dollars of their own money to play. You can't put a value on that experience."

However, there is a view that players raising the payment issue should not be condemned. Jay Haas speaks for some of his countrymen when he says: "It was unfortunate that some of the guys got crucified for saying that we were the show, but we got no money. They heard how the PGA [of America] was earning tens of millions of dollars and we were earning nothing. So they questioned the money and I understand that now. The charity compromise saved face for everybody and is a good formula. I don't think the players should get paid, they make enough money."

The issue is often related back to the Cup's ownership. The American pro golfers, members of the PGA Tour, do not own any portion of the Ryder Cup. Their counterparts on the European Tour own 60% of their "home" matches and so dictate where the profits are spent. Not that Team Europe receives payment either, but they are happier that they have some degree of ownership.

European players overwhelmingly believe that the experiences of being a part of this incredible team event are priceless. Not only that, but the European Tour committee is also smart enough to recognise that its members are not all from Europe and that the Cup needs to work also for golfers from other continents as well. That means development programmes in non-European countries receive money; the Ryder Cup is taken on tour and displayed to fans in countries as far away as China; and key Ryder Cup media events are staged beyond Europe's borders (such as captaincy announcements in the United Arab Emirates) to bring extra golf awareness to the event and the country. European Ryder Cup director Richard Hills insists: "The Ryder Cup is for all members of the European Tour, whether they are from South Africa or Scotland."

Until the American tour players have some element of control over the Ryder Cup, the issue of player payment will never be fully put to rest. However, if fees or prize money for Cup participants are ever instituted, then it's likely the atmosphere at the matches will change forever.

Participants – In 1927, the Ryder Cup helped settle the question about which was the strongest golfing nation of that era: Britain or America. There really were no other contenders in those days and Samuel Ryder never considered expanding the competition to include other countries. When the matches became too one-sided, then Europe took on the mantle of America's opponents in 1979 because that meant the Ryder Cup could become a contest between the two strongest golfing continents in the world. But the forecasters predict that in a few decades time, neither America nor Europe will develop the majority of the world's best players. That title, they say, will go to Asia and, more particularly, China. The theory is that America became golf's supreme nation in the late 1920s simply because it was the country with the most golfers and, by sometime in the 2020s, Asia will hold that position.

The most recent survey in the US in 2010 by the PGA of America set the number of golfers in the country at 26 million, but that number was down from a peak of 30 million five years earlier. Those numbers certainly indicated to the PGA of America that the so-called Tiger Woods Bubble that galvanised the whole sport in America when the Californian emerged onto the scene in 1996 had burst.

The statistics in Asia, by contrast, show incredible growth. The current number of adult (over 18) regular golfers is a little over 400,000 in China, but that figure would have been close to zero a decade ago. Now it is projected that there will be an astonishing 20 million Chinese golfers by 2020 with many more to come. In a country currently populated by 1.5 billion people (around five times that of America), even those forecasts are conservative, especially as the Chinese government announced in November 2013 that it was easing its one-child-only policy for parents.

The world's best players already know what these statistics mean. Greg Norman told The Golf Channel in 2013: "The east will take over the west in the game of golf within a generation. When you have 1.5 billion people getting a taste of golf they will accelerate the progress." Jack Nicklaus and Nick Faldo have also spoken openly about Asian golf supremacy and, for them, it is not just a matter of economics and the growth of the golfing population – the Asian temperament suits the game, they say.

They point to the success of South Korean golfers as the best current example. What K. J. Choi started with his first win on the PGA Tour in 2002, Y. E. Yang then took to a new level by winning the PGA Championship in 2009, reeling in Tiger Woods in the process. More South Korean men are playing at the top level every season and even they are still to reach the heights their female counterparts who dominate the LPGA Tour where five of the top 10 money earners in 2013 were from that single Asian country. In fact, men's pro golf could be overwhelmed by South Koreans in the same way that the women's game has been for a decade – of the 25 women's majors staged from 2008 to 2013, 10 were won by South Korean golfers, while six more were grabbed by other players from the Asian continent, the Taiwanese Yani Tseng and China's Shanshan Feng.

Yet, if there is a possibility of South Korean domination of men's professional golf in the near future, then the odds on an even bigger impact by Chinese golfers are much shorter. The Chinese golf community delivered its first international hero in 2013 when teenage sensation Guan Tianlang qualified for the Masters tournament. The interest in the 14-year-old was huge around the world and this boy from Guangzhou, north west of Hong Kong, even surprised Tiger Woods when they played together on the Monday of the tournament week. "It's frightening to think that he was born after I won my first Masters," commented Woods at the time. "It's a pretty remarkable story. The kid is 14 and he's good."

Guan made the cut and scored no worse than bogey throughout his 72 holes. He was penalised for slow play, but that only added to the number of words written about him. The great Gary Player was one of many to be dumbstruck by the boy's talent: "Mark my words, we are witnessing the most historic moment golf has experienced in my lifetime."

Players like Guan need more top level tournaments in Asia and that is happening too. The first European Tour event on mainland China took place in May 2004 in Shanghai, though Hong Kong had been hosting a top-tier tournament for many years. The PGA Tour finally jumped on the Asian bandwagon in 2010 when it staged an event in Kuala Lumpur, Malaysia, that was given unofficial American tour status. That event became an official part of the American tour three years later and soon after that in spring 2014 Commissioner Finchem announced a deal to launch a satellite tour along with the China Golf Association and the China Olympic Sports Industry. Players on PGA Tour China will get access to American events as a solid connection is created between the two golfing nations.

On top of China and South Korea, other Asian countries are also likely to produce more stars of the future. Japan has long had its own highly successful tour, while Malaysia, Indonesia and the Phillipines have long staged European Tour-sanctioned events. Then there is India, another country with an enormous population that has barely started to discover golf yet can already boast top pros like Jeev Milka Singh and an occasional European Tour event.

So the threat to the Ryder Cup will come if or when Asian players make up the majority of the best golfers in the world, thus reducing the Ryder Cup to a competition between the continents ranking second and third in golf's hierarchy, a situation that would diminish the event's credibility.

Samuel Ryder's vision was for his cup to be contested by the best players in the world, so could the teams change again like they did in 1979? Could America and Europe one day play Asia for the Ryder Cup? Or could three teams – America, Europe and Asia – all take part in a triangular match? These ideas may seem like fantasy, but they are no more incredible than America vs Europe would have been in 1927.

Rivals – The Ryder Cup has been the pre-eminent professional team golf event across nine decades, but in recent years the marketplace for similar tournaments has become more crowded.

When the PGA Tour invented the Presidents Cup in 1994 with an American team taking on one from the Rest of the World (that is, without any Europeans), it was a direct result of both the Ryder Cup's success as well as the Tour's own inability to gain any ownership of the world's most prestigious golf team trophy.

The Presidents Cup is wholly-owned by the PGA Tour and is now established in the non-Ryder Cup years. The match attracts the best players (Woods has not missed an appearance since he first became eligible for the team in 1998) and big-name captains such as Jack Nicklaus, Gary Player, Arnold Palmer and Greg Norman. There is also a growing interest from the fans. The 2013 contest at Muirfield Village, Ohio, was a sellout of 35,000 spectators on each of the four days of competition with around 2,000 fans travelling in from abroad. Most importantly, corporate America and the TV networks have also been enthusiastic about the event, so the PGA Tour has more than balanced the books on the tournament.

Although it sometimes feels like a made-for-TV-event (so-called innovations like contrived pairings were tried but failed to capture the public's imagination), the Presidents Cup has not reached anywhere near the heights of drama delivered by the Ryder Cup. Some American players have gone on record as saying the Presidents Cup is their preferred team event, but that may be partly to irritate the Europeans.

A more likely reason for the Americans' warm feelings about the Presidents Cup is that they won eight, tied one and lost just one of the first 10 contests. For the players and the ambitious PGA Tour commissioner, what could be better than an international team event with players from a dozen or more countries – including many from Asia – playing in front of huge crowds plus a growing TV audience and plenty of sponsors. And the PGA Tour has total control. And America usually wins.

In 2015, the Presidents Cup will be played in Asia for the first time, specifically in South Korea albeit it at the rather non-Asian-sounding Jack Nicklaus Golf Club in Incheon. The only other three non-American venues – two in Australia and one in Canada – have all proved commercially successful, but the Asian match is the true test of this Cup's future. If the Presidents Cup can unlock the Asian market – and a match in China is only a matter of time – then it could catch the wave of growth in that part of the world and overwhelm the interest in its Ryder Cup rival in terms of Asian viewers and commercial revenues.

But it is not just the Ryder Cup and Presidents Cup that are in the market for fans and money. The Royal Trophy has been operated annually since 2006, a match between players from Europe and Asia dreamed up by Seve Ballesteros. Meanwhile in spring 2014, the inaugural EurAsia Cup took place in Malaysia, again featuring players from those two continents. There is already some friction between these events (one is organised by the Ballesteros family and the other by the European Tour), so who knows how long they will be able to exist alongside each other. Then when you factor in the biennial Seve Trophy – Britain against Continental Europe –suddenly, there is a glut of international team golf matches and not a lot of space in the top players' schedules.

Every one of these events is in competition with the Ryder Cup in some way: a threat to funding, the interest of the best players, sponsors, advertisers or TV schedules and rights fees. But only the strongest will survive and the chances of all five of these matches still being in existence in 10 years time are slim.

Over-Friendliness – Nowadays, every professional golfer aspires to reach the world's top 50. Once your ranking sends you into this group, the world is at your feet. Best of all, the top 50 players play in all the best events including the four major titles, the four World Golf Championships. It is almost impossible for a modern-day Ryder Cup player not to come from this elite company and that means the competition's opponents see more of each other than ever before.

The knock-on effect is that the nature of the confrontation between the Ryder Cup teams has changed. Whereas the players were originally virtual strangers who fought tooth and nail without regard for their opponents' feelings, the modern-day contests are often between good friends or, at the very least, golfers who know each other very well.

The old-style relationship between the players was more visceral. When Neil Coles made his Cup debut in 1961 at Royal Lytham, his opponents were often unknown to him. "You met [your opponent] on the first tee and off you went. It was just another golf tournament. I played Gene Littler in the singles and came down the last all square. He holed a putt right across the green to stop me from beating him. 'Bloody Americans' is what I said to one of the officials who replied to me 'He is the US Open Champion'. I didn't have a clue."

Similarly, Howard Clark was certainly not on first-name terms with the likes of Jack Nicklaus, Tom Watson and Ray Floyd when he made his Ryder Cup debut in 1977. Yorkshireman Clark was only 23 and yet to even win his maiden European Tour event. "In 1977, I was intimidated, totally, and it was strange because you were playing golfers who you saw on TV. We were up against icons in golf because in my day, the Americans were often most of the top 12 golfers in the world," says Clark. He was thrown into combat with major champions at a time when he had only played in three Open Championships and had missed the cut twice.

Now a TV commentator, Clark sees a good deal of the top players on a regular basis and is amazed that the intensity levels of the current matches are so high despite the fact that Americans and Europeans mix so regularly. "Now the [Ryder Cup] players are playing people who they see every week. There is less of a divide now [between the players] because of the world golf rankings. I just hope the friendliness won't detract from the intensity."

Clark played only a handful of times in America (including just four US-based majors) whereas an increasing number of European players of today are basing themselves in the States to play more on the PGA Tour. Whereas once upon a time Team Europe was a tightly knit group that travelled to and from matches together, over half the Europeans who played in the 2012 Ryder Cup match at Medinah simply returned to their homes in America rather than fly back with the trophy, their captain, Jose Maria Olazabal, and the other victorious team members.

Former American Ryder Cup players also recognise the difference in the atmosphere between the teams. Kenny Perry played in two matches – 2004 and 2008 – amid worries that there could be too much friendliness among the players rather than a little frisson. "We never hated anyone. We just wanted to represent our country well. But now the Europeans are more our friends. We see with them every day, we play with them every day. We don't have the intimidation factor any more."

The modern-day players are no longer frightened of anyone and claim to be able to put friendships to one side for three days of Ryder Cup competition. They say that their desire to win has never been greater. But while the matches are still incredibly tense and hard-fought, there are observers who worry that the players know each other too well and that the very element that has makes so many great sporting rivalries so watchable – the antipathy between the competitors – is being slowly eroded at the Ryder Cup.

One recent example was the exciting conclusion to a key 2012 singles match, Europe's Justin Rose vs Phil Mickelson. A smile plus thumbs-up from the American when Rose holed a monster putt on the 17th green to level the match was generally viewed as a marvellous act of sportsmanship. But when Rose won a crucial point for his team with a birdie putt on the 18th, every instinct told him to yell, scream and fist pump to his nearby teammates. Instead, he chose to bottle those feelings and shake hands with Mickelson as a mark of respect. Was this an indication of the softening of the battle lines between the two teams?

Rory McIlroy famously said prior to his 2010 Ryder Cup debut that the matches were glorified exhibitions. That is a statement he soon retracted after playing at Celtic Manor, but there is no question that the rivalry has morphed into something more subtle than the simple love-hate relationships of the past.

Fighting a faceless opponent has to be different than battling against a friend. Sometimes the celebrations crossed the line into boorishness in previous matches such as in 1999 in Brookline, but it is the added spice of the rancour and ill feeling between the two teams that makes the Ryder Cup more compelling as a sporting spectacle. Any significant dilution of that feeling, born out of modern-day friendliness towards the opponent, and the event will surely suffer.

Sensible summation

Having talked to dozens of modern players, captains, administrators and others involved, it is clear that the majority of them love the Ryder Cup just the way it is. That is no great surprise. Virtually everything about the matches appears in a healthy condition – crowds, TV, sponsorship and even the plans for its immediate future.

And there are few complaints from Ryder Cup golfers and administrators from the past. A few would prefer more respect among the players and others wonder about controlling the expanding crowds, but most are simply stunned by the contest's development over the last 40 years from one of golf's least lucrative events into its most successful.

In terms of host venues, the Cup finds itself another new American state in 2016 when the matches come to Minnesota for the first time, specifically to Hazeltine National Golf Club while Le Golf National in Paris in 2018 will open up another entire country to the power of the contests on a course that could have been built for matchplay. Whistling Straits, Wisconsin, will be another remarkably picturesque venue for spectators in 2020 and, for fans watching on TV, akin to Kiawah Island in 1991.

With the two sets of Ryder Cup committees becoming increasingly adept at their operational jobs, with the players ever more desperate to take part, and with the media, fans and commercial partners all still fascinated by the matches, it might seem foolish not to predict good times ahead for this series.

Yet, by studying the history of the matches, the laws of the Ryder Cup's own natural development dictate caution in forecasting too much blue sky ahead. If you look back more than 30 years into the past, it was a time when Europe first joined the battle and the Cup's future still looked questionable, so the Cup's current success would have seemed like a fantasy back then. And go back in time another 30 years to the late 1940s and today's matches would have looked like even more like science fiction. Therefore, in over three decades time as we approach 2050 (the end-point of the SWOT analysis), then who can really say for certain what the contests might look like. Placing a bet on particular differences between the make-up of the teams or the schedule or even the format would be utter foolishness. Suffice to say that change will come.

Final fantastical forecast

So it is time for a fantasy forecast, worst-case scenarios, most unlikely outcomes. After a SWOT analysis, not all of the strengths and opportunities will be maximised and some of the weaknesses and threats are bound to have an influence. Not only that, but currently unknown factors will also come along to either help the Ryder Cup's cause, or cause it to stumble. So what might be the fantastical scenarios for the Ryder Cup by the year 2050? Maybe these will be the headlines.

Organisers of the 58th Ryder Cup believe the 20% drop in television income this year will not affect the quality of the tournament if another major sponsor can be found. European Ryder Cup captaincy falls to Italy's 57-year-old Matteo Maneserro while elder statesman Richard "Rickie" Fowler has accepted a third term as captain of Team USA at the age of 62, making him the second oldest skipper after Tom Watson who plans to celebrate his 101st birthday at the event.

Ryder Cup television audiences are expected to be down again this year because there are still no US or European professional players in the world's top 20 and this has particularly hit the global audience figures. TV analysts say that while Chinese, Japanese, Indian and South Korean golfers dominate the majors and the upper echelons of the world rankings, audiences will be less interested in the Cup than a generation earlier. Only a small handful of men from either USA or Europe have reached golf's elite since 2040.

The first staging of the Ryder Cup's new rival team tournament – The Presidents Continental Challenge Cup presented by Google – was judged a huge success as worldwide advertising and other commercial partners piled in. The four-way World Cup-style team event between Europe, The Americas, Asia and Africa/Australasia and was won easily by Asia and prompted record global audience ratings for golf on Google's own digital television network. The match was the brainchild of the PGA Tour as an extension of their highly successful Presidents Cup and brought over 100,000 spectators per day to the Mission Hills golf complex in China.

Players' fees for the next Presidents event in 2051 have been set at $1 million for each winning golfer down to $250,000 for a fourth place team member with 15% of gross merchandising sales within their own regions being shared by the players.

During an interview on YouTube's Global Golf TV news show, 93-year-old Sir Nick Faldo says his calls for the merger of the Ryder Cup and the EurAsia Cup should have been taken seriously because the Presidents Continental Challenge is now a real threat to the future of the two older competitions.

The Seve Trophy – an amalgamation with the Junior Ryder Cup – will continue to be played by golfers aged 18 and under, a change that is now celebrating its second decade.

Could Samuel Ryder have predicted in 1927 that the cup which bears his name would one day be contested by two dozen multimillionaire golfers; in countries like Spain and France; on golf courses approaching 8,000 yards in length; witnessed by 45,000 spectators every day; and broadcast by television companies beaming pictures to over 180 countries along with an extra audience on something called the worldwide web? It would have seemed like a daydream… as ridiculous to him as forecasting a black man would ever become the world's No 1 golfer.

Given that change of all kinds can move so quickly in the 21st century, maybe the next 30 years of the Ryder Cup's story will be more unpredictable than some experts believe. If so, then nothing – not even these fantasy headlines for 2050 – is impossible.

Index

Y

Z

Ryder Cup Results 1927-2012

Winners and Losers

A total of 39 Ryder Cup Matches have been played on a biennial basis between 1927 and 2012. Here are the full results from each of those contests:

1927
WORCESTER COUNTRY CLUB, Massachusetts
Captains: E. Ray (British Isles), W. Hagen (U.S.A.)

BRITISH ISLES		U.S.A.	
Foursomes			
E. Ray & F. Robson	0	W. Hagen & J. Golden (2&1)	1
G. Duncan & A. Compston	0	J. Farrell & J. Turnesa (8&6)	1
A. Havers & H. Jolly	0	G. Sarazen & A. Watrous (3&2)	1
A. Boomer & C. Whitcombe (7&5)	1	L. Diegel & W. Mehlhorn	0
Singles			
A. Compston	0	W. Mehlhorn (1 hole)	1
A. Boomer	0	J. Farrell (5&4)	1
H. Jolly	0	J. Golden (8&7)	1
E. Ray	0	L. Diegel (7&5)	1
C. Whitcombe	½	G. Sarazen	½
A. Havers	0	W. Hagen (2&1)	1
F. Robson	0	A. Watrous (3&2)	1
G. Duncan (1 hole)	1	J. Turnesa	0

Match result: British Isles 2½ U.S.A. 9½

1929
MOORTOWN, Leeds, England
Captains: G. Duncan (British Isles), W. Hagen (U.S.A.)

BRITISH ISLES		U.S.A.	
Foursomes			
C. Whitcombe & A. Compston	½	J. Farrell & J. Turnesa	½
A. Boomer & G. Duncan	o	L. Diegel & A. Espinosa (7&5)	1
A. Mitchell & F. Robson (2&1)	1	G. Sarazen & E. Dudley	o
E. Whitcombe & H. Cotton	o	J. Golden & W. Hagen (2 holes)	1
Singles			
C. Whitcombe (8&6)	1	J. Farrell	o
G. Duncan (10&8)	1	W. Hagen	o
A. Mitchell	o	L. Diegel (9&8)	1
A. Compston (6&4)	1	G. Sarazen	o
A. Boomer (4&3)	1	J. Turnesa	o
F. Robson	o	H. Smith (4&2)	1
H. Cotton (4&3)	1	A. Watrous	o
E. Whitcombe	½	A. Espinosa	½

Match result: British Isles 7 U.S.A. 5

1931
SCIOTO COUNTRY CLUB, Columbus, Ohio
Captains: C. Whitcombe (British Isles), W. Hagen (U.S.A.)

BRITISH ISLES		U.S.A.	
Foursomes			
A. Compston & W.H. Davies	o	G. Sarazen & J. Farrell (8&7)	1
G. Duncan & A. Havers	o	W. Hagen & D. Shute (10&9)	1
A. Mitchell & F. Robson (3&1)	1	L. Diegel & A. Espinosa	o
S. Easterbrook & E. Whitcombe	o	W. Burke & W. Cox (3&2)	1
Singles			
A. Compston	o	W. Burke (7&6)	1
F. Robson	o	G. Sarazen (7&6)	1
W. Davies (4 &3)	1	J. Farrell	o
A. Mitchell	o	W. Cox (3&1)	1
C. Whitcombe	o	W. Hagen (4&3)	1
B. Hodson	o	D. Shute (8&6)	1
E. Whitcombe	o	A. Espinosa (2&1)	1
A. Havers (4&3)	1	C. Wood	o

Match result: British Isles 3 U.S.A. 9

1933
SOUTHPORT & AINSDALE, Lancashire, England
Captains: J.H. Taylor (British Isles), W. Hagen (U.S.A.)

BRITISH ISLES		U.S.A.	
Foursomes			
P. Alliss & C. Whitcornbe	½	G. Sarazen & W. Hagen	½
A. Mitchell & A. Havers (3&2)	1	O. Dutra & D. Shute	0
W. Davies & S. Easterbrook (1 hole)	1	C. Wood & P. Runyan	0
A. Padgham & A. Perry	0	E. Dudley & W. Burke (1 bole)	1
Singles			
A. Padgham	0	G. Sarazen (6&4)	1
A. Mitchell (9&8)	1	O. Dutra	0
A. Lacey	0	W. Hagen (2&1)	1
W. Davies	0	C. Wood (4&3)	1
P. Alliss (2&1)	1	P. Runyan	0
A. Havers (4&3)	1	L. Diegel	0
S. Easterbrook (1 hole)	1	D. Shute	0
C. Whitcombe	0	H. Smith (2&1)	1

Match result: British Isles 6½ U.S.A. 5½

1935
RIDGEWOOD COUNTRY CLUB, New Jersey
Captains: C. Whitcombe (British Isles), W. Hagen (U.S.A.)

BRITISH ISLES		U.S.A.	
Foursomes			
A. Perry & J. Busson	0	G. Sarazen & W. Hagen (7&6)	1
A. Padgham & P. Alliss	0	H. Picard & J. Revolta (6&5)	1
W. Cox & E. Jarman	0	P. Runyan & H. Smith (9&8)	1
C. Whitcombe & E. Whitcombe (1 hole)	1	O. Dutra & K. Laffoon	0
Singles			
J. Busson	0	G. Sarazen (3&2)	1
R. Burton	0	P. Runyan (5&3)	1
R. Whitcombe	0	J. Revolta (2&1)	1
A. Padgham	0	O. Dutra (4&2)	1
P. Alliss (1 hole)	1	C. Wood	0
W. Cox	½	H. Smith	½
E. Whitcombe	0	H. Picard (3&2)	1
A. Perry	½	S. Parks	½

Match result: British Isles 3 U.S.A. 9

1937
SOUTHPORT & AINSDALE, Lancashire, England
Captains: C. Whitcombe (GB), W. Hagen (U.S.A.)

BRITISH ISLES		U.S.A.	
Foursomes			
A. Padgham & H. Cotton	o	E. Dudley & B. Nelson (4&2)	1
A. Lacey & W. Cox	o	R. Guldahl & T. Manero (2&1)	1
C. Whitcombe & D. Rees	½	G. Sarazen & D. Shute	½
P. Alliss & R. Burton (2&1)	1	H. Picard & J. Revolta	o
Singles			
A. Padgham	o	R. Guldahl (8&7)	1
S. King	½	D. Shute	½
D. Rees (3&1)	1	B. Nelson	o
H. Cotton (5&3)	1	T. Manero	o
P. Alliss	o	G. Sarazen (1 hole)	1
R. Burton	o	S. Snead (5&4)	1
A. Perry	o	E. Dudley (2&1)	1
A. Lacey	o	H. Picard (2&1)	1

Match result: British Isles 4 U.S.A. 8

1947
PORTLAND GOLF CLUB, Oregon
Captains: H. Cotton (British Isles), B. Hogan (U.S.A.)

BRITISH ISLES		U.S.A.	
Foursomes			
H. Cotton & A. Lees	o	E. Oliver & L. Worsham (10&9)	1
F. Daly & C. Ward	o	S. Snead & L. Mangrum (6&5)	1
J. Adams & M. Faulkner	o	B. Hogan & J. Demaret (2 holes)	1
D. Rees & S. King	o	B. Nelson & H. Barron (2&1)	1
Singles			
F. Daly	o	E.J. Harrison (5&4)	1
J. Adams	o	L. Worsham (3&2)	1
M. Faulkner	o	L. Mangrum (6&5)	1
C. Ward	o	E. Oliver (4&3)	1
A. Lees	o	B. Nelson (2&1)	1
H. Cotton	o	S. Snead (5&4)	1
D. Rees	o	J. Demaret (3&2)	1
S. King (4&3)	1	H. Keiser	o

Match result: British Isles 1 U.S.A. 11

1949
GANTON, Yorkshire, England
Captains: C. Whitcombe (British Isles), B. Hogan (U.S.A.)

BRITISH ISLES		U.S.A.	
Foursomes			
M. Faulkner & J. Adams (2&1)	1	E.J. Harrison & J. Palmer	0
F. Daly & K. Bousfield (4&2)	1	R. Hamilton & S. Alexander	0
C. Ward & S. King	0	J. Demaret & C. Heafner (4&3)	1
R. Burton & A. Lees (1 hole)	1	S. Snead & L. Mangrum	0
Singles			
M. Faulkner	0	E.J. Harrison (8&7)	1
J. Adams (2&1)	1	J. Palmer	0
C. Ward	0	S. Snead (6&5)	1
D. Rees (6&4)	1	R. Hamilton	0
R. Burton	0	C. Heafner (3&2)	1
S. King	0	C. Harbert (4&3)	1
A. Lees	0	J. Demaret (7&6)	1
F. Daly	0	L. Mangrum (4&3)	1

Match result: British Isles 5 U.S.A. 7

1951
PINEHURST, North Carolina
Captains: A. Lacey (British Isles), S. Snead (U.S.A.)

BRITISH ISLES		U.S.A.	
Foursomes			
M. Faulkner & D. Rees	0	C. Heafner & J. Burke (5&3)	1
C. Ward & A. Lees (2&1)	1	E. Oliver & H. Ransom	0
J. Adams & J. Panton	0	S. Snead & L. Mangrum (5&4)	1
F. Daly & K. Bousfield	0	B. Hogan & J. Demaret (5&4)	1
Singles			
J. Adams	0	J. Burke (4&3)	1
D. Rees	0	J. Demaret (2 holes)	1
F. Daly	½	C. Heafner	½
H. Weetman	0	L. Mangrum (6&5)	1
A. Lees (2&1)	1	E. Oliver	0
C. Ward	0	B. Hogan (3&2)	1
J. Panton	0	S. Alexander (8&7)	1
M. Faulkner	0	S. Snead (4&3)	1

Match result: British Isles 2½ U.S.A. 9½

1953
WENTWORTH, Surrey, England
Captains: H. Cotton (British Isles), L. Mangrum (U.S.A.)

BRITISH ISLES		U.S.A.	
Foursomes			
H. Weetman & P. Alliss	o	D. Douglas & E. Oliver (2&1)	1
E. Brown & J. Panton	o	L. Mangrum & S. Snead (8&7)	1
J. Adams & B. Hunt	o	T. Kroll & J. Burke (7&5)	1
F. Daly & H. Bradshaw (1 hole)	1	J. Burkemo & C. Middlecoff	o
Singles			
D. Rees	o	J. Burke (2&1)	1
F. Daly (9&7)	1	T. Kroll	o
E. Brown (2 holes)	1	L. Mangrum	o
H. Weetman (1 hole)	1	S. Snead	o
M. Faulkner	o	C. Middlecoff (3&1)	1
P. Alliss	o	J. Turnesa (1 hole)	1
B. Hunt	½	D. Douglas	½
H. Bradshaw (3&2)	1	F. Haas	o

Match result: British Isles 5½ U.S.A. 6½

1955
THUNDERBIRD GOLF & COUNTRY CLUB, Palm Springs, California
Captains: D. Rees (British Isles), C. Harbert (U.S.A.)

BRITISH ISLES		U.S.A.	
Foursomes			
J. Fallon & J. Jacobs (1 hole)	1	C. Harper & J. Barber	o
E. Brown & S. Scott	o	D. Ford & T. Kroll (5&4)	1
A. Lees & H. Weetman	o	J. Burke & T. Bolt (1 hole)	1
H. Bradshaw & D. Rees	o	S. Snead & C. Middlecoff (3&2)	1
Singles			
C. O'Connor	o	T. Bolt (4&2)	1
S. Scott	o	C. Harbert (3&2)	1
J. Jacobs (1 hole)	1	C. Middlecoff	o
D. Rees	o	S. Snead (3&1)	1
A. Lees (3&2)	1	M. Furgol	o
E. Brown (3&2)	1	J. Barber	o
H. Bradshaw	o	J. Burke (3&2)	1
H. Weetman	o	D. Ford (3&2)	1

Match result: British Isles 4 U.S.A. 8

1957
LINDRICK, Yorkshire, England
Captains: D. Rees (British Isles), J. Burke (U.S.A.)

BRITISH ISLES		U.S.A.	
Foursomes			
P. Alliss & B. Hunt	0	D. Ford & D. Finsterwald (2&1)	1
K. Bousfield & D. Rees (3&2)	1	A. Wall & F. Hawkins	0
M. Faulkner & H. Weetman	0	T. Kroll & J. Burke (4&3)	1
C. O'Connor & E.C. Brown	0	R. Mayer & T. Bolt (7&5)	1
Singles			
E. Brown (4&3)	1	T. Bolt	0
P. Mills (5&3)	1	J. Burke	0
P. Alliss	0	F. Hawkins (2&1)	1
K. Bousfield (4&3)	1	L. Hebert	0
D. Rees (7&6)	1	E. Furgol	0
B. Hunt (6&5)	1	D. Ford	0
C. O'Connor (7&6)	1	D. Finsterwald	0
H. Bradshaw	½	R. Mayer	½

Match result: British Isles 7½ U.S.A. 4½

1959
ELDORADO COUNTRY CLUB, Palm Desert, California
Captains: D. Rees (British Isles), S. Snead (U.S.A.)

BRITISH ISLES		U.S.A.	
Foursomes			
B. Hunt & E. Brown	0	R. Rosburg & M. Souchak (5&4)	1
D. Rees & K. Bousfield	0	J. Boros & D. Finsterwald (2 holes)	1
C. O'Connor & P. Alliss (3&2)	1	A. Wall & D. Ford	0
H. Weetman & D. Thomas	½	S. Snead & C. Middlecoff	½
Singles			
N. Drew	½	D. Ford	½
K. Bousfield	0	M. Souchak (3&2)	1
H. Weetman	0	R. Rosburg (6&5)	1
D. Thomas	0	S. Snead (6&5)	1
C. O'Connor	0	A. Wall (7&6)	1
D. Rees	0	D. Finsterwald (1 hole)	1
P. Alliss	½	H. Hebert	½
E. Brown (4&3)	1	C. Middlecoff	0

Match result: British Isles 3½ U.S.A. 8½

1961
ROYAL LYTHAM & ST ANNES, Lancashire, England
Captains: D. Rees (British Isles), J. Barber (U.S.A.)

BRITISH ISLES		U.S.A.	
Morning Foursomes			
C. O'Connor & P. Alliss (4&3)	1	D. Ford & G. Littler	0
J. Panton & B. Hunt	0	A. Wall & J. Hebert (4&3)	1
D. Rees & K. Bousfield	0	W. Casper & A. Palmer (2&1)	1
T. Haliburton & N. Coles	0	W. Collins & M. Souchak (1 hole)	1
Afternoon Foursomes			
C. O'Connor & P. Alliss	0	A. Wall & J. Hebert (1 hole)	1
J. Panton & B. Hunt	0	W. Casper & A. Palmer (5&4)	1
D. Rees & K. Bousfield (4&2)	1	W. Collins & M. Souchak	0
T. Haliburton & N. Coles	0	J. Barber & D. Finsterwald (1 hole)	1
Morning Singles			
H. Weetman	0	D. Ford (1 hole)	1
R. Moffitt	0	M. Souchak (5&4)	1
P. Alliss	½	A. Palmer	½
K. Bousfield	0	W. Casper (5&3)	1
D. Rees (2&1)	1	J. Hebert	0
N. Coles	½	G. Littler	½
B. Hunt (5&4)	1	J. Barber	0
C. O'Connor	0	D. Finsterwald (2&1)	1
Afternoon Singles			
H. Weetman	0	A. Wall (1 hole)	1
P. Alliss (3&2)	1	W. Collins	0
B. Hunt	0	M. Souchak (2&1)	1
T. Haliburton	0	A. Palmer (2&1)	1
D. Rees (4&3)	1	D. Ford	0
K. Bousfield (1 hole)	1	J. Barber	0
N. Coles (1 hole)	1	D. Finsterwald	0
C. O'Connor	½	G. Littler	½

Match result: British Isles 9½ U.S.A. 14½

1963
EAST LAKE COUNTRY CLUB, Atlanta, Georgia
Captains: J. Fallon (British Isles), A. Palmer (U.S.A.)

BRITISH ISLES		U.S.A.	
Morning Foursomes			
B. Huggett & G. Will (3&2)	1	A. Palmer & J. Pott	o
P. Alliss & C. O'Connor	o	W. Casper & D. Ragan (1 hole)	1
D. Thomas & H. Weetman	½	G. Littler & D. Finsterwald	½
N. Coles & B. Hunt	½	J. Boros & A. Lema	½
Afternoon Foursomes			
D. Thomas & H. Weetman	o	W. Maxwell & R. Goalby (4&3)	1
B. Huggett & G. Will	o	A. Palmer & W. Casper (5&4)	1
N. Coles & G.M. Hunt	o	G. Littler & D. Finsterwald (2&1)	1
T. Haliburton & B. Hunt	o	J. Boros & J. Lema (1 hole)	1
Morning Fourballs			
B. Huggett & D. Thomas	o	A. Palmer & D. Finsterwald (5&4)	1
P. Alliss & B. Hunt	½	G. Littler & J. Boros	½
H. Weetman & G. Will	o	W. Casper & W. Maxwell (3&2)	1
N. Coles & C. O'Connor (1 hole)	1	R. Goalby & D. Ragan	o
Afternoon Fourballs			
N. Coles & C. O'Connor	o	A. Palmer & D. Finsterwald (3&2)	1
P. Alliss & B. Hunt	o	A. Lema & J. Pott (1 hole)	1
T. Haliburton & G.M. Hunt	o	W. Casper & W. Maxwell (2&1)	1
B. Huggett & D. Thomas	½	R. Goalby & D. Ragan	½
Morning Singles			
G.M. Hunt	o	A. Lema (5&3)	1
B. Huggett (3&1)	1	J. Pott	o
P. Alliss (1 hole)	1	A. Palmer	o
N. Coles	½	W. Casper	½
D. Thomas	o	R. Goalby (3&2)	1
C. O'Connor	o	G. Littler (1 hole)	1
H. Weetman (1 hole)	1	J. Boros	o
B. Hunt (2 holes)	1	D. Finsterwald	o
Afternoon Singles			
G. Will	o	A. Palmer (3&2)	1
N. Coles	o	D. Ragan (2&1)	1
P. Alliss	½	A. Lema	½
T. Haliburton	o	G. Littler (6&5)	1
H. Weetman	o	J. Boros (2&1)	1
C. O'Connor	o	W. Maxwell (2&1)	1
D. Thomas	o	D. Finsterwald (4&3)	1
B. Hunt	o	R. Goalby (2&1)	1

Match result: British Isles 9 U.S.A. 23

1965
ROYAL BIRKDALE, Lancashire, England

Captains: H. Weetman (British Isles), B. Nelson (U.S.A.)

BRITISH ISLES		U.S.A.	
Morning Foursomes			
L. Platts & P. Butler	o	J. Boros & A. Lema (1 hole)	1
D. Thomas & G. Will (6&5)	1	A. Palmer & D. Marr	o
B. Hunt & N. Coles	o	W. Casper & G. Littler (2&1)	1
P. Alliss & C. O'Connor (5&4)	1	K. Venturi & D. January	o
Afternoon Foursomes			
D. Thomas & G. Will	o	A. Palmer & D. Marr (6&5)	1
P. Alliss & C. O'Connor (2&1)	1	W. Casper & G. Littler	o
J. Martin & J. Hitchcock	o	J. Boros & A. Lema (5&4)	1
B. Hunt & N. Coles (3&2)	1	K. Venturi & D. January	o
Morning Fourballs			
D. Thomas & G. Will	o	D. January & T. Jacobs (1 hole)	1
L. Platts & P. Butler	½	W. Casper & G. Littler	½
P. Alliss & C. O'Connor	o	A. Palmer & D. Marr (6&4)	1
B. Hunt & N. Coles (1 hole)	1	J. Boros & A. Lema	o
Afternoon Fourballs			
P. Alliss & C. O'Connor (1 hole)	1	A. Palmer & D. Marr	o
D. Thomas & G. Will	o	D. January & T. Jacobs (1 hole)	1
L. Platts & P. Butler	½	W. Casper & G. Littler	½
B. Hunt & N. Coles	o	K. Venturi & A. Lema (1 hole)	1
Morning Singles			
J. Hitchcock	o	A. Palmer (3&2)	1
L. Platts	o	J. Boros (4&2)	1
P. Butler	o	A. Lema (1 hole)	1
N. Coles	o	D. Marr (2 holes)	1
B. Hunt (2 holes)	1	G. Littler	o
D. Thomas	o	T. Jacobs (2&1)	1
P. Alliss (1 hole)	1	W. Casper	o
G. Will	½	D. January	½
Afternoon Singles			
C. O'Connor	o	A. Lema (6&4)	1
J. Hitchcock	o	J. Boros (2&1)	1
P. Butler	o	A. Palmer (2 holes)	1
P. Alliss (3&1)	1	K. Venturi	o
N. Coles (3&2)	1	W. Casper	o
G. Will	o	G. Littler (2&1)	1
B. Hunt	o	D. Marr (1 Hole)	1
L. Platts (1 hole)	1	T. Jacobs	o

Match result: British Isles 12½ U.S.A. 19½

1967
CHAMPIONS GOLF CLUB, Houston, Texas
Captains: D. Rees (British Isles), B. Hogan (U.S.A.)

BRITISH ISLES		U.S.A.	
Morning Foursomes			
B. Huggett & G. Will	½	W. Casper & J. Boros	½
P. Alliss & C. O'Connor	o	A. Palmer & G. Dickinson (2&1)	1
A. Jacklin & D. Thomas (4&3)	1	D. Sanders & G. Brewer	o
B. Hunt & N. Coles	o	R. Nichols & J. Pott (6&5)	1
Afternoon Foursomes			
B. Huggett & G. Will	o	W. Casper & J. Boros (1 hole)	1
M. Gregson & H. Boyle	o	G. Dickinson & A. Palmer (5&4)	1
A. Jacklin & D. Thomas (3&2)	1	G. Littler & A. Geiberger	o
P. Alliss & C. O'Connor	o	R. Nichols & J. Pott (2&1)	1
Morning Fourballs			
P. Alliss & C. O'Connor	o	W. Casper & G. Brewer (3&2)	1
B. Hunt & N. Coles	o	R. Nichols & J. Pott (1 hole)	1
A. Jacklin & D. Thomas	o	G. Littler & A. Geiberger (1 hole)	1
B. Huggett & G. Will	o	G. Dickinson & D. Sanders (3&2)	1
Afternoon Fourballs			
B. Hunt & N. Coles	o	W. Casper & G. Brewer (5&3)	1
P. Alliss & M. Gregson	o	G. Dickinson & D. Sanders (3&2)	1
G. Will & H. Boyle	o	A. Palmer & J. Boros (1 hole)	1
A. Jacklin & D. Thomas	½	G. Littler & A. Geiberger	½
Morning Singles			
H. Boyle	o	G. Brewer (4&3)	1
P. Alliss	o	W. Casper (2&1)	1
A. Jacklin	o	A. Palmer (3&2)	1
B. Huggett (1 hole)	1	J. Boros	o
N. Coles (2&1)	1	D. Sanders	o
M. Gregson	o	A. Geiberger (4&2)	1
D. Thomas	½	G. Littler	½
B. Hunt	½	R. Nichols	½
Afternoon Singles			
B. Huggett	o	A. Palmer (5&3)	1
P. Alliss (2&1)	1	G. Brewer	o
A. Jacklin	o	G. Dickinson (3&2)	1
C. O'Connor	o	R. Nichols (3&2)	1
G. Will	o	J. Pott (3&1)	1
M. Gregson	o	A. Geiberger (2&1)	1
B. Hunt	½	J. Boros	½
N. Coles (2&1)	1	D. Sanders	o

Match result: British Isles 8½ U.S.A. 23½

1969
ROYAL BIRKDALE, Lancashire, England
Captains: E. Brown (British Isles), S. Snead (U.S.A.)

BRITISH ISLES		U.S.A.	
Morning Foursomes			
N. Coles & B. Huggett (3&2)	1	M. Barber & R. Floyd	0
B. Gallacher & M. Bembridge (2&1)	1	L. Trevino & K. Still	0
A. Jacklin & P. Townsend (3&1)	1	D. Hill & T. Aaron	0
C. O'Connor & P. Alliss	½	W. Casper & F. Beard	½
Afternoon Foursomes			
N. Coles & B. Huggett	0	D. Hill & T. Aaron (1 hole)	1
B. Gallacher & M. Bembridge	0	L. Trevino & G. Littler (2 holes)	1
A. Jacklin & P. Townsend (1 hole)	1	W. Casper & F. Beard	0
P. Butler & B. Hunt	0	J. Nicklaus & D. Sikes (1 hole)	1
Morning Fourballs			
C. O'Connor & P. Townsend (1 hole)	1	D. Hill & D. Douglass	0
B. Huggett & A. Caygill	½	R. Floyd & M. Barber	½
B. Barnes & P. Alliss	0	L. Trevino & G. Littler (1 hole)	1
A. Jacklin & N. Coles (1 hole)	1	J. Nicklaus & D. Sikes	0
Afternoon Fourballs			
P. Butler & P. Townsend	0	W. Casper & F. Beard (2 holes)	1
B. Huggett & B. Gallacher	0	D. Hill & K. Still (2&1)	1
M. Bembridge & B. Hunt	½	T. Aaron & R. Floyd	½
A. Jacklin & N. Coles	½	L. Trevino & M. Barber	½
Morning Singles			
P. Alliss	0	L. Trevino (2&1)	1
P. Townsend	0	D. Hill (5&4)	1
N. Coles (1 hole)	1	T. Aaron	0
B. Barnes	0	W. Casper (1 hole)	1
C. O'Connor (5&4)	1	F. Beard	0
M. Bembridge (1 hole)	1	K. Still	0
P. Butler (1 hole)	1	R. Floyd	0
A. Jacklin (4&3)	1	J. Nicklaus	0
Afternoon Singles			
B. Barnes	0	D. Hill (4&2)	1
B. Gallacher (4&3)	1	L. Trevino	0
M. Bembridge	0	M. Barber (7&6)	1
P. Butler (3&2)	1	D. Douglass	0
N. Coles	0	D. Sikes (4&3)	1
C. O'Connor	0	G. Littler (2&1)	1
B. Huggett	½	W. Casper	½
A. Jacklin	½	J. Nicklaus	½

Match result: British Isles 16 U.S.A. 16

1971
OLD WARSON COUNTRY CLUB, St Louis, Missouri
Captains: E. Brown (British Isles), J. Hebert (U.S.A.)

BRITISH ISLES		U.S.A.	
Morning Foursomes			
N. Coles & C. O'Connor (2&1)	1	W. Casper & M Barber	0
P. Townsend & P. Oosterhuis	0	A. Palmer & G. Dickinson (2 holes)	1
B. Huggett & A. Jacklin (3&2)	1	J. Nicklaus & D. Stockton	0
M. Bembridge & P. Butler (1 hole)	1	C. Coody & F. Beard	0
Afternoon Foursomes			
H. Bannerman & .B. Gallacher (2&1)	1	W. Casper & M. Barber	0
P. Townsend & P. Oosterhuis	0	A. Palmer & G. Dickinson (1 hole)	1
B. Huggett & A. Jacklin	½	L. Trevino & M. Rudolph	½
M. Bembridge & P. Butler	0	J. Nicklaus & J.C. Snead (5&3)	1
Morning Fourballs			
C. O'Connor & B. Barnes	0	L. Trevino & M. Rudolph (2&1)	1
N. Coles & J. Garner	0	F. Beard & J.C. Snead (2&1)	1
P. Oosterhuis & B. Gallacher	0	A. Palmer & G. Dickinson (5&4)	1
P. Townsend & H. Bannerman	0	J. Nicklaus & G. Littler (2&1)	1
Afternoon Fourballs			
B. Gallacher & P. Oosterhuis (1 hole)	1	L. Trevino & W. Casper	0
A. Jacklin & B. Huggett	0	G. Littler & J.C. Snead (2&1)	1
P. Townsend & H. Bannerman	0	A. Palmer & J. Nicklaus (1 hole)	1
N. Coles & C. O'Connor	½	C. Coody & F. Beard	½
Morning Singles			
A. Jacklin	0	L. Trevino (1 hole)	1
B. Gallacher	½	D. Stockton	½
B. Barnes (1 hole)	1	M. Rudolph	0
P. Oosterhuis (4&3)	1	G. Littler	0
P. Townsend	0	J. Nicklaus (3&2)	1
C. O'Connor	0	G. Dickinson (5&4)	1
H. Bannerman	½	A. Palmer	½
N. Coles	½	F. Beard	½
Afternoon Singles			
B. Huggett	0	L. Trevino (7&6)	1
A. Jacklin	0	J.C. Snead (1 hole)	1
B. Barnes (2&1)	1	M. Barber	0
P. Townsend	0	D. Stockton (1 hole)	1
B. Gallacher (2&1)	1	C. Coody	0
N. Coles	0	J. Nicklaus (5&3)	1
P. Oosterhuis (3&2)	1	A. Palmer	0
H. Bannerman (2&1)	1	G. Dickinson	0

Match result: British Isles 13½ U.S.A. 18½

1973
MUIRFIELD, East Lothian, Scotland
Captains: B. Hunt (British Isles), J. Burke (U.S.A.)

BRITISH ISLES		U.S.A.	
Morning Foursomes			
B. Barnes & B. Gallacher (1 hole)	1	L. Trevino & W. Casper	0
C. O'Connor & N. Coles (3&2)	1	T. Weiskopf & J.C. Snead	0
A. Jacklin & P. Oosterhuis	½	J. Rodriguez & L. Graham	½
M. Bembridge & E. Polland	0	J. Nicklaus & A. Palmer (6&5)	1
Afternoon Fourballs			
B. Barnes & B. Gallacher (5&4)	1	T. Aaron & G. Brewer	0
M. Bembridge & B. Huggett (3&1)	1	A. Palmer & J. Nicklaus	0
A. Jacklin & P. Oosterhuis (3&1)	1	T. Weiskopf & W. Casper	0
C. O'Connor & N. Coles	0	L. Trevino & H. Blancas (2&1)	1
Morning Foursomes			
B. Barnes & P.J. Butler	0	J. Nicklaus & T. Weiskopf (1 hole)	1
P. Oosterhuis & A. Jacklin (2 holes)	1	A. Palmer & D. Hill	0
M. Bembridge & B. Huggett (5&4)	1	J. Rodriguez & L. Graham	0
N. Coles & C. O'Connor	0	L. Trevino & W. Casper (2&1)	1
Afternoon Fourballs			
B. Barnes & P. Butler	0	J.C. Snead & A. Palmer (2 holes)	1
A. Jacklin & P. Oosterhuis	0	G. Brewer & W. Casper (3&2)	1
C. Clark & E. Polland	0	J. Nicklaus & T. Weiskopf (3&2)	1
M. Bembridge & B. Huggett	½	L. Trevino & H. Blancas	½
Morning Singles			
B. Barnes	0	W. Casper (2&1)	1
B. Gallacher	0	T. Weiskopf (3&1)	1
P. Butler	0	H. Blancas (5&4)	1
A. Jacklin (2&1)	1	T. Aaron	0
N. Coles	½	G. Brewer	½
C. O'Connor	0	J.C. Snead (1 hole)	1
M. Bembridge	½	J. Nicklaus	½
P. Oosterhuis	½	L. Trevino	½
Afternoon Singles			
B. Huggett (4&2)	1	H. Blancas	0
B. Barnes	0	J. C. Snead (3&1)	1
B. Gallacher	0	G. Brewer (6&5)	1
A. Jacklin	0	W. Casper (2&1)	1
N. Coles	0	L. Trevino (6&5)	1
C. O'Connor	½	T. Weiskopf	½
M. Bembridge	0	J. Nicklaus (2 holes)	1
P. Oosterhuis (4&2)	1	A. Palmer	0

Match result: British Isles 13 U.S.A. 19

1975
LAUREL VALLEY GOLF CLUB, Pennsylvania
Captains: B. Hunt (British Isles), A. Palmer (U.S.A.)

BRITISH ISLES		U.S.A.	
Morning Foursomes			
B. Barnes & B. Gallacher	0	J. Nicklaus & T. Weiskopf (5&4)	1
N. Wood & M. Bembridge	0	G. Littler & H. Irwin (4&3)	1
A. Jacklin & P. Oosterhuis	0	A. Geiberger & J. Miller (3&1)	1
T, Horton & J. O'Leary	0	L. Trevino & J.C. Snead (2&1)	1
Afternoon Fourballs			
P. Oosterhuis & A. Jacklin (2&1)	1	W. Casper & R. Floyd	0
E. Darcy & C. O'Connor Jr	0	T. Weiskopf & L. Graham (3&2)	1
B. Barnes & B. Gallacher	½	J. Nicklaus & R. Murphy	½
T. Horton & J. O'Leary	0	L. Trevino & H. Irwin (2&1)	1
Morning Fourballs			
P. Oosterhuis & A. Jacklin	½	W. Casper & J. Miller	½
T. Horton & N. Wood	0	J. Nicklaus & J.C. Snead (4&2)	1
B. Barnes & B. Gallacher	0	G. Littler & L. Graham (5&3)	1
E. Darcy & G.L. Hunt	½	A. Geiberger & R. Floyd	½
Afternoon Foursomes			
A. Jacklin & B. Huggett (3&2)	1	L. Trevino & R. Murphy	0
C. O'Connor Jr & J. O'Leary	0	T. Weiskopf & J. Miller (5&3)	1
P. Oosterhuis & M. Bembridge	0	H. Irwin & W. Casper (3&2)	1
E. Darcy & G.L. Hunt	0	A. Geiberger & L. Graham (3&2)	1
Morning Singles			
A. Jacklin	0	R. Murphy (2&1)	1
P. Oosterhuis (2 holes)	1	J. Miller	0
B. Gallacher	½	L. Trevino	½
T. Horton	½	H. Irwin	½
B. Huggett	0	G. Littler (4&2)	1
E. Darcy	0	W. Casper (3&2)	1
G.L. Hunt	0	T. Weiskopf (5&3)	1
B. Barnes (4&2)	1	J. Nicklaus	0
Afternoon Singles			
A. Jacklin	0	R. Floyd (1 hole)	1
P. Oosterhuis (3&2)	1	J.C. Snead	0
B. Gallacher	½	A. Geiberger	½
T. Horton (2&1)	1	L. Graham	0
J. O'Leary	0	H. Irwin (2&1)	1
M. Bembridge	0	R. Murphy (2&1)	1
N. Wood (2&1)	1	L. Trevino	0
B. Barnes (2&1)	1	J. Nicklaus	0

Match result: British Isles 11 U.S.A. 21

1977
ROYAL LYTHAM & ST ANNES, Lancashire, England
Captains: B. Huggett (British Isles), D. Finsterwald (U.S.A.)

BRITISH ISLES		U.S.A.	
Foursomes			
B. Gallacher & B. Barnes	o	L. Wadkins & H. Irwin (3&1)	1
N. Coles & P. Dawson	o	D. Stockton & J. McGee (1 hole)	1
N. Faldo & P. Oosterhuis (2&1)	1	R. Floyd & L. Graham	o
E. Darcy & A. Jacklin	½	E. Sneed & D. January	½
T. Horton & M. James	o	J. Nicklaus & T. Watson (5&4)	1
Fourballs			
B. Barnes & T. Horton	o	T. Watson & H. Green (5&4)	1
N. Coles & P. Dawson	o	E. Sneed & L. Wadkins (5&3)	1
N. Faldo & P. Oosterhuis (3&1)	1	J. Nicklaus & R. Floyd	o
A. Jacklin & E. Darcy	o	D. Hill & D. Stockton (5&3)	1
M. James & K. Brown	o	H. Irwin & L. Graham (1 hole)	1
Singles			
H. Clark	o	L. Wadkins (4&3)	1
N. Coles	o	L. Graham (5&3)	1
P. Dawson (5&4)	1	D. January	o
B. Barnes (1 hole)	1	H. Irwin	o
T. Horton	o	D. Hill (5&4)	1
B. Gallacher (1 hole)	1	J.W. Nicklaus	o
E. Darcy	o	H. Green (1 hole)	1
M. James	o	R. Floyd (2&1)	1
N. Faldo (1 hole)	1	T. Watson	o
P. Oosterhuis (2 holes)	1	J. McGee	o

Match result: British Isles 7½ U.S.A. 12½

1979

THE GREENBRIER, White Sulphur Springs, West Virginia

Captains: J. Jacobs (Europe), W. Casper (U.S.A.)

EUROPE		U.S.A.	
Morning Fourballs			
A. Garrido & S. Ballesteros	o	L. Wadkins & L Nelson (2&1)	1
K. Brown & M. James	o	L. Trevino & F. Zoeller (3&2)	1
P. Oosterhuis & N. Faldo	o	A. Bean & L. Elder (2&1)	1
B. Gallacher & B. Barnes (2&1)	1	H. Irwin & J. Mahaffey	o
Afternoon Foursomes			
K. Brown & D. Smyth	o	H. Irwin & T. Kite (7&6)	1
S. Ballesteros & A. Garrido (3&2)	1	F. Zoeller & H. Green	o
A. Lyle & A. Jacklin	½	L. Trevino & G. Morgan	½
B. Gallacher & B. Barnes	o	L. Wadkins & L. Nelson (4&3)	1
Morning Foursomes			
A. Jacklin & A. Lyle (5&4)	1	L. Elder & J. Mahaffey	o
N. Faldo & P. Oosterhuis (6&5)	1	A, Bean & T. Kite	o
B. Gallacher & B. Barnes (2&1)	1	F. Zoeller & M. Hayes	o
S. Ballesteros & A Garrido	o	L. Wadkins & L. Nelson (3&2)	1
Afternoon Fourballs			
S. Ballesteros & A. Garrido	o	L. Wadkins & L. Nelson (5&4)	1
A. Jacklin & A. Lyle	o	H. Irwin & T. Kite (1 hole)	1
B. Gallacher & B. Barnes (3&2)	1	L. Trevino & F. Zoeller	o
N. Faldo & P. Oosterhuis (1 hole)	1	L. Elder & M. Hayes	o
Singles			
B. Gallacher (3&2)	1	L. Wadkins	o
S. Ballesteros	o	L. Nelson (3&2)	1
A. Jacklin	o	T. Kite (1 hole)	1
A. Garrido	o	M. Hayes (1 hole)	1
M. King	o	A. Bean (4&3)	1
B. Barnes	o	J. Mahaffey (1 hole)	1
N. Faldo (3&2)	1	L. Elder	o
D. Smyth	o	H. Irwin (5&3)	1
P. Oosterhuis	o	H. Green (2 holes)	1
K. Brown (1 hole)	1	F. Zoeller	o
A. Lyle	o	L. Trevino (2&1)	1
M. James (halved, match not played)	½	G. Morgan (halved, match not played)	½

Match result: Europe 11 U.S.A. 17

1981
WALTON HEATH, Surrey, England
Captains: J. Jacobs (Europe), D. Marr (U.S.A.)

EUROPE		U.S.A.	
Morning Foursomes			
B. Langer & M. Pinero	0	L. Trevino & L. Nelson (1 hole)	1
A. Lyle & M. James (2&1)	1	B. Rogers & B. Lietzke	0
B. Gallacher & D. Smyth (3&2)	1	H. Irwin & R. Floyd	0
P. Oosterhuis & N. Faldo	0	T. Watson & J. Nicklaus (4&3)	1
Afternoon Fourballs			
S. Torrance & H. Clark	½	T. Kite & J. Miller	½
A. Lyle & M. James (3 &2)	1	B. Crenshaw & J. Pate	0
D. Smyth & J.M. Canizares (6&5)	1	B. Rogers & B. Lietzke	0
B. Gallacher & E. Darcy	0	H. Irwin & R. Floyd (2&1)	1
Morning Fourballs			
N. Faldo & S. Torrance	0	L. Trevino & J. Pate (7&5)	1
A. Lyle & M. James	0	L. Nelson & T. Kite (1 hole)	1
B. Langer & M. Pinero (2& 1)	1	R. Floyd & H. Irwin	0
J.M. Canizares & D. Smyth	0	J. Nicklaus & T. Watson (3&2)	1
Afternoon Foursomes			
P. Oosterhuis & S. Torrance	0	L. Trevino & J. Pate (2&1)	1
B. Langer & M. Pinero	0	J. Nicklaus & T. Watson (3&2)	1
A. Lyle & M. James	0	B. Rogers & R. Floyd (3&2)	1
D. Smyth & B. Gallacher	0	T. Kite & L. Nelson (3&2)	1
Singles			
S. Torrance	0	L. Trevino (5&3)	1
A. Lyle	0	T. Kite (3&2)	1
B. Gallacher	½	B. Rogers	½
M. James	0	L. Nelson (2 holes)	1
D. Smyth	0	B. Crenshaw (6&4)	1
B. Langer	½	B. Lietzke	½
M. Pinero (4&2)	1	J. Pate	0
J.M. Canizares	0	H. Irwin (1 hole)	1
N. Faldo (2&1)	1	J. Miller	0
H. Clark (4&3)	1	T. Watson	0
P. Oosterhuis	0	R. Floyd (1 hole)	1
E. Darcy	0	J. Nicklaus (5&3)	1

Match result: Europe 9½ U.S.A. 18½

1983
PGA NATIONAL GOLF CLUB, Palm Beach Gardens, Florida
Captains: A. Jacklin (Europe), J. Nicklaus (U.S.A.)

EUROPE		U.S.A.	
Morning Foursomes			
B. Gallacher & A. Lyle	o	T. Watson & B. Crenshaw (5&4)	1
N. Faldo & B. Langer (4&2)	1	L. Wadkins & C. Stadler	o
J.M. Canizares & S. Torrance (4&3)	1	R. Floyd & B. Gilder	o
A. Ballesteros & P. Way	o	T. Kite & C. Peete (2&1)	1
Afternoon Fourballs			
B. Waites & K. Brown (2&1)	1	G. Morgan & F. Zoeller	o
N. Faldo & B. Langer	o	T. Watson & J. Haas (2&1)	1
S. Ballesteros & P. Way (1 hole)	1	R. Floyd & C. Strange	o
S. Torrance & I. Woosnam	½	B. Crenshaw & C. Peete	½
Morning Fourballs			
B. Waites & K. Brown	o	L. Wadkins & C. Stadler (1 hole)	1
N. Faldo & B. Langer (4&2)	1	B. Crenshaw & C. Peete	o
S. Ballesteros & P. Way	½	G. Morgan & J. Haas	½
S. Torrance & I. Woosnam	o	T. Watson & B. Gilder (5&4)	1
Afternoon Foursomes			
N. Faldo & B. Langer (3&2)	1	T. Kite & R. Floyd	o
S Torrance & J.M. Canizares	o	G. Morgan & L. Wadkins (7&5)	1
S. Ballesteros & P. Way (2&1)	1	T. Watson & B. Gilder	o
B. Waites & K. Brown	o	J. Haas & C. Strange (3&2)	1
Singles			
S. Ballesteros	½	F. Zoeller	½
N. Faldo (2&1)	1	J. Haas	o
B. Langer (2 holes)	1	G. Morgan	o
G.J. Brand	o	B. Gilder (2 holes)	1
A. Lyle	o	B. Crenshaw (3&1)	1
B. Waites	o	C. Peete (1 hole)	1
P. Way (2&1)	1	C. Strange	o
S. Torrance	½	T. Kite	½
I. Woosnam	o	C. Stadler (3&2)	1
J.M. Canizares	½	L. Wadkins	½
K. Brown (4&3)	1	R. Floyd	o
B. Gallacher	o	T. Watson (2&1)	1

Match result: Europe 13½ U.S.A. 14½

1985
THE BELFRY, Warwickshire, England
Captains: A. Jacklin (Europe), L. Trevino (U.S.A.)

EUROPE		U.S.A.	
Morning Foursomes			
S. Ballesteros & M. Pinero (2&1)	1	C. Strange & O'Meara	0
B. Langer & N. Faldo	0	C. Peete & T. Kite (3&2)	1
A. Lyle & K. Brown	0	L. Wadkins & R. Floyd (4&3)	1
H. Clark & S. Torrance	0	C. Stadler & H. Sutton (3&2)	1
Afternoon Fourballs			
P. Way & I. Woosnam (1 hole)	1	F. Zoeller & H. Green	0
S. Ballesteros & M. Pinero (2&1)	1	A. North & P. Jacobsen	0
B. Langer & J.M. Canizares	½	C. Stadler & H. Sutton	½
S. Torrance & H. Clark	0	R. Floyd & L. Wadkins (1 hole)	1
Morning Fourballs			
S. Torrance & H. Clark (2 &1)	1	T. Kite & A. North	0
P. Way & I. Woosnam (4 &3)	1	H. Green & F. Zoeller	0
S. Ballesteros & M. Pinero	0	M. O'Meara & L. Wadkins (3&2)	1
B. Langer & A. Lyle	½	C. Stadler & C. Strange	½
Afternoon Foursomes			
J.M. Canizares & J. Rivero (7&5)	1	T. Kite & C. Peete	0
S. Ballesteros & M. Pinero (5&4)	1	C. Stadler & H. Sutton	0
P. Way & I. Woosnam	0	C. Strange & P. Jacobsen (4&2)	1
B. Langer & K. Brown (3&2)	1	R. Floyd & L. Wadkins	0
Singles			
M. Pinero (3&1)	1	L. Wadkins	0
I. Woosnam	0	C. Stadler (2&1)	1
P. Way (2 holes)	1	R. Floyd	0
S. Ballesteros	½	T. Kite	½
A. Lyle (3&2)	1	P. Jacobsen	0
B. Langer (5&4)	1	H. Sutton	0
S. Torrance (1 hole)	1	A. North	0
H. Clark (1 hole)	1	M. O'Meara	0
N. Faldo	0	H. Green (3&1)	1
J. Rivero	0	C. Peete (1 hole)	1
J.M. Canizares (2 holes)	1	F. Zoeller	0
K. Brown	0	C. Strange (4&2)	1

Match result: Europe 16½   U.S.A. 11½

1987
MUIRFIELD VILLAGE, Columbus, Ohio
Captains: A. Jacklin (Europe), J. Nicklaus (U.S.A.)

EUROPE		U.S.A.	
Morning Foursomes			
S. Torrance & H. Clark	o	C. Strange & T. Kite (4&2)	1
K. Brown & B. Langer	o	H. Sutton & D. Pohl (2&1)	1
N. Faldo & I. Woosnam (2 holes)	1	L. Wadkins & L. Mize	o
S. Ballesteros & J.M. Olazabal (1 hole)	1	L. Nelson & P. Stewart	o
Afternoon Fourballs			
G. Brand Jr. & J. Rivero (3&2)	1	B. Crenshaw & S. Simpson	o
A. Lyle & B. Langer (1 hole)	1	A. Bean & M. Calcavecchia	o
N. Faldo & I. Woosnam (2&1)	1	H. Sutton & D. Pohl	o
S. Ballesteros & J.M. Olazabal (2&1)	1	C. Strange & T. Kite	o
Morning Foursomes			
J. Rivero & G. Brand Jr.	o	C. Strange & T. Kite (3&1)	1
N. Faldo & I. Woosnam	½	H. Sutton & L. Mize	½
A. Lyle & B. Langer (2&1)	1	L. Wadkins & L. Nelson	o
S. Ballesteros & J.M. Olazabal (1 hole)	1	B. Crenshaw & P. Stewart	o
Afternoon Fourballs			
N. Faldo & I. Woosnam (5&4)	1	C. Strange & T. Kite	o
E. Darcy & G. Brand Jr.	o	A. Bean & P. Stewart (3&2)	1
S. Ballesteros & J.M. Olazabal	o	H. Sutton & L. Mize (2&1)	1
A. Lyle & B. Langer (1 hole)	1	L. Wadkins & L. Nelson	o
Singles			
I. Woosnam	o	A. Bean (1 hole)	1
H. Clark (1 hole)	1	D. Pohl	o
S. Torrance	½	L. Mize	½
N. Faldo	o	M. Calcavecchia (1 hole)	1
J.M. Olazabal	o	P. Stewart (2 holes)	1
E. Darcy (1 hole)	1	B. Crenshaw	o
J. Rivero	o	S. Simpson (2&1)	1
B. Langer	½	L. Nelson	½
A. Lyle	o	T. Kite (3&2)	1
S. Ballesteros (2&1)	1	C. Strange	o
G. Brand Jr.	½	H. Sutton	½
K. Brown	o	L. Wadkins (3&2)	1

Match result: Europe 15 U.S.A. 13

1989
THE BELFRY, Warwickshire, England
Captains: A. Jacklin (Europe), R. Floyd (U.S.A.)

EUROPE		U.S.A.	
Morning Foursomes			
N. Faldo & I. Woosnam	½	T. Kite & C. Strange	½
H. Clark & M. James	o	L. Wadkins & P. Stewart (1 hole)	1
S. Ballesteros & J.M. Olazabal	½	T. Watson & C. Beck	½
B. Langer & R. Rafferty	o	M. Calcavecchia & K. Green (2 &1)	1
Afternoon Fourballs			
S. Torrance & G. Brand Jr. (1 hole)	1	C. Strange & P. Azinger	o
H. Clark & M. James (3&2)	1	F. Couples & L. Wadkins	o
N. Faldo & I. Woosnam (2 holes)	1	M. Calcavecchia & M. McCumber	o
S. Ballesteros & J.M. Olazabal (6&5)	1	T. Watson & M. O'Meara	o
Morning Foursomes			
I. Woosnam & N. Faldo (3&2)	1	L. Wadkins & P. Stewart	o
G. Brand Jr. & S. Torrance	o	C. Beck & P. Azinger (4&3)	1
C. O'Connor Jr. & R. Rafferty	o	M. Calcavecchia & K. Green (3&2)	1
S. Ballesteros & J.M. Olazabal (1 hole)	1	T. Kite & C. Strange	o
Afternoon Fourballs			
N. Faldo & I. Woosnam	o	C. Beck & P. Azinger (2&1)	1
B. Langer & J.M. Canizares	o	T. Kite & M. McCumber (2&1)	1
H. Clark & M. James (1 hole)	1	P. Stewart & C. Strange	o
S. Ballesteros & J.M. Olazabal (3&2)	1	M. Calcavecchia & K. Green	o
Singles			
S. Ballesteros	o	P. Azinger (1 hole)	1
B. Langer	o	C. Beck (3&1)	1
J.M. Olazabal (1 hole)	1	P. Stewart	o
R. Rafferty (1 hole)	1	M. Calcavecchia	o
H. Clark	o	T. Kite (8&7)	1
M. James (3 &2)	1	M. O'Meara	o
C. O'Connor Jr. (1 hole)	1	F. Couples	o
J.M. Canizares (1 hole)	1	K. Green	o
G. Brand Jr.	o	M. McCumber (1 hole)	1
S. Torrance	o	T. Watson (3&1)	1
N. Faldo	o	L. Wadkins (1 hole)	1
I. Woosnam	o	C. Strange (2 holes)	1

Match result: Europe 14 U.S.A. 14